THE
CHATSWORTH VILLAGES
AT PEACE AND WAR

LIFE IN EDENSOR, PILSLEY AND BEELEY

KEITH TAYLOR

FOREWORD BY THE DOWAGER DUCHESS OF DEVONSHIRE

Keith Taylor

COUNTRY BOOKS

Published by Ashridge Press / Country Books
Courtyard Cottage, Little Longstone, Bakewell, Derbyshire DE45 1NN
Tel: 01629 640670
e-mail: dickrichardson@country-books.co.uk
www.countrybooks.biz

ISBN 978-1-906789-92-3

© 2014 Keith Taylor

British Library Cataloguing in Publication Data.
A catalogue record for this book is available from the British Library.

FRONT COVER:
*Personnel from the Royal Naval Convalescent Hospital
at Edensor Institute, Chatsworth, early 1915.
George Edward Siddall stands third from the left,
in civilian clothes, before he joined up.
He would be killed on active service, later in the War*

BACK COVER:
*Andrew and Deborah Cavendish, the future 11th Duke and Duchess of Devonshire,
with their children, Peregrine and Emma, at 'The Rookery', Ashford in the Water, 1945*

Printed and bound in England by 4edge Ltd. Hockley, Essex. Tel: 01702 200 243

CONTENTS

ACKNOWLEDGEMENTS

The Dowager Duchess of Devonshire, for kindly supplying the foreword.
Ruth Gordon and the knowledgeable, friendly, helpful staff at Matlock Local Studies Library (special mention for John Taylor, for help with photographs).
The Records Office, Matlock.
Ian Else at Chatsworth Estate Office.
Cliff Housley, in connection to the Sherwood Foresters Regiment.
Frank Dickens for work with the computer.

Special thanks for their time, information, memories and loan of photographs to the following people (I apologise if any person's name has been omitted from the list):

Davina Askey, Jean Bamfield, Julie Beswick, Bernard Birds, Anne Boot, Jean Blackwell, Jean Boulsover, Gordon Bowering, Edna Boyce, Leonard Broome, Eileen Bradley, Doris Brightmore, Martin W. Brightmore (Bsc. (Hons) SHEM CMIOSH), Trevor Brown, Kath Burnett, Margaret Buxton, Sandy Caudwell, Steven Coates, Pam Cobley, David Critchlow, Derby Museum, Derbyshire County Council, Derbyshire Libraries and Heritage, Derbyshire Times, Dowager Duchess of Devonshire, J. Duncan, Delhi Eades, Peter Eades, Ian Else, Ethel Eyre, Fred Fearn, Margaret Fearn, Dr. Kate Fielden, Susan & Max Fischer, Mark Fuller, James Furness, Rachel Gadsby, Bob Gilbert, Ken Gilbert, Lewis Gilbert, Edna Goodwin, Joyce Gowen, Lesley Gregory, Sylvia Gregory, John Grindey, Nell Hall, Pamela Halliwell, Pauline and Vernon Harrison, Barbara Hawksworth, Chris Heathcote, Cyril Heathcote, Mary Heathcote, Mr. Henshaw, High Peak News, Tony Holmes, Mrs. Homer, Josie Hone, Cliff Housley, Dorothy Howard, Graham Howard, Richard Jeacock, Judith Jones, Lord Lansdowne, Jim Link, Ralph Lord, Jennifer Lovett, Manchester Evening News, Helen Marchant, Vernon Mather, Winnie McGregor, Fred Morton, Peter Morton, Edwin Mosley, Virginia Moyse, Mr. Mulvey, Diane Naylor, Derek Neave, Stan Oliver, Tony Ollivant, Pamela Paget, Betty Peacock, Potter & Compnay, Margaret Race, Kay Reeve, Duncan Rhodes, Dick Richardson, J. Richmond, Cyril Robinson, Norman Rosser, Vera Russell, Colonel Sainsbury, Dudley Salmon, Ann Salmon, Kay Schurer, G. Scott, Frank Sheldon, Geoffrey Sheldon, Mary Sheldon, Margaret Sheldon, P. Shimwell, Margaret Slin, Alan Smith, David Spencer, John Strutt, John Taylor, Sheila Taylor, Michael Thompson, Harry Towndrow, Kenneth and Carol Trickett, Leonard Twigg, Glyne Waite, Raymond and Crystal Wallage, Betty Waterhouse, Gill Watson, Barbara and Bill Wild, S. Wiltshire, Pat Wragg.

BIBLIOGRAPHY AND SOURCES

Squadron Histories by Peter Lewis, Putnam and Company.
Fighter Squadrons of the RAF by John Rawlins, Macdonalds and Janes.
Bomber Squadrons of the RAF by John Rawlins, Macdonalds and Janes.
Bomber losses of the Second World War.
Battalion war diaries and Regimental histories.
Pen and Sword publications on various battles.
The Salient - Ypres, 1914 - 1918 by Alan Palmer, Constable, London.
The Face of Battle by John Keegan, Jonathan Cape.
History of the First World War by Liddell Hart.
The Grenadier Guards in the Great War by Sir Frederick Ponsonby,
    Macmillan and Company.
The Second World War – Winston Churchill.
Information from the 1871, 1881, 1891 and 1901 Census.
Ancestry website.
Parish Baptism, Marriage and Burials Registers.
Newspapers, including the *High Peak News*, *Derbyshire Times*,
    Matlock Mercury and *Buxton Advertiser*.
Information on the Commonwealth War Graves Commission website.
CD Rom of *The Soldiers Died in the Great War*.
Through Limestone Hills by Bill Hudson, Oxford Publishing Company.
Trust, Chalkdust and Wanderlust by Ron Whitehead, Hamilton and Co.
Schooldays at Chatsworth by Nancie Park.
Calver Record.

The most valuable sources of information and many accompanying photographs have been generously provided by people connected to the areas being studied.

Chatsworth House from the west
Cyril Robinson

The State Drawing Room at Chatsworth House
Chris Heathcote

FOREWORD

THE DOWAGER DUCHESS OF DEVONSHORE

There cannot be a church in these islands that does not keep the names of the men and women lost to their parishes.

The villages described in this book are no exception, in spite of being engaged mainly in agriculture. Some families were cruelly affected, with more than one son dying for their country.

My husband's family suffered the loss of his elder brother, on whom all the hopes of his parents were centred. My parents-in-law never recovered from Billy Hartington's loss.

The effects were felt more than on similar estates because his loss was followed so closely by the death of my father-in-law, necessitating the sale of more than half the Derbyshire estate to pay the vast tax bill imposed by the then government.

My only brother was killed and so was another brother-in-law. My mother and father were sorely affected by these tragedies that were suffered by so many more.

One of the saddest deaths at Chatsworth was that of the eldest son of the head keeper, who was killed on the last day of the war.

At least Chatsworth itself was well used between 1939-45. Three hundred girls from Penrhos College, North Wales, with their teachers lived and worked there. That marvellous building seems to adapt itself to any circumstance, and the old girls look back with pleasure and a certain pride on their schooldays in this unusual place.

In spite of these blows, we survived and, I am happy to say, Chatsworth with us.

Deborah Devonshire

A group of Edwardians about to arrive at the House, Chatsworth c1905
Derek Neave

Chatsworth House stands beyond the bridge
Chris Heathcote

INTRODUCTION

Remembrance Day, November 11th 2014, falls in the year in which "Chatsworth Villages Through Peace and War" has been published and comes exactly 100 years after the guns that had killed more than 900,000 British and Empire servicemen during the First World War finally fell silent. The Kaiser had abdicated and the Armistice ending hostilities was signed by the German High Command and German politicians. But the "war to end all wars" turned out only to be a prelude to an even more murderous and devastating conflict.

The titanic clashes of 1914-1918 and 1939-1945 remain the dominating presence in our collective memory of war. Inevitably, as the survivors of those terrible struggles become fewer in number, it becomes ever-more important to remember what they went through and why they went through it. It required a willingness to make sacrifices of a kind which most of us would do almost anything to avoid. We owe the freedom and prosperity we enjoy today partly to the fact that these previous generations did not shirk those sacrifices. To be their inheritors is our greatest privilege, and it is one none of us should ever forget.

Within the following pages I have taken, as a "snapshot" of this period, three villages from the rural idyll of the Derbyshire countryside – Edensor, Pilsley and Beeley – and attempted to discover the stories of the lives and deaths of the men from these villages who went off to war, but lost their lives and whose names are now to be found on the parish war memorials.

Connected as they are to the Chatsworth estate of the Duke of Devonshire, it might be supposed that these villages and their inhabitants would be spared the horrors and sacrifices of war, but very few families were immune to war's stranglehold on the life of the country.

Thirty five servicemen from these villages lost their lives during the Great War and another eight men are commemorated after paying the supreme sacrifice during the Second World War.

The arrival of the Midland Railway in the 1850's and 60's linked up this district to the outside world, with easy access north and south.

The villages, however, remained relative oases of peace and tranquillity in the Edwardian era, leading up to the start of the Great War. For the majority of their inhabitants, they worked, married, raised families and played within the narrow confines of village life. Rowsley's railway connections witnessed a turnover of personnel from outside Derbyshire, as did the employment of gardeners, servants and staff at Chatsworth, whilst Baslow's proximity to Sheffield and the arrival of the railway in the Wye Valley, resulted in certain "well-to-do" families coming to live in the village and commuting to the nearby cities.

Yet these villages would not be spared the consequences of war, for we find that the harbinger of death would reap both "high" and "low" between 1914 and 1919. Whether it be the Duke of Devonshire's brother, his brother-in-law or his Agent's son, the son of a tenant farmer, an estate worker toiling in the kitchen gardens, sawmill, quarry, woods and house, the engines of war showed no favours as officers and other ranks were slaughtered side by side on the battlefields of the Western Front or in other theatres of the Great War.

When final relief came with the Armistice of November 11th 1918, at tremendous cost to human life, the people of Edensor, Pilsley and Beeley must have looked with hope to peaceful times ahead (although the flu pandemic was still claiming victims throughout the later stages of 1918 and into 1919).

Sadly, just 21 years later, these aspirations were shattered when Neville Chamberlain broadcast to the nation on Sunday September 3rd 1939 that Britain was once again at war with Germany. Further names would be added to the village war memorials.

In writing this book I have attempted to reveal the backgrounds to these men, as well as show what happened to them when they went off to war. However, I have also set these men back into the three villages and surrounding landscapes they would have been familiar with, either before the Great War or during the inter-war years of the 1920's and 1930's.

Through words and photographs, a picture hopefully emerges of life in the relative backwater of the Chatsworth villages before events on the world scene were to rudely intervene and take so many of these men away from their families and to their deaths during the two world-wide conflicts of the 20th century.

The First World War is passing from human memory into history, whilst many of those who survived the Second World War have passed away. It is the aim of this book to celebrate the lives of these lost generations (and their colleagues who were fortunate to survive those conflicts). It is the author's hope that it will help others to appreciate their supreme sacrifice.

Keith Taylor 2014

THE WEEKEND OF JUNE 27TH/28TH 1914

The weekend of June 27th/28th 1914 was pleasantly sunny and warm throughout the Chatsworth area of the Peak District. Sunday June 28th was for many folk from the Chatsworth villages, a day of rest from their toil in either the corn mill, sawmill, gardens, quarries or on the railway. Some residents would be attending the church services, such as those of the Reverend Joseph Hewetson at Beeley, whilst others worshipped in chapels. Not all could escape the tedium of work that weekend, for tasks on the farm were plentiful and visitors discovering the delights of this rural area had their needs to be catered for.

On the Friday, there had been the 16th Annual Sports of the Lady Manners School, held on Bakewell Recreation Ground in ideal weather and the following Tuesday (June 30th) was the hottest day recorded since August 9th 1911, 120 degrees Fahrenheit having been recorded. Considerable progress had been made in the hayfields, as a large number of Irish labourers had arrived in the district.

On the previous Saturday, June 20th, the annual feast of the Benign Friendly Society, associated with the Manchester Unity of Oddfellows, had taken place at Beeley in glorious weather.

Darley Brass Band was in attendance and entertainment for those assembled included hurdy-gurdeys, swings, coconut shies and donkey rides. The annual service was held in St. Anne's Church at 11-45a.m., whilst at 1p.m. a substantial dinner, supplied by the landlord of the Devonshire Arms, Lewis Reeves, was served in the Lodge premises, the Reverend Joseph Hewetson presiding. The village of Beeley then went en-fete.

On Thursday July 9th, Beeley Mothers' Outing, including the Reverend and Mrs. Hewetson, visited Hardwick Hall. The Duke of Devonshire allowed them the use of his private road through Chatsworth Park. The brakes were supplied from Wall's Posting Stables at Bridge House Farm, Rowsley. A start was made at 10-15a.m. via Baslow and Chesterfield. A halt was made at Chesterfield to rest the horses and have light refreshments, before continuing and reaching Hardwick Hall at 2p.m. A capital sandwich tea was served at the beautiful old inn, nearby, before they visited the Hall and its gardens. The return journey was begun at 5p.m. and Beeley was reached at 10p.m., bringing to a conclusion an enjoyable day's outing.

There seemed no justifiable reason why these idyllic scenes of Edwardian life should not continue through the remainder of the summer months.

It was however, with the sound of two gun shots ringing out in a mid-European town that the fate of men with Edensor, Pilsley and Beeley connections was to be sealed and the lives of many others affected by hardship and sadness.

These reassuring scenes of Edwardian past times in the beautiful setting of the Chatsworth estates were to be swept aside as a result of the consequences of those pistol shots ringing out in the far-away Bosnian town of Sarajevo. They came from the gun of a Serbian student nationalist, Gavrilo Princip. His assassination of the heir to the Austro-Hungarian Empire, Archduke Franz Ferdinand and his wife, the Duchess of Hohenberg, on that same sunny morning of Sunday June 28th would result in village folk finding their lives changed dramatically as Britain and the European Powers became enmeshed on the road to violent conflict, during the long, hot days of July.

In the following chapter I have attempted to bring to life a view of the Chatsworth estate villages that these men and women would have been familiar with during the years before the Great War and into the 1930's. Fascinating images emerge of parochial life in a rural setting – the harshness of working conditions, the feeling of community, everyday aspects of village life, and yet also the changes taking place in their world in this relative backwater of the British Isles.

CHAPTER ONE

LIFE IN THE CHATSWORTH VILLAGES OF EDENSOR, PILSLEY AND BEELEY

CHATSWORTH HOUSE AND THE CAVENDISH FAMILY

Originally the home of the formidable Bess of Hardwick and her second husband, Sir William Cavendish, Treasurer of the King's Chamber, Chatsworth was transformed into the magnificent palace one sees today by the 1st Duke of Devonshire. It became a statement of the Devonshires' wealth and power, the interior embodying the Baroque interpretation of the Classical era.

The house was built on land purchased by Sir William Cavendish in 1549 for £600. Construction was begun in 1552 but he did not live to see its completion when he died in 1557. His widow, Bess of Hardwick, completed the building work in the 1560's and lived there with her fourth husband, the 6th Earl of Shrewsbury. In 1568 Shrewsbury was entrusted with the custody of Mary, Queen of Scots and brought his prisoner to Chatsworth House several times from 1570 onwards. She lodged in the apartment above the Great Hall, which is now known as the Queen of Scots Room. Bess bequeathed the house to her son, Henry Cavendish. Henry sold the house to his younger brother, William, who became the 1st Earl of Devonshire in 1618. The 4th Earl of Devonshire became the 1st Duke in 1694.

The 1st Duke of Devonshire rebuilt Chatsworth in Classical style between 1686 and 1707, with the Library and North Wing added by the 6th Duke between 1790 and 1858. The Park was landscaped by the 4th Duke (1720 - 1764), who engaged "Capability Brown" to reshape the formal garden into the more natural one that is seen today. The 6th Duke engaged Joseph Paxton as the Head Gardener, resulting in the enrichment of the gardens and the creation of the Emperor Fountain, as well as the now demolished Great Conservatory (situated where the Maze is today).

Rooms inside the House include the Library, originally the 1st Duke's Long Gallery, which was refitted as a Library by the 6th Duke. The Painted Hall, with its vast wall and ceiling paintings depicting scenes from the life of Julius Caesar, was once the 1st Duke's ceremonial entrance hall. The first meal served in the Great Dining Room was for the Princess (later Queen) Victoria and her mother, the Duchess of Kent, in 1832. She returned to Chatsworth as Queen, with Prince Albert, in 1843, when she was entertained by a large array of illuminated fountains. The stunning Chapel was built between 1688 and 1693 by the 1st Duke and has remained unaltered ever since.

The 105 acres of gardens included the giant rockeries (1692), the Cascade (1696) and the Canal (1702). The Cascade, a man-made waterfall, built by Grillet for the 4th Duke, drops down over 200 vertical feet in a fall of 24 steps, each step being of a different size.

It was during the 4th Duke's occupancy of Chatsworth that Capability Brown worked on the park and the gardens. The open tree-flecked landscape is not natural. Brown straightened the river and constructed a network of drainage channels under the grass. He filled in most of Bess of Hardwick's fish ponds. James Paine designed the new bridge to the north of the House and also the Stables (1760), with originally stalls for 80 horses, plus black-smiths' shops. The first floor was occupied by granaries and accommodation for the stable staff. The last horses left the stables in 1939.

Most of the houses of the original village of Edensor, sited by the river and in full view of the House, were demolished and the village rebuilt out of sight of the House. The hedges between the fields on the west bank of the river were grubbed up to create open park land and woods were planted on the horizon. These were arranged in triangular clumps so that the screen of trees could be maintained when each planting had to be felled.

Around 1775 the 5th Duke had an elegant red brick inn built at Edensor to accommodate the increasing number of visitors coming to see Chatsworth (nowadays the Edensor Institute/Cavendish Club). The Devonshires also built the Newhaven Hotel on the Ashbourne - Buxton road and the Snake Inn on the Sheffield - Glossop road.

On the hills at the eastern side of Chatsworth Park is Stand Wood, in which is found the "Hunting Tower", originally called Stand Tower (built in the 1580's). At the top of the wood is a plateau which is the source of water for all the gravity fed waterworks in the gardens. The Swiss Lake feeds the Cascade and the Emperor Lake feeds the Emperor Fountain, built in 1843/1844.

In 1826, William Cavendish, the 6th Duke, began his partnership with 23 year-old Joseph Paxton, as his Head Gardener, and the creation of the gardens (Paxton had trained at Kew Gardens). The Great Conservatory was constructed, designed in glass, iron and wood, which would serve as the inspiration for his later design of the Crystal Palace for the Great Exhibition

The old Peacock Hotel, Baslow, before it was altered and renamed the Cavendish
Tony Holmes

of 1851. 84 metres by 37 metres and 19 metres high, it was begun in 1836 and completed in 1841. It was demolished in the early 1920's as it needed 10 men to run it and huge quantities of coal to heat it. All the plants had died during the Great War when no coal had been available for non-essential purposes.

Paxton also designed the Emperor Fountain in the Canal Pond. In 1843 Tsar Nicholas I of Russia informed the Duke that he was likely to visit the following year. The Duke decided to build the world's highest fountain and Paxton set to work. Working throughout the next six months, by the light of flares at night, it was finished on time, but sadly the Tsar did not pay a visit (the jet of water can reach a height of 90 metres, but usually reaches half that height, running on partial power).

The 4th Duke had decided to demolish the houses of old Edensor village, which were visible from Chatsworth House, and re-house the tenants in the nearby estate villages of Pilsley and Beeley. The 6th Duke continued this work, dismantling the old village and beginning the task of building the new Edensor. Joseph Paxton chose the site for the new village but John Robertson, an architect from Derby, provided the designs.

The different houses from his book of designs, ranging from Norman to Jacobean, Swiss style to Italian villa, were all to be seen at Edensor.

The north of the Park still remained a challenge to the 6th Duke. Though a

The Library at Chatsworth House
Chris Heathcote

*The Duke of Devonshire reviews the Territorials of the 6th Battalion Sherwood Foresters
in Chatsworth Park before the Great War*
Chris Heathcote

Lying-in-state of the 9th Duke of Devonshire, March 28th 1908
Chris Heathcote

Aerial view of Chatsworth House

17

Billy Bond, Baslow postman in the 19th century.
He travelled by donkey on his round and delivered the post to Chatsworth
Margaret Sheldon

The mill on the Edensor Chatsworth Estate was damaged in 1962 when two beech trees crushed it
Pauline Harrison

minor road connected Chatsworth House to the new Chesterfield Turnpike, it was not the gracious entrance required by the Duke.

The breakthrough came in 1820 when the Dukes of Devonshire and Rutland decided to exchange several estates in North Derbyshire. The 6th Duke acquired 3366 acres, including 1002 acres in Baslow, 1273 in Hathersage and 409 in Aldwark. The exchange allowed the Devonshires to extend the Park to the north, with a new approach road running through it.

At Baslow, the lowland area, occupied by farms, fields and houses, became part of the Park. Once the land had been cleared of people and the turnpike road had been diverted, the Duke had the major task of landscaping his Park. The middle section of land between the Robin Hood Inn and Park Gate Farm remained as farmland whilst the largest section, the 652 acres of Gibbet Moor, could be used for shooting and country pursuits.

BEELEY

The village of Beeley, which is today a mixture of Chatsworth estate and privately owned property, is of Anglo-Saxon origin. Godric, an Anglo-Saxon, cultivated a small royal manor at the time of the Norman Conquest, and the name "Begelie" was recorded in the Domesday Survey of 1086, consisting of 90 acres of taxable land.

The village was sited away from the Derwent, since the river was prone to flood and wash away the nearby pasture. By the end of the 17th century the open fields and common land in Beeley were enclosed, including nearly all the village green near the church.

The proximity of Chatsworth and its park land has had a major influence on Beeley and the surrounding landscape, ever since the Chatsworth estate was bought by Sir William Cavendish in 1549. However, it was the 4th Duke of Devonshire who was mainly responsible for bringing Beeley under the control of the Chatsworth estate when his agent bought much property and land during his improvement of Chatsworth Park. Before 1620, only 80 acres of land had belonged to the Cavendish family and the village itself remained independent of any control by Chatsworth until the 3rd Duke of Devonshire purchased "Beeley Hill Top" in 1747, when Chatsworth became the greatest employer of people in the parish, with farming being the main occupation.

The Old Hall, situated in the village, was the first manor house in Beeley, but when John Greaves, a yeoman, bought the manor of Beeley in 1559, just ten years after Bess of Hardwick and her husband purchased Chatsworth, his own home, "Greaves House", dating from 1250, became the new manor house. This property is outside the village and stands 700 feet above sea level, besides a steep narrow lane leading to Beeley Moor. It was rebuilt during the early years of the 17th century and was renamed **"Beeley Hill Top"** around

Beeley Church of England School c1910. BACK ROW: *X, X, X, Frances Grafton, Alice Bond, X, X, X, X*
NEXT ROW: *Miss Evans, X, X, X, X, X, X, X, X, X.* NEXT ROW: *Miss Leah Ratcliffe, X, Lois Bond,*
Edith Hulley, Nellie Hutchinson, Milly Bond, Grace Fearn, Muriel Hulley, Eileen Hulley,
Evelyn Hutchinson. FRONT ROW: *X, Charlie Stone, Jack Bond, Sam Bond, Rollin Hawksworth,*
Rose Hutchinson

Pauline Harrison and Joyce Gowen

Beeley School 1916.1917. BACK ROW: *Nora Fearn, X, Dorothy Drinkwater, X, X, Rose Hutchinson,*
Alice Beard, Peggy Hilson, X, Irene Holmes. NEXT ROW: *Miss Ratcliffe, Madge Holmes, X, X, X,*
Elizabeth (Bess) Hulley, Eva Hulley, X, Evelyn Hutchinson, X, Muriel Newnes, Gwen Smedley,
Edith Hulley, Miss Evans. NEXT ROW: *X, X, Margaret Newnes, X, X, X, X, Ena Holmes,*
Nancy Hilson, Olive Newnes, Nell Hulley, X, Louise Bond. FRONT ROW: *X, X, X, Bob Hutchinson,*
Harry Hulley, George Elliott, Vernon Stone, X. Headmistress of Beeley School for seventeen years,
Miss Leah Ratcliffe married George Hawksworth in October 1922. They left to reside in
Chapel-en-le-Frith

Pauline Harrison and Joyce Gowen

20

Beeley School c1892. BACK ROW: *Miss Clarke, Edith Hawksworth, Ethel Buckley, ? Holmes, ? Holmes, Emily Hawksworth, George Hulley, teacher.* NEXT ROW: *X, Hilda Stone, Ginny Morton, Alice Holmes, Edith Clay, Alice Burdekin.* NEXT ROW: *Becky Hawksworth, Millie Brown, X, Emily Grafton, X, Minnie Morton, May Grafton, Mois Buckley.* FRONT ROW: *Billy Gilbert, ? Bond, Alfred Grafton, Wilfred Grafton, Sam Burdekin, Nellie Burdekin*

Pauline Harrison and Joyce Gowen

Beeley School photo c1901. Standing: second from left is Polly or Alice Beard. First right is Annie Muriel Burdekin and second from right is Lily Styling. Seated: third from left is Annie Hutchinson

Pauline Harrison and Joyce Gowen

The senior girls at Beeley School c1926
BACK ROW: *Olive Reeve, Doris Bond X, X, Gladys Fearn, Barbara Fearn, Mary Reeve, Evelyn Haynes*
FRONT ROW: *Margaret Hutchinson, Elizabeth Grafton, Doris Fearn, Emily Hulley, Melissa Grafton,*
Mary Elliott, Nancy Wall, Olive Newnes (or Muriel Newnes)
Mrs Homer and Vera Russell

Beeley School group in 1936
BACK ROW: *Marjorie Hill, Joan Parker, Vera Hutchinson, Joyce Reeve, Mary Berrisford,*
Gwenny Cummings, Alice Stewardson. SITTING ON MAT: *Harry Towndrow*
Joyce Gowen

Boys at Beeley School c1937
LEFT TO RIGHT: *Joe Smith, Tom Grafton (or Colin Smith), Frank Downes, Ronald Grafton, Harry Towndrow, Bob Fearn, Geoff Kerry*
Harry Towndrow

Mother, baby and child group at Beeley c1925
Meetings were held with the nurse to see if they were healthy and check for head lice, etc.
People from Rowsley also attended
BACK ROW: *X. X. Mrs Hilson, X, X, X, X, X*
MIDDLE ROW: *X, Mrs Grafton, X, X, X, Mrs Fearn and Doreen, Bert Reeve, Alice Reeve with Phyllis Reeve*
X, Harry Reeve
FRONT ROW: *X, X, X, X, X, X, X*
Joyce Gowen

23

Teas were served in the marquee, erected in the field, during the celebrations for Queen Victoria's Golden Jubilee at Beeley, in 1887

Barbara Hawksworth

The Golden Jubilee Celebrations for Queen Victoria in 1887 were held in a field at the back of Duke's Barn (stabling) and Yard, Beeley. The banner in the far distance is over the Duke's Barn and reads "Long Live Our Duke"

Barbara Hawksworth

24

On the evening in April 1977, a Jubilee tree was planted by the Duchess of Devonshire in the grounds of the Village Hall to commemorate the Queen's Silver Jubilee. The village hall was built by men from the village in 1924

LEFT TO RIGHT: *Myra Critchlow, Dennis Hopkins, Duchess of Devonshire, X, Joan Parker, Sandra Gregory, Lily Grindey, Bill Grindey, X, X, X, Maud Fearn, Bernard Godwin, X, X, Mrs Towndrow*

Barbara Hawksworth

Silver Jubilee Celebrations for George V at Beeley in 1935
STANDING: *Ivy Stewartson, Vera Ward, Philip Thraves, Colin Smith*
The girl sitting on the left side of the see-saw is Phyllis Reeve
Vera Russell

The first Chapel in Beeley was erected in 1806
J Richmond

1667, under the ownership of the Saville family. The south wing was demolished in the early years of the 18th century, when it reverted to being a farmhouse, and in 1747 it became part of the Chatsworth estate when the property was purchased by the 3rd Duke of Devonshire.

As the 4th Duke embarked on his grand plan to develop and landscape Chatsworth, Beeley then started to become part of the estate. Land and buildings were purchased as they came on the market, but this task took some time and was completed by the 6th Duke. The buildings in the village have remained much the same for the last 200 years but their uses have changed. The post office, reading room, school, school house and chapel have now become private dwellings.

The good-looking, hard wearing, honey-coloured sandstone for these buildings came from the quarries at nearby Fallinge Edge and these same quarries provided many of the local villagers with employment over the years. The two Bruntwood Quarries provided stone for some of the principal buildings in Manchester.

"**Norman House**", containing its own purpose built cheese house, is probably the oldest dwelling in the village, named after the family who lived there during the 17th century and through into the 1850's. Their wealth came from a number of sources, for they owned quarries at Fallinge Edge and Beeley Moor, as well as a coal pit there, together with a tan yard alongside Beeley Brook and a lead smelter between Beeley and Rowsley. The tannery

In the far distance is the newly rebuilt Beeley Chapel, situated on Chapel Hill. The rebuilding took place in 1891. In the foreground on the left is the thatched village shop

J Richmond

was in a former corn mill, powered by the water from Beeley Brook. Water was drawn off and there were tan pits for washing the skins.

William Hodkin, who operated Paine's corn mill in Chatsworth Park, lived in Norman House from the 1860's, with family descendants residing there until 1960. A circular horse walk is in a yard behind the house and provided power to operate crushing and chopping machinery that dealt with cereals.

The Corn Mill in the Park had been built to a design of James Paine in 1761/1762. During the 4th Duke's landscaping of the Park it replaced the main

A view of Devonshire Square c1894. The Devonshire Arms Inn is on the right. Facing the camera, in the middle distance, are the three Y-shaped 'Paxton' cottages, designed by GH Stokes, the husband of one of Joseph Paxton's daughters. Edensor was being redeveloped in 1856 and villagers from Edensor were rehoused in these cottages

Joyce Gowen

27

Two horses and carriages outside the Devonshire Arms, Beeley, c1909
Joyce Gowen

The Devonshire Arms, Beeley, on the occasion of Beeley Club Feast, June 1912
LEFT TO RIGHT: *Harry Reeve, F. Reeve, R. Hill, B. Reeve, X, Ernest Reeve, Lewis Reeve (landlord),*
J. Downs, C. Buckley, X, X, X, G. Bond, Frank Grafton, X, X, X, H. Fearn, X. X

The back-leaded range and fireplace at Beeley Post office, typical of so many cottages
Pauline Harrison

The village post office, Beeley, with its thatched roof. The Methodist Chapel is shown on Chapel Hill
Pauline Harrison

Beeley c1915. This house was built for the Holmes family c1845, on Devonshire Square facing the Devonshire Arms Inn. The thatched shop and post office is on the corner of Chapel Hill, at its junction with Devonshire Square. The trap nearest to the post office contains Lewis Reeve, landlord of the Devonshire Arms and his son, Frank

Joyce Gowen

Beeley Post Office, shop and Refreshment Room when Harry Reeve was in charge, c1930s. Harry Reeve and daughter Joyce stand in the doorway. Motor vehicles could be hired by this time and the shop had one of the few phones in the village. The thatched roof was removed in 1949, the roof level was raised and the dormer window also removed

Pauline Harrison and Joyce Gowen

Beeley Post Office and Refreshment Room in July 1902. It was run by Mary and Thomas Burdekin. In the doorway stand Nelly Louise Burdekin and Emily Burdekin, their daughters. The newspaper in the window declares "The King's Illness". The coronation of Edward VII should have been held but had to be postponed due to his illness. However, the village celebrations went ahead

Joyce Gowen

Beeley c1951. The village post office and shop, run by the Massheder family, has just had its thatched roof replaced with tiles

Joyce Gowen

Devonshire Square, Beeley, in the late 1940s
Joyce Gowen

estate flour mill which was close to Chatsworth House. The lower weir to the mill was built in 1774, to raise the water level in the river where a headrace took water underground to within a short distance of the mill, where it was joined by a small stream running from a spring. The present weir of millstone grit was built in 1838. The mill was finally used to store animal food until 1952, but in 1962, a severe storm brought two trees crashing down upon it to demolish part of the structure.

The old road from Matlock to Chatsworth used to go through the heart of the village of Beeley. It left by **Pig Lane** (so named because of a group of pig sties located there, which were converted into part of a dwelling in the 1980's) and crossed the River Derwent by Mill Bridge, near the old ruined mill building in Chatsworth Park.

However, in 1761, James Paine designed and built the **One Arch Bridge** that we see and use today. The road that enters Beeley from Chesterfield via Beeley Moor was a new road made early in the 19th century. Virtually the only "new" houses in Beeley are to be found at the bottom of this road, in the form of council houses, some of which were built in the years after the Great War and others in the 1960's.

The bottom of Chapel Hill, Beeley, c1905. The smithy, (now a village shop and café), is the building on the right, in the middle distance. By the 1930s it was still in operation and was run by the village blacksmith, Tom Wall, who also had premises at Rowsley and Pilsley

Pauline Harrison and Joyce Gowen

'The Croft' or 'Thatched Cottage', off Pig Lane, c1905. Frances Roose is shown standing. At the time of publication of this book, the refurbished cottage is the home of former Labour Cabinet Minister, David Blunkett

Joyce Gowen

33

*William Harrison
of Beeley
('Woodbine Willy')
with horse and cart at
Fallinge Farm. Later he
worked in the sawmills
at Calton Lees, Edensor*
Pauline Harrison

Beeley Football Team playing on the meadow across the road from Devonshire Square, c1906
BACK ROW: *X, S. Hallowes, C. Buckley, S. Grafton*
MIDDLE ROW: *G. Burdekin, R. Morton, E. Morton*
FRONT ROW: *G. Hawksworth, W. Gilbert, F. Wagstaff, T. Stone, G. Buckley*
Gordon Bowering

The Reverend Howard Chadwick, vicar of Beeley (1917-1925), had presided over a parish council meeting in May 1919 at which he castigated the condition of certain housing and the resulting overcrowding, as well as the lack of reasonable sanitation in parts of the village of Beeley. He caused some controversy when he claimed that these conditions could result in the settlement being classed as a slum village (in the summer months there was often a shortage of adequate water). It is probably as a result of these problems that the earlier group of council houses was eventually constructed.

At the far end of Brookside was an area of land owned, not by the Chatsworth estate, but by the Odd Fellows Manchester Unity Friendly Society, who rented out the land and properties on it. This area became known as the "Club Yard", but nowadays all these properties are privately owned.

We have seen how the various Lodges of the Friendly Societies in the different villages raised money for the local hospitals, but also on their own account, so that members of the Lodge who had paid their subscriptions could draw upon the money raised to pay for visits to the doctor and hospital in time of need, or if they were out of work for a period. The "Club Feast Day" at Beeley was a special occasion in the village, featuring a special service, a parade around the streets and lanes behind a brass band, with the Lodge banner proudly unfurled, followed by a meal and sports. During the first three decades of the 20th century, Timmy Ray, together with his wife and daughters, arrived in his gypsy-style caravan and set up the swing boats, coco-nut shies and stalls. Two large traction engines called "Big Sally" and "Little Sally" drove the various attractions and at the end of their stay the two thirsty engines would drain the troughs of water alongside the country lanes as they progressed to their next venue and their eventual "wintering" quarters at Hartington.

The building in the village known as **"Duke's Barn"** was built in 1791 as stabling for the 5th Duke's shire horses, whilst cart horses and drays that provided transport for the estate farms were also housed there. A shed at the rear of the building housed a traction engine which transported damsons to the Tansley Dye Works of Drabbles Mill and ice to Cromford Canal, returning with a load of coal from Cromford wharf, in the days before this fuel could be obtained from the newly built railway station and sidings at Rowsley.

Duke's Barn and a large playing field were given by the 11th Duke of Devonshire to the Derby Royal School for the Deaf in 1987 and the School restored and re-fitted out the Barn as a countryside centre for the deaf and disabled. This changed in 2001 when, as the Ron Beddoes Outdoor Centre, it was funded and run as an independent charity, enabling schools and other groups to use the centre for outdoor pursuits.

"**Beeley School**" was built alongside Duke's Barn in 1841, as a gift of the Duke of Devonshire, for the education of the younger estate workers. By the mid 1870's, just over 90 children of school age lived in the village, with the older boys being transferred to Edensor School, situated on the green at Edensor.

A bell dating from 1670, having hung in the chancel of Beeley Church until 1841, was now hung in a small belfry on the roof of the school and called the children to attend. When the school closed in 1968 and was converted into two bungalows, the bell was eventually returned to the church. Until the 1870 Education Act was passed, it was the Duke of Devonshire who paid the teachers' salaries, having provided and maintained the buildings since 1841.

During this period we hear of absenteeism at the school due to the children helping out on the farms during the busy times of the farming calendar, such as hay making, or when bilberries and blackberries were ready to be gathered from the moors and hedgerows, and school numbers were low during the many occasions when epidemics of measles, diphtheria, scarlet fever and sickness in general, struck the village.

However, we also read in school accounts that during the 1870's and 1880's there were cases of absenteeism by pupils who were attempting to obtain money from the visitors to Chatsworth who had arrived at Rowsley Station and were making their way through Beeley. On a number of occasions, groups of girls were absent attempting to invite visitors to partake of tea, at a price, at their parents' homes in the village, whilst it was known for boys to go absent for a number of days at a time as they begged from the passing visitors.

It was in a field near the school that the celebrations for Queen Victoria's Golden and Diamond Jubilees were held.

Golden Jubilee Celebrations, 1887. A sum of £30 had been collected for jubilee day celebrations. A service was held in church at noon on June 21st 1887, the vicar, Reverend C. Sculthorpe officiating. The Birchover Band was engaged and preceded the procession around the village, hymns being sung en route. Dinner was served in a large room lent by Mr. Grafton, to which everyone in the village was invited. Again, on the Wednesday night, there was a tea for all who chose to partake of it. The vicar and his wife were energetic in making the arrangements. At night, a beacon was set ablaze by Mr. B. Morton on Beeley Hill Top.

On the day of the **Coronation of King George V and Queen Mary**, 1911, Beeley children received two Coronation souvenir mugs (one the gift of Her Grace, the Duchess of Devonshire, and the other from the Committee). Reverend J. Hewetson held a service at the church, followed by a tea for

Beeley schoolchildren pose as Carnival 'Royalty' during Coronation Year, 1953, close to Beeley Village Hall. Life was getting back to normal after the years of the Second World War
BACK ROW: *Doris Parker, Barbara Bond, Pamela Mayfield, Sandra Critchlow, Queen Beverley Allsop, Gwen Fearn, Heather Gilbert, Joy Hammersley*
FRONT ROW: *Janet Holmes, Geoffrey Fearn, Shirley Marsden*
Pauline Harrison

children and adults. Sports and dancing were held in the evening, the music supplied by Mr. J.E. Sutton's band.

The Church of St. Anne dates back to Saxon times, although the present structure shows evidence from the Norman period. It was originally a chapelry of Bakewell but became united with Baslow when the Duke of Devonshire purchased the living in 1764. After 1852 we find that both Edensor and Beeley churches were ministered by a priest-in-charge. In 1856, Joseph Paxton's son-in-law, G.H. Stokes, designed a new vicarage, at the cost of £1200.

The Norman pillars with Early English arches were removed from the church in 1869 when the nave was rebuilt, as it was also in the major restoration in 1883 by H. Cockbain, costing £2500. Only the Norman South doorway survived this restoration. Memorial windows to the 7th Duke and his third son, Lord Edward Cavendish, were included.

It is a long standing custom at weddings in St. Anne's Church, that the bride and groom must not use the west gate and must pay to leave by the narrower east gate, the wider one being used for funerals.

A **Wesleyan Methodist Chapel** was built at Beeley in 1806, at a cost of £95, after ten shillings had been paid to farmer William Brown for a plot of land. There had been competition with the Church of England in Beeley for some time. Some parishioners felt neglected spiritually because Beeley had to share its vicar with two other parishes and the vicar lived at Baslow between 1778 and 1852. Sometimes there would be no service at all and at most, only once a Sunday (the bell rang to warn the parishioners that a service would be taking place).

The chapel that was built on Chapel Lane, Beeley, in 1806, was considered unsafe by 1890 and so the building was demolished that year. It was rebuilt on the same site the following year at a cost of £912, with the 7th Duke providing additional land for the larger building. Built by W. Toft and E. Evans of Youlgreave, it was even provided with stabling for the preacher's horse in the basement (later, this area was used as a fuel store). The chapel sadly closed in 1996 and the premises became a private residence.

The Devonshire Arms dates from the 18th century and was possibly converted into a coaching inn and farm from three cottages in 1747. In the decade before the Great War and in the years immediately after that conflict, its proprietor was Lewis Reeve, who we shall find lost two sons during the war.

The area in front of the inn is called Devonshire Square and across from the building are the three Y-shaped "Paxton Cottages", designed by G.H. Stokes, son-in-law of Joseph Paxton. They were built to re-house villagers from Edensor, when that settlement was re-developed in 1856.

Also across the Square from the inn, and at the bottom corner of Chapel Lane, was the Post Office and village shop, run in the late 19th century and into the 1930's by members of the Burdekin and Reeve families. During the time it was operated by Harry Reeve and his wife during the 1920's and 30's, Harry ran a taxi business from the premises and also provided hospitality at a tea room that was attached. During the short period when navvies were improving the water scheme from the Derwent Dams along the Derwent Valley, he even converted part of the tea room into sleeping accommodation for the workmen. As with so many other villages, Beeley lost its Post Office and shop when it closed in 1990.

The Village Blacksmith and Forge was also to be found on Chapel Lane, just a little higher up the lane from the Post Office and on the opposite side of the road (nowadays the premises are used as a café and gift shop). During the years after the Great War it was being worked by Sam Wall and then into the 1930's by his son, Tom. The family also ran similar premises in Rowsley and Pilsley.

EDENSOR

Following the Norman Conquest of 1066, the settlement of Edensor was given by the King to Henry de Ferrers, but in Tudor times, in 1549, Bess of Hardwick and her husband, Sir William Cavendish, bought it, together with the settlement of Chatsworth. The old village lay between the river and a road through the Park, and was set out in a straggling line down to the Derwent.

We have already seen that in the 18th century, in the time of the 4th Duke of Devonshire, Capability Brown, the landscape developer, and architect James Paine, were employed to straighten out the river, beginning in 1757, and to extend the Park to the west. Prior to this, the Derwent had formed the western boundary of Chatsworth Park, with Edensor being outside the Park, as it lay on the west bank and up the hill beyond.

A new road was built above the west bank and it was during this period that those houses within view of the West Wing of Chatsworth House were demolished. The old mill and Edensor bridge were demolished and James Paine designed the new One Arch Bridge near Beeley and the 5th Duke

Edensor Church of England School, July 1912, situated on the village green
Derek Neave

Edensor Boys School, on the green in front of the church. Built in 1841, on the site of a former school,
it was demolished in 1950, the stone being used to build the first pair of Hartington Memorial
Cottages in Pilsley, in 1950. A tree, planted by the Dowager Duchess of Devonshire,
now marks the site
Derek Neave

removed the few houses still remaining in view from the House.

After removing Edensor tenants to new or temporary housing at Pilsley and Beeley in the period around 1838 - 1840, the 6th Duke of Devonshire decided to demolish the rest of the houses in Edensor old village, with the exception of "Park Cottage", the house nowadays standing to the east of the road running through the Park. The work was supervised under the direction of Joseph Paxton, the Duke's Head Gardener. "Park Cottage" is the only building to remain that used to be on the High Street of the old village. Enclosed by stone walls, it is said that the 6th Duke did not demolish it because it was occupied by an elderly employee. The new road through the Park no longer passed through the village.

Paxton employed John Robertson as architectural assistant from 1840 to 1846, and then George Henry Stokes took over this role (he also became Paxton's son-in-law after marrying Emily Paxton). Paxton now began to make Edensor a model village, enclosing it and remodelling the existing houses. Most of the original houses in the eastern part of the old village were demolished, with the exception of a few that were re-roofed and faced.

The village was now arranged around two uphill roads, either side of the old church (it would be a few years later that a new church was constructed,

A group of pupils from Edensor Boys School c1890
J. Richmond

Edensor Church of England School in July 1912. A number of the older children in the photograph would serve in the forces during the Great War. The teachers are school mistress K. Hutchinson and headmaster, A. E. Wragg
Derek Neave

41

Entrance Lodges to Chatsworth Park in 1915
Chris Heathcote

dominating the village). The houses were designed and built in a wide variety of styles from Robertson's architectural patent book. Norman, Gothic, Jacobean, Italianate and castellated all appeared and one can see a Swiss Cottage, a Norman house and a Tudor cottage amongst many others.

At the entrance to the model village is a triangular green upon which the village school was built in 1841. To the right, inside the entrance gate, is a **Castellated Entrance Lodge** built in 1842 to Robertson's design and which was once the post office, whilst to the left, on the left side of Japp Lane, Paxton and Robertson altered the roof and facade of the old Talbot Inn to form a Swiss Chalet style design, the house nowadays being called "**The Italian Villa**". The nearby **Norman Fountain**, designed by Robertson in 1841, was on the site of the Talbot Inn Yard and brew house.

The **Post Office** (sadly recently closed), **Tearoom and Post Office Cottage** were originally a large farmhouse which was remodelled by Paxton. The Tea-room used to be an outbuilding to the farmhouse.

Continuing up Japp Lane, the present **Vicarage** was in the Georgian style, but into the 20th century it became the home of Gerry Hartopp, one of the agents to the Duke of Devonshire, when he arrived in 1920, and then the home of Francis Thompson, the Chatsworth librarian. It then became the Vicarage in 1973 when the Old Vicarage lost its former role and was divided into two properties. The Old Vicarage had once been the principal house in

Edensor from the west, c1906
Derek Neave

Chatsworth Hotel, at Edensor, in 1906.
Today, it is the site of the Edensor Institute (Cavendish Club) and the Estate Offices
Derek Neave

the old village during the 18th century.

As one views the village from the entrance gate, the lane to the right of the church is known as Edensor Lane and many of the houses on its right hand side were new houses, designed afresh by Robertson and Stokes, not old ones simply updated. It is interesting to note that all these houses were designed for their appearance to the outside world, to be on show, whilst the insides consisted of lots of small rooms that today tend to pose problems for modern living. The houses on **Daisy Bank**, to the left of Edensor Lane, had new facades built on to the old back walls and new roofs were added.

To preserve the idea of a model village, a common drying ground and laundry area had to be hidden away from view. This area was on flat ground behind the house known as **Deerlands**, on the right of Edensor Lane. The same desire to "hide away" was deemed necessary with regards to vegetable gardens and pig sties, with the allotments being incorporated into the design by being placed at the very top of the village, with buildings also included there to house the livestock.

Edensor Village School for boys was sited on the village green, near to the entrance, and was built in 1841 for 60 boys and 20 infants. There had been an earlier school and adjoining cottage and workshops on the same site but this was demolished, ready for the construction of the new school. Robertson's design was in the Italian style. The roof had two belfries and at the west end was a wall concealing a yard in which the fuel store and toilets were located. The boys from Beeley School attended Edensor when they were nine years of age, whilst the girls remained at Beeley. Mr. Wragg was the last school headmaster, living at the School house, and for 50 years he was also the choir master and organist at the church.

The School was demolished in 1950, as the building was no longer required and the Duke of Devonshire requested that the stone be used to build the first pair of the **Hartington Memorial Cottages** in Pilsley that same year, as a memorial to his eldest son, William Cavendish, Marquis of Hartington, who was killed in action in 1944, whilst serving in the Coldstream Guards. On one gable end of the Memorial Cottages is the crest of the Coldstream Guards in an oval, and in a second oval is the Cavendish crest. A second pair of matching cottages were built in 1970.

Edensor House, at the lower end of Edensor Lane, was originally a single storey farmhouse, designed by Decimus Burton in 1836. It remained a farm-house until 1853, but after the 6th Duke's death in 1858, the building was altered and the house enlarged. It became the home of the Duke of Devon-shire's agent, John Gregory Cottingham, and by 1909 the agent living there was John Pepys Cockerell and his wife (we shall find that they would lose their son in the Great War).

This tradition of agents of the Dukes of Devonshire living there continued into the 1940's. Gerry Hartopp was one of four agents working under the chief agent, Sir Roland Burke, looking after the outlying estates. Eventually, Gerry Hartopp left Edensor House to live at Barbrook, and from 1947 until 1959, the 11th Duke and Duchess of Devonshire lived there until they moved into Chatsworth House.

The outbuildings of Edensor House were used to stable draught horses until 1910, when these buildings were converted into the estate offices for Chatsworth. The horses were then kept in the newly built Stud Farm at Pilsley (nowadays the site of Pilsley Farm Shop and restaurant). In 1958 the estate offices were eventually moved from the former stable block to their

The Chatsworth camp of the Derbyshire Imperial Yeomanry in 1905. The camera is looking towards the 'Golden Gates'. Nine years later, the Yeomanry would depart for service at Gallipoli and later Salonika

Derek Neave

Sawmill staff at Calton Lees Sawmill on the Chatsworth Estate in 1910

J. Duncan

Between 1901 and 1916, the Howden and Derwent Reservoirs were constructed for the Derwent Valley Water Board by construction workers living in the temporary tin village of Birchinlee (Howden opened in 1912 and Derwent in 1916). A water pipeline was constructed through the Derwent Valley by gangs of navvies. Here, the pipeline is being laid through Chatsworth Park in March 1906. Temporary rail lines were constructed and small locomotives used

Chris Heathcote

Another view of the laying of the pipeline for the Derwent Valley Water Scheme through Chatsworth Park, March 1906

Chris Heathcote

Navvies working on constructing the water pipeline across Chatsworth Park in 1906.
Mrs. Windle from Rose Cottage (now Nailstone Cottage), Baslow, is ready to serve out refreshments
for the men. Mrs. Windle was the sister of Robert Bates, who would be killed during the Great War
Doris Brightmore

One of the locomotives used on the temporary railway line through Chatsworth Park, helping in the
construction of the water pipeline
Derek Neave

Two Chatsworth Inter-Departmental Teams are ready for their game of cricket, 1890
BACK ROW: *? Read, W. Brightmore, H. Wall, ? Lomas, H. Fletcher, ? Baker, C. Bacon, J. Hudson,*
J. Edge, J. Evans, X
MIDDLE ROW: *C. Bestwick, ? Kenworthy, C. Watson, A. Foster, X, J. Staley*
FRONT ROW: *R, James, F. Dale, H. Brightmore, W. Evans, R. Broomhead*
Gordon Bowering

present premises in the Edensor Institute building, and at this time the old estate offices were converted into the Cavendish Flats, which still perform that role today for employees and former employees of the estate.

The Park Lodge Houses are sited at the entrance to the Park and consist on the left, in the direction of Pilsley, of "**Tudor Lodge**", built in the style of an Old English lodge and on the right of "**The Lodge**", built in an Italian style, both houses being designed by Jeffrey Wyattville and built in 1837. Two similar lodges were planned for the Beeley end of the Park but never materialised. It is an interesting fact that the gates at both ends of the Park were locked at 10p.m. each night until the Council took over the upkeep of the roads.

The Edensor Inn, just outside the Park gates, was designed by Joseph Pickford of Derby and was known also as the Chatsworth Inn, later becoming the Edensor Institute and later still the Cavendish Club. It was built between 1776 and 1777 of red brick, the brick earth being dug from the Park and burned in kilns that had been specially constructed for this task. There had been an older inn near the Park gates but its reputation became poor and it had been demolished.

The new Edensor Inn or Hotel, though of red brick, was originally rendered. It was spared during the re-modelling of the village and in 1827 was enlarged as more visitors arrived to view Chatsworth House and its newly built West Wing.

The Inn had 12 bedrooms and stabling for 40 horses near the end of its time as an inn. Early in the 20th century the inn became the village institute, with the kitchen wing being demolished and a ballroom took its place. The rendering was now removed and in buildings behind the Institute, there was communal bathing facilities provided and accommodation for single men employed on the estate. Part of the Institute was used as a cinema, showing silent films during the 1920's.

Early in the 20th century, **Teapot Row**, a group of four houses, opposite the Institute, was built. They were believed to have got this name because of the large quantities of tea drunk by the builders, employed by the Ashford firm of Cox-Wilson.

A medieval church stood on the same site as the present **Church of St. Peter**. It had a lead roof, a square, squat tower and battlemented parapets. Although we have seen that it was the 6th Duke of Devonshire who had the village of Edensor re-modelled, in the 1840's and 50's, it was the 7th Duke who rebuilt the church. It took two years to demolish the old church and prepare the foundations, for the Cavendish Memorial to the 1st Earl of Devonshire had to be carefully dealt with. A quarry was reopened locally to supply the necessary stone. There had been four bells in the old tower. One dated 1669, now hangs over the Stable Block at Chatsworth House. The other

Chatsworth Football Club, 1912
Standing: *Allan Bowering, ? Staley, Richard Morton, ? Evans, J. Hibbert, ? Ford*
Kneeling: *F. Sheldon, S. Holmes, W. Gilbert, S. Burdekin, C. Brightmore*
Gordon Bowering

Chatsworth playing at home to Bolton Abbey team, 1920s
Gordon Bowering

Cricket at Chatsworth, c1929
FRONT ROW: *X, X, X (three Duke's sisters), Duchess of Devonshire, 9th Duke of Devonshire, William Cavendish, Lord Hartington, Elizabeth Cavendish, X, X*
Andrew Cavendish sits on the grass
Gordon Bowering

three were recast in 1867 and form part of the six bells in the new tower.

The eminent Victorian architect, George Gilbert Scott, was appointed for the church's design, shortly after he had just won the competition for the designs of both the Albert Memorial in London and the Home and Foreign Offices in Whitehall. It was he who had also designed St. Pancras Station and Hotel.

By September 1864 the design had been approved and work began in December of that year. Certain stones from the old church were included in its construction, whilst the South Porch, with its semicircular Norman door-head, was dismantled and included, several feet to the west. It was also Scott who designed many of the interior furnishings and fittings.

The Early English tower and spire rose to a grand height of 166 feet, dominating the village. The Cavendish Chapel was built both as a semi-private family chapel and also to house the Jacobean monument to William, 1st Earl of Devonshire and his brother, Henry Cavendish, two sons of Bess of Hardwick. Lord Frederick Cavendish, murdered in Phoenix Park, Dublin, in 1882, also lies here.

The magnificent timber roof to the nave resembled the hull of a great ship turned upside down, whilst the pulpit, designed by Scott, displayed a fine range of local marbles. Meanwhile, the old churchyard was extended south-wards and included a Cavendish Burial Ground. Here lie members of the present Duke's ancestors, including the 6th Duke of Devonshire, whilst nearby is the grave of his Head Gardener, Joseph Paxton. Also close by lies the grave of Kathleen Cavendish, sister of President John F. Kennedy and wife of William Cavendish, Marquis of Hartington, who was killed during the Second World War, shortly after their marriage. Sadly, she was killed in an air crash, four years after the death of her husband.

The cost of the new church of St. Peter's, paid for by the 7th Duke of Devonshire, was £14,000, a vast sum of money for that period. Completed in 1870, the new church was consecrated in that same year.

Just beyond Teapot Row and the gate lodges lies the small hamlet of **Dunsa**, consisting of six houses. Its most prominent building is Dunsa Villa (now called Dunsa House), an Italianate villa with similarities to the style of Barbrook, the former home of Sir Joseph Paxton, and Park Lodge, Baslow. It was built to a design by Joseph Paxton around 1848 for the 6th Duke's friend, Miss Thornhill.

The Kennels are a pair of cottages, with the outbuildings behind them being part of Dunsa Farm. These outbuildings are now used by the game-keepers on the estate for storing the deer larder, and the Head Gamekeeper now lives at Dunsa. All the tractors for Chatsworth estate are stored centrally at Dunsa Farm, whilst the pheasant chicks on the estate are reared in incubators at Dunsa.

In June 1887, the model village of Edensor joined with Pilsley for the holding of **Queen Victoria's Golden Jubilee Celebrations**. The arrangements were taken in hand by Mr. G. Martin, Steward to the Duke of Devonshire, Mr. Whitehead, Mr. E. Swain, the vicar, the Reverend J. Hall, Mr. Turnbull and others.

Two large marquees were erected near Edensor, one for dancing and the other providing the venue for a meal. The children met at the Chatsworth Hotel and from there proceeded to church, where the vicar preached a thanksgiving service. Headed by the Baslow Band they returned to the tents subsequently and partook of a good dinner, provided solely by Mrs. Harrison. Those over 15 years of age had dinner at the expense of the Committee. About £60 had been subscribed for the festival. There were sports, fireworks and a beacon fire in the evening. The children were presented with medals in commemoration of the jubilee.

Edensor was again en fete on the occasion of **King George V's Coronation**, 1911. At 10a.m. a presentation of Coronation medals and mugs was made, the latter being a gift of the Duchess of Devonshire to the children. Afterwards, a church service was held and at 12-30p.m. a luncheon was served in the Chatsworth Hotel. Sports were arranged and a tea taken. At night, a bonfire was lit and fireworks set off and proceedings ended with a dance in the school, to music supplied by Robertson's Estate Band.

PILSLEY

Known as Pirelaie at the time of the Domesday Book, 1086, and belonging to Henry de Ferrers and then the Foljambe family as part of the ecclesiastical parish of Edensor, the village was known as Pilsley by the 1570's.

The village was on an old packhorse route and once consisted of houses along a single street (High Street). The rest of the village was planned, especially when it was extended to re-house estate workers in the 18th century after the 4th Duke demolished their houses in Edensor. The school, school house and some of the buildings around the green date from construction work in the time of the 6th Duke, when he also re-located other Edensor folk during the 1840's period of building by Joseph Paxton.

The High Street went past **Top House** and nowadays splits into three paths or tracks. In the past, these were packhorse routes, with salt and lead being carried, and on this street were once three inns or ale houses to cater for these travellers and often the "jaggers" or packhorse men would change the packhorses at Pilsley before starting off again over the moors.

Farming was the chief occupation, for by the 1830's, of the 45 families in the village, nearly 30 were employed on the land. Many of the cottages were smallholdings, with strips of land at the rear of the premises.

Some alterations came in the 1840's as the 6th Duke bought land and properties and he and Paxton made their additions. The 60 houses that make up the village today are all owned by the Chatsworth estate. The Chapel was built during this period and was used until its closure in the 1940's, when it has since been used as a village hall, school canteen, store and is now used as an annexe to the school, housing a computer suite.

We have already seen that in much earlier days there were three ale houses on High Street and even in 1835 there was the "Snake and Crown" to keep the "Devonshire Arms" company. However, by 1850, only the Devonshire Arms remained as a hostelry in Pilsley.

Built in 1739, the **Devonshire Arms** was originally run by the Harrison family, who were also farmers, and the small farmyard at the rear of the premises remained until the 1950's, operating on 20 acres of land. From 1852 to 1937 the Newton family kept the inn, with John Newton, his wife and daughter, running it throughout the 1920's and into the late 1930's.

The present **Post Office and Village Shop** has played this role in village affairs for many years. It has also functioned as a bakery until 1962. From the early 1890's to the mid 1920's, George Siddons was the baker, even delivering bread to Chatsworth House, as well as supplying to local shops and houses, by means of his horse and trap.

After a period in the late 1920's and early 1930's, when it was operated by baker and Wesleyan local preacher, Mr. Garfoot, George Simpson arrived

The Devonshire Arms Inn, Pilsley. the man in the doorway is Johnnie Newton, the innkeeper.
His wife and daughter continued to run the inn until 1937

J. Duncan

from Horncastle in Lincolnshire, to take over the bakery and shop. It was he who combined the bakery with the running of a village shop and post office. Helping him in the bakery were his wife, grandfather and son.

The bake house was at the rear of the building and contained two ovens and a stoke hole. Steam was used to heat the ovens, with coke being the fuel used to provide the heat, which rose to a temperature of 450 degrees. The bake house consumed up to three barrows of coke per day.

In the second storey of the bake house was the dough mixing machine run by a two stroke motor, and then, before the Second World War, by electricity. The building eventually had a metal railway line inserted to strengthen it because the action of the mixer caused the floorboards to shake in a worrying manner. The narrow lane alongside the shop was known as Bun Alley and at the end of it were sheds, where delivery vehicles could be stored.

Around 250 loaves were baked daily, as well as cakes and pastries. A hand-cart was taken round the village by Ken Simpson to deliver to the households. Cliff College, between Calver and Baslow, was supplied with large sandwich loaves before the Second World War, whilst the Still Room at Chatsworth House was supplied daily with 40 loaves. George Simpson was kept extra busy during the war years supplying bread to the staff and girl pupils of Penrhos College, who had been evacuated to Chatsworth House from

The bakery and shop of George S. Siddons, Pilsley.
He had made bread for Chatsworth House since 1894
J. Duncan

Colwyn Bay, in September 1939 and remained at the House until 1946.

The village green at Pilsley would have looked somewhat different before the Second World War. It was only in 1959 that the eight Mary Devonshire cottages (named after the 10th Duke's wife) were built facing the green to accommodate extra office staff on the estate. They were built from local materials on the site of former farm buildings, including a joinery shop. During the Second World War, the upper parts of these outbuildings had been used to store food stuffs and paper for re-cycling for the war effort.

Mains water is now supplied to the village, but only from 1966. Prior to this it came by pipe from Park Gate Farm via the Paddocks, with the pipe crossing the Derwent on an old metal footbridge between Home Farm and Hare Park. On the green, across the road from the cottages near the post office, was where the water bore came into the village and taps were attached to stone posts that were sited around the village.

The village blacksmith lived at Smithy House and nearby, at the green, was the smithy itself, consisting of a room where horses were shod, including those from Pilsley Stud Farm (now the site of Pilsley Farm Shop and restaurant). Two huge fire places were always kept going, by means of bellows. Alongside was a yard where wheels and park gates were made.

Sam Wall, the last blacksmith to operate the forge, made the metal tyre for the wooden wheels, which were produced elsewhere. The steel rims were heated and bent in the forge and this ring was then again heated on a fire on the green. The white hot rim was then lifted by means of rods onto the wooden wheel, causing the wood to become alight, and the flaming wheel was plunged into the huge water trough, nine feet square, that was sited on the green. The metal shrank as it cooled and settled firmly onto the rim of the wheel. Sadly, as the Stud Farm became converted into a dairy and tractors replaced horses, Sam Wall's business declined.

The Stud Farm had been built in 1910 for the 9th Duke to stable his shire horse stud. It was built of stone from the local quarry at the top of High Street, off Bradley Lane. The head groom lived at Top House, on High Street. In springtime, stallions were walked by their horsemen to farms all around the county to serve the mares, and mares were sometimes brought to the Stud Farm.

This continued into the 1950's, but with the arrival of the tractor the Stud horse was phased out of work on the farm and, as we have seen, the Stud Farm was converted first into a dairy (containing 40 Jersey cows that had been kept until then at Churchdale Hall, Ashford) and then to its present role as a farm shop and restaurant.

Duck Row, Pilsley, was once the route north east out of the village and the cottages on the lane are the oldest in the village (one dates from 1709 and

Pilsley Well Dressings in 1898. Looking down High Street towards Duck Row
Gordon Bowering

Pilsley, c1910. The cottage that once stood in the middle of the photograph is now a pile of rubble. To the right is Duck Row, with the bay-windowed house having once been a coaching inn
Chris Heathcote

Pilsley well dressing, c1882
The cottage behind the well dressing was demolished between 1900 and 1912
J. Duncan

Well dressing in Pilsley village, c1898.
LEFT TO RIGHT: *W. Moore, J. Bark, J. Sheldon, W. Evans, Fred Newton, S. Newton*
Gordon Bowering

Well dressing at Pilsley, c1912/1913
LEFT TO RIGHT: *Bill Vickers, Jim Bark, E. Evans, F. Haynes, B. Gill*
The Cavendish coat-of-arms figured prominently
J. Duncan

Pilsley, c1900. Looking down from the top end of the High Street. Behind the lady with the dog is the
Alphabet Stone, set into the high wall. The house next to the wall, is believed to have been used as
Pilsley School and was called 'School House', before changing its name to Rock Cottage
Gordon Bowering

The Alphabet Stone set into the wall next to School House (now called Rock Cottage), Pilsley
Gordon Bowering

Performing the maypole dance on May Day 1933 at Pilsley School.
Fred Fearn stands in the centre of the photograph
Fred Fearn

Pilsley School, c1932
BACK ROW: *X, X, X, X, X, X, Gordon Bowering, X, X*
NEXT ROW: *X, X, X, X, X, X, Gwen Duffy, X*
NEXT ROW: *X, X, X, Elizabeth Booth, X, X, X, X, X*
NEXT ROW: *Cyril Brumby, Fred Fearn, Charles Roose, X, X, X, X, X*
FRONT ROW: *Ted Bond, Fred Bater, Billy Roose, Trevor Parry, Eric Bowering*
Gordon Bowering

Pilsley High Street, c1941
Gordon Bowering

1953 Pilsley Coronation Day Fancy Dress
BACK ROW: *Joan Harris, Betty Ward, Leonard Broom, Ian Shimwell, Ernest Evans*
NEXT ROW: *Gwen Duffy, Mrs. Clegg, Joyce Turner, Carol Holmes, Margaret Hadfield*
NEXT ROW: *Elaine Broom, John Holmes, X, David Clegg, X*
NEXT ROW: *Norman Turner, X, Susan Ward, Robert Lee, Owen Jones, Dennis Bond, John Holmes,*
Derek Neave
FRONT ROW: *X, X, Jimmy Hulley, X, Carol Edmundson, Neil Edmundson, ? Rowland*
Gordon Bowering

another from 1753). Pig sties can be found at the bottom of the gardens.

It is known that the property with a large bay window was once a coaching inn. In the early days of well dressing activities, a duck made from flowers stood at the end of the row, spouting water from its beak. The first known such festivities date from 1840, and from early days the well design had the Cavendish coat of arms depicted. The clay, into which the flowers and foliage were pressed, came from a wood near Hassop, called "Clay Pits".

On June 22nd 1897, Pilsley, from the earliest hours, was one mass of bunting as it celebrated **Queen Victoria's Diamond Jubilee (60 years as monarch)**. Large flags were floating from the prominent buildings, as well as on the Recreation Ground, where the sports took place.

A huge marquee had been erected on the Green, in the centre of the village. At 12 o'clock, the whole of the adult population, 14 years of age and upwards, sat down here to a roast beef meal. The band rendered a selection of music during the meal. A royal toast was drunk and a procession formed, headed by the band. Everyone received a medal and they marched to the Recreation Ground where sports were performed.

At 5p.m. a meat tea was provided for all 250 inhabitants, in the large marquee. By 6p.m., everyone was again on the Recreation Ground where various amusements took place, especially for the children. Dancing to the strains of the band took place at 7-30p.m. until 9-30p.m., when, preceded by the tones of Highland bagpipes, a procession formed, but this time the Pilsley Town Head was the destination and here, an enormous bonfire, 20 feet in diameter, was lighted at the firing of a rocket signal at 10p.m. The *National Anthem* was sung, fireworks followed and dancing was then resumed until the early hours.

Rock House on High Street is believed to have once been a school in the village, with a stone in the nearby wall containing the inscriptions of letters of the alphabet. The present **Village School** was built on a design by Joseph Paxton for 122 pupils, in 1849, at a cost of £513. There was one main classroom, warmed originally by a fireplace, with another classroom sited underneath the school. The clock on the gable end was from J. Smith and Sons of Derby.

As the chapter now draws to a conclusion, it is hoped that these impressions of Beeley, Edensor and Pilsley, as portrayed through words and photographs in the previous pages, will give some idea of what life in these five villages was like in the years before the Great War and during the inter-war years. The men whose lives are told within the following pages of this book were connected in one way or another with the Chatsworth villages and the landscape round about. As the momentous events of July and early August 1914 unfolded in Europe, leading to war, the happiness of many families within these villages was shattered as news came back of the loss of their loved ones on the battlefields of the Great War.

CHAPTER TWO

1914 – INTO THE MAELSTROM

We have already seen that the assassination by Gavrilo Princip of Archduke Franz Ferdinand, heir to the Austro-Hungarian Empire, and his wife, the Duchess of Hohenberg, in Sarajevo, triggered the march towards hostilities. The assassination on June 28th 1914 was the 9/11 moment of the early 20th century. One terrorist attack and the world shifted on its axis, bringing war and chaos in its wake.

From a Serb peasant family, Princip was radicalised by reading Nietzsche as well as nationalist and socialist literature after being rejected from military service for physical weakness. He fell in love with his co-conspirator's sister but was rejected because of his lack of sophistication. He hung around cafés and fell in with equally aimless young men politically.

Almost everything about the Sarajevo assassination of 1914 was driven by fate and accident. It was a malign destiny that placed Princip outside Moritz Schiller's delicatessen on the riverside road in Sarajevo only six feet away from where the archduke's car momentarily stopped to change gear into reverse, because the chauffeur had taken a wrong turning. Princip fired twice, killing the archduke and his wife. "Sophie! Sophie! Don't die," were Franz Ferdinand's anguished words. "Live for our children."

(*** *Princip tried to commit suicide after the shooting, yet the revolver was wrenched from his hand, the bomb in his pocket fell out as he was held by the crowd, and the cyanide capsule he swallowed merely left him vomiting. After his trial, he was committed to prison and it was there that he died from tuberculosis in 1918, aged 23*).

It is true to say that enthusiasm for war was high amongst the populations of the belligerent nations. Throughout the European capitals, vast crowds swept onto the streets, each voicing support for their country's hostile stance. The belief in a successful, brief but bloody war was held by all armies.

The primary reason that the incident turned into a global war was Austria's suspicion that Serbia was behind the murder. The assassination had resulted in Austria presenting Serbia with impossible conditions to avoid annexation; Russia immediately mobilised in support of her fellow Slavs, Germany responded at once and France followed suit. Mobilisation plans were fully dependent on the railway timetable and once this was initiated, it was difficult for the diplomats to halt the process.

On Tuesday August 4th, 4,300 trains, decorated with flowers and tricolour flags, overflowed with a noisy, enthusiastic mass of young men in old fashioned uniforms and resounded with an endless chanting of the "Marseillaise". The trains were carrying the French Army towards the German Army, which was moving to meet it in 11,000 trains.

Hopes that Great Britain could somehow stay out of the conflict were dashed, when, following the long prepared Schlieffen Plan, German forces entered neutral Belgium, en route to Northern France.

The days before war was declared by Britain had been the Bank Holiday weekend and Monday August 3rd was the day for a trip out. The weather was beautiful, with brilliant blue skies and a warm temperature, ideal for a visit to the seaside. Thousands flocked to the railway stations across Britain to catch special trains bound for the coast. However, the First Lord of the Admiralty, Winston Churchill, had mobilised the fleet and all excursion trains were taken over by naval reservists.

Sunday August 2nd witnessed church services at Beeley providing special

Gatherings of the Oddfellows Societies, similar to this one at St Mary's Church, South Darley, were taking place in the three Chatsworth villages during the weeks leading up to the Great War
Keith Taylor

hymns, psalms and prayers, with sermons preached on the imminent perils.

At 4p.m. on August 4th the British Army was mobilised. Britain demanded that the German Army be withdrawn from Belgium by midnight August 4th or a state of war would exist between the British Empire and Germany. The ultimatum was ignored and war was declared at 11p.m. The Great War had begun.

In British cities everywhere, excitement reigned. On August 5th 1914 the pride of London's famous streets poured into the recruiting offices at Great Scotland Yard and elsewhere. They had come from watching Surrey play Notts at the Oval. Some still carried memories of the scene outside Buckingham Palace the previous night when they had sung *God Save The King*.

Reverend Joseph Hewetson of Beeley 1911-1917
Vernon Mather

The nearby market town of Bakewell always attracted crowds of visitors on August Bank Holiday Monday, but owing to the shadow of war, the town was unusually quiet, with fewer visitors than usual, owing to the fact that certain railway facilities had been curtailed. Thoughts for the forthcoming 66th Bakewell Show on Wednesday August 5th were also to the forefront of the minds of show officials.

The news of war was announced to Bakewell and district folk at a large gathering in Rutland Square, Bakewell, on Wednesday August 5th. That same day the Bakewell Show went ahead, despite the war clouds, but the entries of cattle were affected when the Midland Railway Company wired to the effect that they were unable to convey cattle to the Show owing to the uncertainty of the train service (there would be no further Bakewell Shows until 1920).

In 1914 Britain was essentially a maritime power, with only a small, if highly trained and professional army. Only 120,000 men would initially make up the British Expeditionary Force (BEF) that embarked for France, compared with some four million Frenchmen and four and a half million Germans.

Lord Kitchener shocked a meeting of the War Council on August 6th by predicting a long war; countering the popular cry of, "It will be all over by Christmas!" On August 7th, Kitchener publicly called for 100,000 volunteers. By September 12th, an amazing total of 480,000 men had enlisted as volunteers.

These are some of the local Territorials of the Sherwood Foresters at their summer camp, near Filey,
Yorkshire in late July, 1914, just before the declaration of war
Cliff Housley

A line of mounted Derbyshire Imperial Yeomanry troops
at the Chatsworth Annual Summer Camp, c1909
Derby Museum

Derbyshire Imperial Yeomanry mounted at summer camp, Chatsworth, pre-1914
Derby Museum

Map reading exercise for Derbyshire Imperial Yeomanry at summer camp, Hardwick Hall, 1913
Derby Museum

Church Service for Derbyshire Imperial Yeomanry at their summer camp, Hardwick Hall, 1913
Derby Museum

Derbyshire Imperial Yeomanry troops on reveiew at summer camp, Hardwick Hall, 1913
Derby Museum

Derbyshire Imperial Yeomanry kit inspection summer camp, c1900
Derby Museum

Bakewell and the district round about had fostered strong relations with the military. The old "Volunteers" had been around since Napoleonic times. The Derbyshire Imperial Yeomanry, an irregular mounted force, was raised in 1899 and served in South Africa during the Boer War. Chatsworth House and Hardwick Hall estates were used as summer training camps for the Yeomanry, whilst by 1900, a Territorial Company of the 6th Battalion Sherwood Foresters was also based in Bakewell, stationed in a camp on Coombs Road. Many men from Edensor, Pilsley and Beeley were members of either the Territorials or the Yeomanry and gave some of their spare time to training with these units, and as part time soldiers, were to be called up once war broke out.

On Sunday July 26th the local Territorials had left Bakewell Station by special train for their fifteen day annual camp at Hunmanby, three miles from Filey, Yorkshire. As war became almost certain, they returned early, on Tuesday August 4th, having left the north east coast on Monday night at 10p.m. Tuesday night also saw the King's proclamation posted in Buxton, Bakewell and Tideswell and the members of the Yeomanry prepared themselves and their horses in the various villages, ready to ride to Bakewell

Station, to be transported to their military destination.

After a night's rest, Beeley immediately sent their Territorials to gather in Bakewell. On the morning of departure, the vicar, the Reverend Joseph Hewetson (vicar 1911-1917), visited each personally and wished him God-speed and a safe return (the vicar was a breeder and exhibitor of poultry and on the previous weekend had won awards at the Liverpool and Hexham Shows).

The Duke of Devonshire had decided to take in, if necessary, 60 convalescents at Chatsworth from the start of the war. The beautiful little theatre at Chatsworth House would also be got ready as a temporary hospital. A course of ambulance lectures was being given daily by Dr. Edleston of Park Lodge, Baslow, son-in-law of Dr. Wrench. Those who were attending the classes were the women servants of the household and also the ladies at Baslow and Edensor who had volunteered to act as nurses or as ward maids (Voluntary Aid Detachment nurses or VAD's for short). Classes were also being held for the male servants.

On the outset of war, the 9th Duke had offered to the Red Cross the use of the ground floor of Devonshire House in Mayfair, London (probably the grandest of the great London mansions, between Berkeley Square and Picadilly). At the end of hostilities he was no longer able to afford the upkeep of the house, which was sold in 1920, and the Duke and Duchess then moved to a smaller house at 2 Carlton Gardens, off The Mall, the former residence of Lord Kitchener.

It had been arranged that the Stockdale Institute at Baslow should be held in readiness to be used as a convalescent home, with accommodation for 20 beds.

From 9p.m. to long after midnight on the evening of August 4th, large crowds had gathered outside the *Buxton Herald* newspaper office. During the evening, bulletins were continually posted in windows of the Herald Office, giving the latest developments. At 11-10p.m., an exclusive telephone message was published to the effect that there was every indication that war would be declared at midnight. This announcement was received with loud cheers, which were only surpassed by those which were accorded on the announcement that Buxton Territorials and Yeomanry had received orders to leave for active service on Wednesday morning. There followed lusty singing of *Rule Britannia* and the *National Anthem*.

One member of the Yeomanry received his orders at 11p.m. on Tuesday evening. At 11-10p.m. he had notified his employer and five minutes later he had made out his time sheet and was paid up with the assurance that his place would be kept open for him until his return.

Wednesday August 5th saw Buxton alive with excitement as the khaki-clad

Territorials and Yeomanry met at the drill hall on Rock Terrace to receive their medical inspection. At 11-25 a.m. the Yeomanry departed from Buxton's Midland Station, with horses, saddles and equipment on board. To the strains of *Rule Britannia* and the waving of handkerchiefs, they began their journey to Bakewell, where they would draw their main supply of horses. From village after village close to Bakewell, other members of the Yeomanry were setting off for the same destination, many on horseback. The Territorials began their march to Chesterfield, finding billets for the night in the Ashford Schoolrooms.

After assembling on Bakewell Recreation Ground, 70 members of the High Peak Squadron of the Yeomanry left the town by road on Monday August 10th at 9-30 a.m., after being billeted there as they awaited horses. 20 others, who were without horses, left by train. Four days later, on Thursday August 13th, it was the turn of the local Territorials (100 members of the 6th Battalion Sherwood Foresters) to depart Bakewell in full marching order.

One of the largest crowds seen in Rutland Square assembled to see them off, with the Bishop of Derby (who was also vicar of Bakewell), Dr. Abraham, conducting an eloquent and stirring service from on top of a landau, drawn up in the Square. Bakewell Brass Band had paraded the streets with the Territorials, whilst the Boy Scouts took up their position by the open stage. *The National Anthem* having been sung with great fervour, the Bishop of Derby gave his address.

Prayers were offered by the Bishop on behalf of the troops and three cheers were next given for the Territorials. The troops filed up, and headed by the Brass Band and the Scouts with their drum and bugle band, set out on their long march to Chesterfield, the Brass Band dropping out at Castle Hill and the Boy Scouts at a later stage.

Horses for the Cavalry, Artillery and Army Service Corps were at a premium and in the weeks following the outbreak of war, many owners from this rural area were required to bring their animals into various centres to see if they were suitable, with the main collection centre being in the Rutland Arms Hotel Stable Yard, Bakewell.

Great excitement was caused on Saturday August 8th when it became known that the local police had arrested German spies at Rowsley. In reality, the Germans had been members of a German firm employed by Caudwell's Corn Mill to re-modernise part of the machinery. Fifty Germans had been involved, but six months before war began, the majority were withdrawn, leaving just a few men behind to complete the work. It was these three men who were arrested and interned. They were brought to Bakewell police station for the night and then conveyed next day to York by train, accompanied by Police Sergeant Maguire and Police Constable Platts of

Bakewell and placed in a military compound for Germans in that city.

Mr. C.H. Glossop, J.P., of Bakewell, said that if any man who was physically fit did not help his country at this time, then he was not a true Englishman.

We find that on the night of August 22nd the Duke of Devonshire presided at a meeting held in the Stockdale Institute, Baslow. The newspaper report indicates that he gave a rousing speech, announcing the capture of Ostende by the Germans, only 136 miles distant from London. The audience was told that in the Baslow district were fine sturdy men of exactly the type that Lord Kitchener was appealing for, "not the narrow-chested kind of youth brought up in a London slum, but the type of men who were used to hard, honest work in the country". The paper reports that as a result, "a really good fine number" of men from Baslow offered themselves for military service.

Meanwhile, the Village Institute at Edensor, recently remodelled from the old Chatsworth Hotel, had been prepared for a party of Belgian refugees. They arrived on Monday September 21st, consisting of a man and his wife who were in charge of eleven children. Mrs. Adams, wife of A.J. Adams, manager of Crompton and Evans Bank, Bakewell, had taken a kind, motherly interest in the party, being herself a native of the ill-fated Belgian town of Louvain and able to speak Flemish fluently. The Belgians had travelled from Malines to Antwerp and then on to England.

The Duke of Devonshire had sent motor cars to Rowsley Station to bring them to Edensor and he was there when they arrived. Meanwhile, at Bolton Abbey, Lady Blanche Cavendish was receiving 25 Belgian refugees.

By October 1914 the Belgians at Chatsworth were accommodated in cottages at the rear of the Edensor Institute, formerly tenanted by unmarried workmen.

September 24th 1914 and the following Sunday saw a Thanksgiving Service for the safe gathering of harvest at Beeley Church. The service was characterised by an even greater fervour than usual, for at this special time of national stress and crisis, the yield of corn and vegetables had been unusually good. The church was resplendent in its festival attire. Choice flowers and grapes were sent for the occasion by the Duke of Devonshire from the Chatsworth conservatories (these would soon be closed down because the use of coal in wartime for such purposes, and the expense, could not be justified). A happy feature of the festival was the presence in uniform of a number of soldiers attached to the Notts. and Derby Mounted Brigade, who returned for the weekend from their training quarters to keep the thanksgiving service in their own native village.

Amidst all the war fever, however, certain items went ahead as normal. During the first week in October, buyers from all parts of the county attended the 6th Annual Chatsworth Sale of cattle, fed by the Duke of Devonshire during the summer in Chatsworth Park. 126 blue grey heifers and steers and West Highland steers were sold, realising a total of £2576. Forty five animals fed on the Duke of Rutland's estate brought £716. The Duke of Devonshire and Lady Maude Cavendish were present at the sale.

Meanwhile, the professional and territorial units of the British Expeditionary Force (BEF) had crossed the English Channel on declaration of war and moved into Belgium. Near Mons the British were struck by the full weight of the aggressive German First Army Group. Outnumbered, the British fought back stoutly, their rifle power discipline taking heavy toll of the close German formations, but they were forced back onto a long retreat during August.

According to the historian of *The History of the First World War*, Liddel Hart: "During the 13 days of the retreat, five of the seven German armies scythed down towards Paris, on a 75 mile front. For the troops on both sides they were days of endless marching under a scorching sun, marching until nearly every man seemed to have nails through the soles of his boots into his blistered feet, and the horses had worn their shoes wafer thin. Every movement was hampered by refugees. Order and counter order plagued both sides.

"In the days between Mons and the Battle of the Marne, the BEF, smallest of the Allied armies, played a vital role, for it found itself at the outset right across the axis of advance of Kluck's army, the most powerful of all the German armies, with 320,000 men."

An important holding action took place at the Battle of Le Cateau, August 26th, when the BEF earned its place in history for the desperate and dogged resistance that took place when no one on either side could possibly have expected it. Again, the disciplined fire power of the professional British Army amazed the oncoming German soldiers as the British riflemen pumped out bullets at the rate of 16 to the minute.

At the Battle of the Marne, September 5th to the 10th, the German advance was brought to a halt, and then turned back, with the BEF severely mauled but showing great powers of recuperation, playing a vital role. Now came the "Race to the Sea", between September 15th and November 24th, as each side tried to outflank the other in a bid to take the Channel ports.

The final action of the "Race to the Sea" was the bloody First Battle of Ypres, October 30th to November 24th, in which the BEF was nearly wiped out in a successful, gallant defence against a heavily reinforced German drive that was expected by them to capture the Channel ports.

It was during this crucial battle in and around Ypres that the Chatsworth villages received news of the first fatal casualties killed during these opening days of the conflict.

On October 14th the first British troops reached the ancient cloth centre of Ypres, in Belgium. Here it was decided by the Allies to make a stand. Beyond was barely 20 miles of open countryside to the Channel ports. If the German Army broke through at Ypres, the war could be lost.

The First Battle of Ypres proved to be the graveyard of the old regular British Army. The Germans threw huge numbers of barely trained conscripts, many of them students, at the defending British and so terrible were the German casualties that the battle would be known to the Germans as the "Slaughter of the Innocents".

British casualties, too, were enormous, and despite a heroic defence, the enemy advanced from three sides to within a few miles of Ypres. The fighting for Messines Ridge, to the south east of the town, began in earnest on October 20th/21st, with the Cavalry Corps to the east of Messines village, and on the first day, October 20th, Major Lord John Spencer Cavendish was killed in action.

MAJOR LORD JOHN SPENCER CAVENDISH
(DSO) 1ST LIFE GUARDS (HOUSEHOLD CAVALRY)
DIED OCTOBER 20TH 1914 AGED 42

Born in Picadilly, London, on March 25th 1875, John Spencer Cavendish (known as "Lord John") was the third and youngest son of Lord Edward Cavendish, MP for Lancashire, and Lady Emma Elizabeth Cavendish (daughter of the Right Honourable William Lascelles and grand daughter of the 3rd Earl of Harewood). He was the grandson of the 7th Duke of Devonshire (William S. Cavendish), who favoured living at Holker Hall, four miles west of Grange-over-Sands, rather than at Chatsworth. The house is famous for the local craftsmanship shown in the interior wood carving. A 17th century structure, it was partly rebuilt in 1873, after a fire.

Lord John Spencer Cavendish
High Peak News
courtesy of Potter and Company, Solicitors

The 7th Duke had three sons: Spencer Compton, who became the 8th Duke, Frederick, who was assassinated in Dublin by Irish nationalists, and Edward, the youngest, who died in 1891.

It was Edward Cavendish's eldest son, Victor, who became the 9th Duke of

Devonshire, whilst his youngest son, John Spencer Cavendish, would be killed in action in 1914.

John Spencer Cavendish was educated at Eton and Trinity College, Cambridge. He opted for a military career, first serving in the Militia, before being given a commission in the 1st Life Guards on February 3rd 1897 and gradually gaining promotion to Lieutenant, April 2nd 1898, Captain August 23rd 1902 and Major April 12th 1911. He served with distinction on the Staff in the South African (Boer) War 1899-1902, acting first as Divisional Signalling Officer to the Second Infantry Division, October 9th 1899 to June 18th 1900, and then as Brigade Signalling Officer from June 19th to October 12th 1900.

"Lord John" was involved in the relief of Ladysmith, including action at Colenso, whilst also taking part in actions during 1900 at Spion Kop, Vaal Kranz, Tugela Heights and engagements at Pieter's Hill. Further action saw him involved in the march from Bloem-fontein to Pretoria, with actions at Zand River, near Johannesburg and at Pretoria and Diamond Hill, whilst more fighting was accomplished in the Orange Free State, at Eland's River, Bethlehem and Wittebergen.

He was mentioned in despatches, first under General Buller in Natal, and subsequently under Lord Roberts in the Free State and Transvaal. He received the Distinguished Service Order (DSO) at the end of the war and the Queen's and King's Medals with 6 clasps.

Lord John Spencer Cavendish

Later, he held a military appointment in Northern Nigeria, where he was employed with the West African Frontier Force from June 29th 1907 to September 6th 1910. He was a great sportsman and when not engaged with his military duties, travelled far and wide in search of big game. The trophies which adorned the Institute at Carke were collected by him from North America, West Africa and East Africa.

After his brother Victor's succession to the title of 9th Duke of Devonshire, he was granted precedence as son of a Duke of Royal Warrant, in 1908.

At the outset of the Great War, Major Lord John Spencer Cavendish was serving as an officer in the 1st Life Guards. The Life Guards is the senior Cavalry Regiment of the British Army and with the Blues and Royals, they made up the Household Cavalry.

Many serving in the Life Guards were not sent across the Channel straight away, having to wait until October 6th before they were despatched to Zeebrugge and into Belgium. However, a Composite Regiment of Life Guards, including Lord John, joined the 6th Carabineers and the 3rd Hussars to form the 4th Cavalry Brigade and this was despatched on August 15th and was coming into contact with German patrols by the 21st. His second in command was the Honourable Edward Wyndham.

The British fought outstandingly well in the opening moves of the war but were forced onto a defensive retreat. The 4th Brigade were on the left wing of the BEF and saw action at Halte, Saultain, Compiegne and Nery.

One of the most heroic actions fought by the BEF during the retreat from Mons to the Marne was that at Nery, a village near Compiegne, where, on September 1st, a single battery of Royal Horse Artillery, which, with the protection of a Cavalry Brigade, was covering the withdrawal of III Corps, held off for several hours the whole of the German 4th Cavalry Division. Three VC's were won by the Artillery battery during the hours of battle and this combined action virtually destroyed the 4th German Cavalry Division as a fighting force.

Ominously, the Composite Regiment of Household Cavalry was already finding the usefulness of trenches in defending against an enemy and even strategic movement was more effective by using trains. When the Germans turned north, after their attack towards Paris faltered, they were outrun by the British forces' effective use of the trains. The days of the Cavalry Regiments were numbered.

By train and on horseback, the Composite Battalion arrived in the vicinity of Ypres by October 14th, joining with other members of the 1st Life Guards who had arrived by sea at Zeebrugge on October 6th. The fighting for Messines Ridge, to the south east of Ypres, began in earnest on October 20th/21st, with the Cavalry Corps to the east of Messines village.

On Monday October 19th, the Cavalry had been pushed out of the town of Roulers by force of numbers and by the end of the day they were to be found on the high ridge, spread in a thin line that stretched from Roosebeke to Passchendaele, waiting and watching and patrolling and looking down on the fires burning in the plain. Under the cover of darkness, a whole new German army was moving into position, ready to strike forward at daybreak on Tuesday October 20th, the day on which Lord John Spencer Cavendish would be killed.

In overwhelming numbers, the Germans were encircling the saucer's rim and the British troops were struggling to maintain a foothold. The Cavalry men were driven out of their rudimentary trenches and back towards Hollebeke.

Orders came for them to abandon their horses and dig in and prepare defences for another German attempt to push them off the Ridge. It was during the desperate fighting on this day that "Lord John" lost his life, when he was spotted by a German machine-gunner whilst issuing orders to the

Cavendish Squadron. News of his death reached Chatsworth on Thursday October 22nd.

His body was recovered and eventually he was buried in grave XX1. C. 26. Cabaret-Rouge British Cemetery, Souchez, 4 kilometres north of Arras.

A memorial service was held on Thursday November 5th at the Grosvenor Chapel, South Audley Street, London. The congregation included the Duke and Duchess of Devonshire, Lady Edward Cavendish, Lady Blanche Cavendish, Lady Lansdowne and the Marchioness of Crewe.

Tired but determined, the cavalrymen and infantry held the defence over the 22nd and 23rd October, with rifles and a limited number of machine-guns. For a week, the Germans attacked other parts of the line but then made a concerted effort to press the British again. A number of heavy guns had been placed and came into action again on October 29th/30th, pounding the defences and hoping to annihilate the British cavalry and infantry who had dug in. It was during this period of severe bombardment on October 30th that Lord John Spencer Cavandish's brother-in-law was killed.

MAJOR LORD CHARLES GEORGE FRANCIS MERCER NAIRNE (MVO) 1ST (ROYAL) DRAGOONS, ATTACHED TO THE STAFF OF THE 6TH CAVALRY BRIGADE DIED OCTOBER 30TH 1914 AGED 40

Born on February 12th 1874, Charles was the second son of Henry Charles Keith Petty-Fitz-maurice, 5th Marquis of Lansdowne and of Maude Evelyn, Marchioness of Lansdowne, of Bowood Park, Calne, Wiltshire. Lord Lansdowne had been a former Viceroy of India and Secretary of State for Foreign Affairs.

Lord Charles Mercer Nairne
Lord Lansdowne

The eldest son, Henry Fitzmaurice, the Earl of Kerry, was educated at Eton and Balliol College, Oxford, serving in the Grenadier Guards 1895-1900, including participation in the Boer War, when he gained a DSO and was Extra ADC to Field Marshal Lord Roberts, Commander-in-Chief. He later joined the Irish Guards until 1906 and during the Great War was Lieutenant Colonel 1914-1916. He was the Unionist MP for West Derbyshire from 1908 to 1918 and succeeded his father in 1927.

His younger brother, Lord Charles Fitzmaurice, joined the 1st Dragoons from the Militia in 1895. From 1897 to 1899 he was ADC to the General Officer Commanding Forces in Ireland and was promoted to Captain in 1901 and Major 1910. He served in South Africa 1901-1904 and during the Boer War was ADC to the Commander-in-Chief, being present at the Relief of Ladysmith, and received the Queen's Medal with five clasps.

In 1909, Lord Charles Fitzmaurice married Lady Violet Mary, a daughter of the 4th Earl of Minto, Viceroy of India, in Calcutta, and the couple had two children, a girl and a boy. At some point before the Great War he inherited an estate in Scotland and subsequently became known as Lord Charles Mercer Nairne. His sister, Lady Evelyn Fitzmaurice, had married the 9th Duke of Devonshire, Victor Cavendish, in 1892.

Lord Charles became an Equerry to His Majesty, George V, when Prince of Wales, and continued to discharge the duties of that office until the outbreak of war in 1914, when he requested to be relieved of his attendance at Court that he might go with his regiment on active service. His brother officers included the Honourable Julien Grenfell and the Honourable J.L.R. Schlater-Booth.

The 1st Royal Dragoons arrived in England from South Africa on September 19th and were attached to the 6th Cavalry Brigade, 3rd Cavalry Division. Lord Charles and the Dragoons moved to Belgium in the first week of October, landing at Zeebrugge. They were to be involved in the defence of Antwerp but arrived as the Belgian evacuation was beginning and instead were sent to help in the defence of Ypres.

On October 25th/26th the Germans attacked against the 7th Division on the Menin Road, north of Ypres, and the line crumbled and then held. The Germans now attacked the British line further south, between Ploegsteert Wood and Gheluvelt, in the battle known as the Battle of Gheluvelt, October 29th/31st. It was at Brigade Headquarters at nearby Klein-Zillebeke that Lord Charles was attending to his duties as Brigade interpreter.

After a preliminary attack on October 29th, which captured a key crossroads close to Gheluvelt, the main attack began on October 30th with a terrible bombardment of the defences by the German artillery. The hard-pressed British line fell back, but did not break. The crisis came on October 31st. A German attack broke through the line and reached Gheluvelt. The entire British line was close to collapse and orders were drafted for a retreat to the Reserve Line, on the outskirts of Ypres, but a counter-attack by 364 men of the 2nd Worcestershire Regiment restored the situation.

Sadly, however, Lord Charles Mercer Nairne was killed by shellfire at Brigade HQ at Klein-Zillebeke on October 30th during the initial German artillery bombardment. He was buried in grave E.1.10. In Ypres Town Cemetery.

After the war his original Flanders grave-cross was returned to Bowood, where it is displayed in the chapel. His name is also listed on the war memorial at St. Peter's, Edensor, because we have seen that his sister Evelyn was married to the 9th Duke of Devonshire. Lord Bertie, British Ambassador to France for most of the war, on hearing of Lord Charles' death, noted in his diary entry of November 2nd: "Poor Charlie Fitzmaurice! I was very fond of him: he was such a nice, cheery creature. Lady Lansdowne adored him."

Lord Lansdowne had offered the grounds of Bowood Park to the Yeomanry for training purposes and in 1915 the South Western Mounted Brigade, comprising 2500 men, spent the summer there. He also established a hospital in the servants' quarters of the house. After he received the news of his younger son's death in November, Lord Lansdowne's health began to decline and he never really recovered from this tragedy.

*** *Lord Charles George Mercer Nairne's elder brother, Henry William, became the 6th Marquis of Lansdowne in 1927 and when he died in 1936, his eldest son, Charles Hope, became the 7th Marquis.*

However, the 7th Marquis, an officer in the Wiltshire Yeomanry, was killed near Arezzo, in Italy, on August 20th 1944 and his name was commemorated on the Monte Cassino Memorial. Just nine days earlier, on August 11th 1944, his younger brother, Edward Norman (Ned), a Lieutenant in the Irish Guards, had been killed in Normandy.

It is interesting to note , therefore, that the succession passed to their cousin, the son of Lord Charles George Mercer Nairne. George John Charles became the 8th Marquis of Lansdowne in 1944, whilst he was serving with the Free French Army.

The actions of the Cavalry at the First Battle of Ypres was to see the death of many lords, earls, viscounts, marquises and baronets, and even a duke, whilst mere honourables were rather commonplace. The roll-call of the officers of the 7th Cavalry Brigade at Passchendaele and Messines Ridge consisted of many sons of the aristocracy of Britain, for this was the Household Cavalry. Amongst the great families represented were the Cavendishes, Castlereaghs, Stanleys, Wyndhams, Astors and Grosvenors. Indeed, Debrett's "Peerage" did not appear as it usually did in early Spring 1915 because so many sons of the aristocracy were dead, so many baronets and lords and knights and heirs to lands and titles. It took the editors many months to revise the entries of most blue-blooded families in the United Kingdom. When it did appear, the 1915 edition of Debrett made sorry reading.

Just before dawn on October 31st, the day on which a Beeley man, Alfred Ernest Earl, lost his life, and with the German Kaiser Wilhelm himself present to direct operations, Germans of the 119 Grenadiers and 125 Infantry Regiment, cheering and blowing horns, made a sudden attack. They captured some of the British line, which was not a continuous trench, but a series of short lengths. By now, the front was along the main village street in Gheluvelt, with hand to hand fighting taking place and both the defenders and attackers were getting tired and desperate. Both sides fought hard, with the battle going on into the night, but the British were forced at last to withdraw from the village.

PRIVATE ALFRED ERNEST EARL No. L/8611 "C" COMPANY
1ST BATTALION THE QUEEN'S (ROYAL WEST SURREY REGIMENT)
DIED OCTOBER 31ST 1914 AGED 27

In 1901 the Earl family was living in the district of Chelsea, London, with 13 year old Alfred the eldest of the four children of Alfred Earl senior and Sarah Ellen Earl (known as Ellen). Alfred senior had been born in Norfolk, in 1864, where he had started his working life as a farm labourer but journeyed to London and joined the police force as a police constable.

It was in Chiswick, Middlesex, that he married Ellen Earl, a native of Devon, and it was there that Alfred junior was born, before his father was transferred to Chelsea.

In the next few years, another transfer saw Alfred policing south of the Thames, in Surrey, and Alfred junior began spending some of his spare time training with the Territorials of the West Surrey Regiment.

However, at some point before the start of the Great War, Alfred Earl senior was transferred to Derbyshire and to the Matlock Green area of Matlock. Meanwhile, their son, Alfred junior, had spent some time serving as a regular soldier in the 1st Battalion Royal West Surrey Regiment, but just before the commencement of war in 1914, he had come out of the Army and had travelled to Derbyshire to live near his parents. He settled down in nearby Beeley and possibly worked in some capacity on the Chatsworth Estate.

On declaration of war, Alfred re-enlisted and returned to the 1st Battalion. They landed at Le Havre as part of the British Expeditionary Force, in August 1914. The Battalion was up to strength with highly skilled professional soldiers.

The 1st Battalion was at Mons, the first battle of the war, in action from August 25th and held up three Jaeger Battalions and a cavalry brigade all that day, giving such a display of rapid rifle fire that the enemy mistook it for machine-gun fire.

During the retreat from Mons, they covered 136 miles in 13 days of fierce fighting. Following the Battle of the Aisne, the Battalion took part in the "Race to the Sea" and by October 22nd were in position at Hooge, near Ypres, ready to participate in the bloody battle that was to take place.

In heavy fighting on the 23rd they lost 165 casualties. The night passed quietly but there was a good deal of shelling on the 24th, while in the evening the enemy attempted two attacks, at 6-30p.m. and 8-30p.m., but was repulsed, and then at 11p.m. the Battalion was relieved, 15 men at a time, by French troops, despite the fact that the German lines were only 100 yards away. During the night they marched back to Hooge.

The 25th was a Sunday and all were glad of a day of rest. On October 26th the Battalion moved into Veldhock Wood, north east of Zandvoorde, on the side of the Menin Road. At this time the 22nd Infantry Brigade held a line between Gheluvelt and Kruiseecke, and thence towards Zandvoorde, and news came on October 29th that this line had been penetrated.

The Battalion was in support but about 10a.m., on arrival at Gheluvelt, and stationed near a windmill 500 yards south east of the village, "D" and "C" Companies (with Alfred in the latter) advanced some 200 yards north and entrenched. The enemy made a light-hearted counter-attack at 7p.m., but were repulsed.

On October 30th the Battalion helped in covering the withdrawal of the 22nd Infantry Brigade and in repulsing the attacks by the enemy.

October 31st, the day of Alfred Earl's death, was one of the worst days experienced by the 1st Battalion during the whole war.

Before dawn, an attack was made on "C" and "B" Companies but was repulsed and the enemy dug in within 300 yards of Battalion lines. At 7a.m. the Battalion line was subjected to a very heavy bombardment, to which Allied guns were unable to reply. The enemy then worked their way into the orchard and men of the Battalion had to retire, bringing the Germans to within 150 yards of the line.

The Battalion was holding its own when, about 10a.m., "B" Company was driven out of its trenches by machine-gun fire from both flanks. Soon after this a message was received from "D" Company reporting that the Germans were all about "C" Company's trenches (Alfred's Company) and no report was forthcoming from them. "B" Company's trenches were evacuated and the men were retiring from the farm as the Germans were entering it, whilst the Germans were seen to be in the village behind "D" Company.

It was now about 11-30a.m. and two remaining officers rallied what few men they could find of different regiments and got them into the trenches. This Battalion of the West Surrey's, now only 32 men strong, fought on, on the southern side of the chateau, near Gheluvelt, remaining in support until dusk on October 31st and spending the whole of the next 24 hours in the trenches.

The casualties this day had been terribly heavy. 10 officers and 624 Other Ranks were killed, wounded or missing. On November 1st the following were found to constitute the 1st Battalion West Surrey Regiment: "A" Company (2 corporals, 2 lance-corporals, 20 privates), "B" Company (4 privates), "C" Company (2 privates), "D" Company (1 lance corporal, 1 private), giving a total of 32 men and they included cooks and transport men collected from the Quarter-master.

The whole Battalion had been decimated in the fierce fighting against over-whelming odds and Private Alfred Ernest Earl of "C" Company was one of the many who lost their lives. His body was never recovered and his name is honoured on the Menin Gate Memorial at Ypres.

On October 31st, the day that Alfred Earl died, the Grenadier Guards were "holding on by their eyelids" to the south east of Ypres. Casualties were high and the situation desperate. Regiments, battalions, all units became mingled and at one point in the afternoon, a message came from First Corps Commander, Sir Douglas Haig, that the Grenadiers were to hold their ground at all costs. They held their ground and heroic actions elsewhere by the BEF blunted any further German advance. The Germans would continue to batter the thin line of defenders around Ypres, but the crisis had passed. The "immortal Ypres Salient" had been created.

Three men from the Chatsworth villages had already paid the supreme sacrifice during these desperate days defending Ypres.

At the beginning of November 1914, when the BEF was fighting so valiantly at Ypres, and the position was becoming desperate, the 3rd Dragoon Guards arrived as part of the reinforcements which were being drawn from all parts of the British Empire. They belonged to the 6th Cavalry Brigade of the 3rd Cavalry Division, commanded by Major-General Julian Byng and were brigaded with the 1st Royal Dragoons and the 10th Hussars.

We have seen that the 3rd Dragoon Guards had been in Egypt since 1912 and at Cairo they had been held for the defence of the Suez Canal, as there was felt to be a considerable danger of the Turks marching against it – as eventually they did.

Until it was relieved by troops from India and Yeomanry forces from England, the regiment had its headquarters at Ismailia, and was responsible for both sides of the Canal between Kantara and Lake Timsah.

Sailing for home on September 29th they arrived in Liverpool on October 18th. The regiment mobilised at Ludgershall, Buckinghamshire, 8 miles north west of Aylesbury, receiving horses from the Yeomanry. The regiment brought from Egypt one squadron of Arab horses, which, when replaced, were sent to the infantry to become officers' chargers.

The regiment sailed for France on October 31st, landing at Le Havre on November 1st. On November 5th the regiment dismounted at Hooge and entered the trenches south of the Ypres-Menin road, on the eastern front of Herontage Woods.

For the next fortnight, in bitter cold and drenching rain, the regiment was to hold its position against assault after assault of German troops attempting to break through to Ypres. Their positions, shallowly entrenched and rapidly becoming water-logged, were repeatedly shelled and many troopers were killed by snipers as they attempted to move around.

About 150 yards in front of the 3rd Dragoon Guards, the enemy was also entrenched, but the position was by no means static. The trenches were not connected up, and had no barbed wire in front. The enemy was extremely aggressive and the regiment was under constant threat of attack.

Like most other cavalry regiments at this time, their mobility was used for moving them quickly to places of danger, where they could dismount a few hundred yards in the rear, send back their horses and occupy scattered rifle-pits, knee deep in liquid mud.

On Friday November 6th, a sudden assault was made by the Germans, with the British Household Cavalry, mud splashed and on their feet, charging with the bayonet through the streets of the village they were defending. During this action, Captain John Hodgkinson was severely wounded in the head by a bullet, whilst in charge of the regimental machine-guns. In just two days they lost 22 men killed and 36 wounded, in this, their first experience under fire.

It was during the ferocious actions of September-November 1914, when thousands of battlefield casualties were returning to England to receive medical attention and recuperation, that Bakewell Red Cross Hospital had been established and the first wounded soldiers (8 British and 6 Belgian) arrived in November. The Bakewell Stretcher Bearer Company, which was formed on the outbreak of war, and now numbered about 35 members, had been officially recognised by the military authorities and was now included as a Men's Voluntary Aid Detachment under the British Red Cross Society, meeting in the Territorial Drill Hall on Castle Street. The Red Cross Hospital was staffed by VAD nurses who had been in training since before the war. By March 12th 1915 there were 35 wounded soldiers recuperating at Bakewell.

It had finally been decided to set up the Royal Naval Convalescent Hospital at Chatsworth in the Edensor Institute (until recently, the former Edensor Hotel), with Medical Corps Staff and wounded arriving at Hassop Station. 72 recovering sailors could be accommodated at a time and the

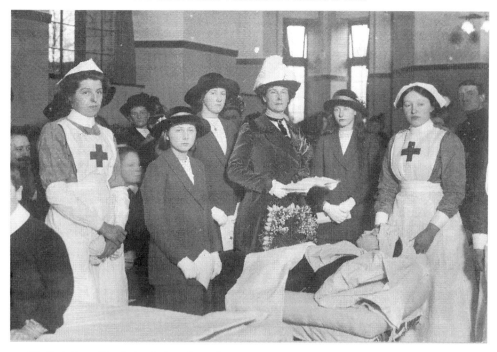

The Red Cross Hospital at Bakewell Workhouse Infirmary (nowadays part of Newholme) 1915,
which tended the wounds of Belgian and British servicemen. Evelyn Gyte is the VAD nurse on the
extreme left, whilst the Duchess of Devonshire stands by the bed, in the middle
Margaret Slin

establishment was under the watchful eye of the Chatsworth Agent, John Pepys Cockerell, with his wife Florence acting as the Quartermaster. The Chief of Staff was SPS W.J. McGuiness, aided by SPS G.W. Knight and Sergeant R. A. Yates (the latter also acting as cinema operator). Dr. Edelstone of Baslow was the Medical Officer of Health and was in attendance whenever required.

The recreation room had been fitted with a billiards table and various games were introduced, whilst outside, there was a canteen. The hospital was divided into three sections, bearing the names of three ships : "The Lion", "The Tiger" and "Canada". To help in the process of recuperation and rehabilitation, art, needlework, wool, wood, fretwork, painting, sketching, macramo and model making classes were provided. There was also a miniature rifle range for which competitions were arranged. Similar convalescent hospitals were set up throughout the dales, including one in the Whitworth Institute building at Darley Dale.

In November 1914 the Reserve Regiment of the Derbyshire Imperial Yeomanry took up their winter quarters for training at Chatsworth and

The Royal Naval Convalescent Hospital, outside the Edensor Institute
(formerly the Chatsworth Hotel) in 1916. Doctors and VAD nurses pose with the patients
Derek Neave

Baslow and by December it was reported in the *High Peak News* that considerable progress had been made. Nearly 500 officers and men were billeted in the two locations. The officers' headquarters were at the Edensor Institute, whilst many of the men were billeted at Baslow in the various hotels and in the Stockdale Institute. Others found excellent quarters near the Chatsworth Stables.

Eighty men of the Yeomanry were billeted at the Devonshire Arms Hotel in Baslow. Their presence meant extra trade for the proprietor but the local police were ever vigilant regarding the breaching of the licensing laws and at the first Bakewell Petty Session after Christmas 1914, Frank Vick, the landlord of the Devonshire Arms Hotel, was fined £5 with £1. 2s. 6d. costs for "keeping his house open for the sale of drink during prohibited hours." Five soldiers of the Derbyshire Yeomanry and a civilian had been found with glasses of beer after closing time. Later in the war we shall find that Frank Vick's son, Frank junior, would lose his life whilst serving his country.

The men of the Yeomanry would find themselves embarking for action in the Gallipoli Campaign the following year, and by 1916 many would be fighting the Bulgarians in Salonika. When the Derbyshire Imperial Yeomanry finally helped defeat the Bulgarians in September 1918, they brought one of the white flags used by the Bulgars to surrender, back to Bakewell as a trophy and it can now be found at The Old House Museum, Bakewell.

No. 3 Troop of the Derbyshire Imperial Yeomanry, who were billeted at the Wheatsheaf Hotel, Baslow,
in the winter of 1914/1915, whilst they trained on the Chatsworth estate
Gill Watson

We have already seen that Chatsworth and the Cavendish family had been heavily affected by the onset of war. The Duke's brother and brother-in-law had both been killed in action in October 1914. Chatsworth House and other properties were closed up and male servants of military age went off to fight. There would be no more special trains for the family, their servants and their ponies and no more visits by the Royal Family during the war years. There would be no more early carnations grown in the Paxton conservatories at Chatsworth, since wartime fuel was in short supply and expensive. Indeed, the conservatories became so ruined from neglect during the war that restoration would have been too expensive at its conclusion. Evelyn, Duchess of Devonshire, suggested that to avoid the expense of painstaking demolition, the strong structures should be blasted by dynamite. It still took two attempts to raise them to the ground, but un-perturbed by the loss of these most original buildings, the Duchess immediately organised her gardens to create rose beds on the site.

Victor Cavendish, 9th Duke of Devonshire, had become Honorary Colonel of the 5th Battalion Sherwood Foresters and formerly served as a major in the Derbyshire Imperial Yeomanry. During the war he was Civil Lord of the Admiralty in 1915 and we shall see that he became Governor General of Canada and Commander-in-Chief of Canadian forces between 1916 and 1921.

Edward Cavendish, his son and heir (Lord Hartington), was born in 1895 and educated at Eton and Trinity College, Cambridge. In 1912 he had joined the Derbyshire Imperial Yeomanry as a Second Lieutenant and was mobilised on August 5th 1914. He embarked for Egypt in March 1915 and served for some months as a Special Intelligence Officer at Cairo, before arriving in Gallipoli in 1915 when he was Aide-de-Camp to Brigadier-General Paul Kenna VC, Commander of the Sherwood Foresters until his death in August 1915. He took part in the Battle of Chocolate Hill on August 21st and was mentioned in despatches. However, in December 1915, Lord Hartington was invalided home to England, suffering from dysentery. After recovering, he went out to France in July 1916 and with his knowledge of French, he became the representative of the British Intelligence Service

Edward Cavendish,
Lord Hartington
High Peak News

with the French Army and by 1917 represented British interests with the French Ministry of Blockade. He married Lady Mary Gascoyne-Cecil, daughter of the 4th Marquis of Salisbury. Their two sons were William, born 1917 (we shall see later that William Cavendish was killed in action during the Second World War) and Andrew, born 1920. Edward would succeed his father Victor in 1938.

Lord Richard Cavendish, brother of the 9th Duke, was MP for a Lancashire seat from 1895 to 1906 and lived at Holker Hall. Later, he became Lieutenant Colonel of the 5th Royal Lancaster Regiment and served on the Western Front between 1914 and 1915, being wounded and mentioned in despatches.

We have seen that men with connections to the area had been killed in the space of three weeks of desperate fighting around the town of Ypres, in Belgium, in the Autumn of 1914. Sadly, throughout the next few years, Edensor, Beeley and Pilsley would not be spared its share of the nation's heartache, for we shall see that in the year 1915 alone, the death count for these villages rose.

In France and Belgium, throughout December 1914, an Allied offensive beat unsuccessfully for ten bloody days against the rapidly growing German system of field fortification. The era of stabilised trench warfare from the North Sea to the Swiss border had begun.

The enormity of the conflict became apparent to everyone as casualty lists were posted. By this time, operations on the Western Front had already cost the Allies nearly one million casualties, with German losses almost as great. The Germans had not won a quick victory and now the Western Front would settle down to four years of bloody attrition.

CHAPTER THREE

1915 – HOPES ARE DASHED

The widening of the conflict to new theatres of war in 1915, especially at the Dardanelles and Gallipoli, together with the vast casualties resulting from the early campaigns, brought home to the British public the increasing sacrifice they would have to make in order to achieve victory for the Allied cause. Nevertheless, the feeling still persisted that once Kitchener's "New Army" of volunteers was ready in 1915, the combined efforts of the Allies would then soon defeat the enemy.

When the Government proposed the setting up of Rifle Clubs and the formation of Home Guard contingents in towns and villages throughout the land in 1915, the three villages responded well. In connection with the Derbyshire Volunteer Regiment of Home Guards, a public meeting was convened on a Saturday evening in January in the Recreation Room of the Grand Hotel and Hydro, by its proprietor, Mr. Mabbott. There was a moderate attendance, with the names of those agreeing to join being taken and a committee formed.

On New Years Day, 1915, a Parochial Church Tea was held in Beeley Elementary School. Great interest was taken in the Belgian refugee families of Messrs. Aug Van der Veken and De Vadder, invited from Alport and Edensor.

The former, whose home was in Antwerp, related most touchingly the sad experience of himself and family during the great German bombardment of the Belgian port and of their flight, first to Holland and then to England. The latter's experience was equally tragic.

A further great element of interest was added by the attendance of a large number of soldiers who were stationed at Chatsworth and Baslow and who entered heartily into the enjoyment of the evening. There was entertainment in the form of singing and recitations and on the stroke of midnight, the *National Anthem* was sung.

On the following day the children of the parish assembled in the church for tea, after which a happy evening was spent in games and listening to gramophone selections kindly provided by Mrs. Rollinson. At the conclusion,

*On May 10th 1915 a Sheffield based charabanc crashed into the parapet of the Old Bridge, Baslow.
Most of the people peering over the parapet are Derbyshire Imperial Yeomanry troops stationed at
Chatsworth Park and billeted at Baslow. It was due to such incidents on the narrow bridge, that the
Devonshire Bridge was constructed in 1925*

Peter Eades

the *National Anthem* was sung, when each child was presented with either a
bag or stocking full of sweets by Mrs. Hewetson (provided by Mrs. Burdekin).

In mid January 1915, Mr. Mabbott J.P. and his wife, of the Grand Hotel and
Hydro, Baslow, set apart their well appointed Assembly Room for a concert
on Thursday evening, the proceeds being split between the Red Cross and
the Comforts for Servicemen's Fund. The evening had been organised by Mrs.
Stockdale and the solicitor's wife, Emily Jane Burdekin (sadly, Mrs. Burdekin
would receive news of the death of her son a few days later, on January 26th).

In April, the *High Peak News* reported that the Derbyshire Imperial
Yeomanry soldiers billeted at Baslow got on well with the villagers. But sixty
of their horses were stabled at the four hotels in the village and the proprietors
of these hotels grumbled loudly about the pay they received for each horse,
which at the present time, and in view of the high cost of foodstuffs, was
deemed to be quite inadequate. The Military Authorities only allowed 1
shilling and six pence for the keep of each horse per day and 3 pence for
stabling in Baslow, whilst the real cost was 1 shilling and 11 pence, apart from
stabling.

On a more mundane, parochial level, attention at Baslow was suddenly drawn in May to a long running problem. With the advent of motor transport, the old narrow road bridge proved to be inadequate for accommodating the new mode of transport and various incidents over the years raised concerns about its safe use.

On Monday evening, at 5-45 p.m. on May 10th 1915, a Belsize charabanc belonging to the firm of Joseph Tomlinson and Sons of Sheffield, returning to the city with 13 passengers and driven by Mr. Honey, ran into the parapet of the bridge. The steering gear got locked with the accelerator pedal, which caused the car to jump forward. It was saved from crashing into the River Derwent below by the presence of a large stone under the gear box, which brought the vehicle to a standstill.

Despite the crash, Baslow villagers would have to wait until May 1925 before the construction of the new Devonshire Bridge took place.

We find that in mid June 1915 the officers and soldiers of the Derbyshire Imperial Yeomanry left Chatsworth and Baslow for training elsewhere, before they were despatched to far away Gallipoli and eventually Salonika. They assembled at Baslow on Saturday June 19th and rode to Rowsley, to be entrained there. For those who thankfully survived the conflicts across the waters of the Mediterranean, it would be 1919 before they saw England again, with many of them suffering from the effects of malaria, contracted whilst members of the Salonika Expeditionary Force.

On Tuesday evening, June 15th 1915, a party of 80 munitions workers from Sheffield was provided with an enjoyable visit to Baslow and Monsal Head. Through the generosity of Thomas Wheater of Grimesthorpe, Sheffield, they were conveyed in motor charabancs, just after they had finished work, at which they had been almost night and day. They were only able to spare a few hours from their important work and would be on duty at 6a.m. next day. Mr. Wheater and the men called on an old friend, Mr. Fred Swindin, proprietor of the Royal Hotel, Baslow, where an impromptu concert was held.

Afterwards, the Home Guards and the Boy Scouts marched to the neighbouring village of Beeley, where a similar meeting was held, the Reverend Joseph Hewetson presiding, supported by E. Fearn and G. Wall.

At Beeley, on August 4th, a public meeting was held in front of the Devonshire Arms Hotel, simultaneously with meetings held throughout the length and breadth of the British Isles, to pass a resolution to prosecute the war with an inflexible determination to a successful conclusion.

Reverend Hewetson presided at the meeting. Mr. Cooper from the Peacock Hotel, who was Commandant of the Rowsley Home Guards, paraded the

Company, which looked very smart, wearing their arm brassards and marching to Beeley. Practically the whole village turned out. The Resolution was proposed by Tom Wall, the village blacksmith, and seconded by Lewis Reeves, proprietor of the Devonshire Arms, and it was carried with unanimity.

Red Cross Flag Day was held across the country in October 1915. The school children of Pilsley, Beeley and Edensor, who had been busily engaged in selling the little Red Cross Flags, assembled in front of the Estate Institute, Edensor. The Duchess of Devonshire, as County President of the Red Cross Society, was present and explained briefly the splendid objective which the Society had in attending to the needs of wounded soldiers. The proceedings ended with the singing of the *National Anthem.*

At Baslow, on that same day, Benjamin and Emily Jane Burdekin of the "Beeches", were in charge of the special day's proceedings, when £25 was raised. Ropes were stretched across the road in one part of the village and motorists and others had to pay a toll in the stage of purchasing a flag.

Meanwhile, at Beeley Day School, on the evening of November 19th, there was a Social Meeting promoted by "Mothers Meeting", assisted by the Girls' Friendly Society, with the proceeds meeting the costs of Christmas presents for the troops. Soldiers stationed at Chatsworth Park attended and musical items were provided by Misses N. Hawksworth, Sutton, Holmes, F. Holmes and Messrs. Earl, J. Stone and several soldiers, whilst the cake guessing competition was won by Mr. Benjamin Stone. Dancing also took place, accompanied by Misses N. Hawksworth and Sutton. At midnight, the *National Anthem* was sung.

By November 1915, Chatsworth Park and the Baslow area again became like a military centre as 600 officers and men from several Yeomanry Regiments and Scottish Horse Regiments, some of the latter wearing the kilt when walking round the village, arrived for winter training. Saturday December 18th witnessed a football match between the soldiers billeted at Baslow and those from Chatsworth, with Baslow coming out on top by four goals to one. Afterwards, they sat down to an excellent tea at the Royal Hotel, Baslow, whilst in the evening, an enjoyable concert was held.

In late December, a "Smoking Concert" was put on in the Stockdale Institute, Baslow, by the Yeomanry from Chatsworth Park, for the entertainment of 200 men and NCO's. This included songs sung by five of the men. A five round boxing exhibition was held between Privates Bowles and Spencer, with Bowles the winner, whilst Private Crossland was champion in a three round contest against Private Needham. Wrestling bouts were also held, the winner getting the best of three falls. At 9-45p.m., proceedings closed with the singing of the *National Anthem.*

All communities within the area, especially the women, were also eager to play their part in the war effort by forming Comfort Funds for local servicemen. Money was raised and knitting circles made clothes so that gift parcels could be sent to servicemen fighting in the war or to those who had been wounded, in order to raise their morale.

A National Egg Collection Scheme (NECS) was organised early in 1915, aiming to collect eggs for distribution to the hospitals and convalescent homes tending to the needs of the wounded servicemen. In the Bakewell district the scheme was organised by the Red Cross and local schools were often used as collecting points. Weekly or monthly lists appeared in the local newspapers highlighting the number of eggs collected by each town or village.

It was reported in late 1916 that Baslow had responded most handsomely since the start of the scheme. Out of the 15 depots in the Bakewell district, Baslow had the honour and distinction of supplying the largest total (5844), with Alport and Youlgreave contributing 5307 and Bakewell 5010.

Many of the men who volunteered for service in 1914 or early 1915 were destined for service overseas and 1915 saw continued British involvement on the Western Front and in other theatres of war. Turkey's entrance into the war on Germany's side in October 1914 had changed the war's complexion. Russia, already shaken by the reverses of 1914, was now virtually cut-off from Franco-British war supplies.

In an attempt to help Russia, a naval expedition was mounted to clear the Dardanelles for Russian ships in the Black Sea. When this venture stalled, an attack was planned on a little known peninsula called Gallipoli.

On the Western Front during 1915, the BEF extended its front southwards across the wet levels of the River Lys into the dreary coalfields west of Lille, where, during 1915, it fought a series of murderous trench to trench battles (Neuve Chapelle in March, Festubert May to June and Givenchy) and also mounted one major, miscarried offensive at Loos in September to October.

British casualties mounted as these attacks were launched during 1915 and increased again when the Germans launched their own major assault at the Second Battle of Ypres (April to May), this latter assault seeing poisonous gas being used by the Germans for the first time in the west.

Increase of lethal fire-power had given the advantage to the defence, for a continuous battle line prevented classical offensive manoeuvres. The Germans had adopted an elastic defence, in two or more lines, highly organised with entrenchments and barbed wire heavy in machine-guns and supported by artillery. Assaulting troops broke through the first line only to be decimated by the fire from the succeeding lines. As a consequence of these facts, we find that the number of men from the Devonshire and Rutland villages who died on the fields of battle or succumbed to their wounds throughout 1915, rose dramatically to fifteen.

The first of these casualties was a young officer with connections to the village of Baslow, who became one of the thousands of victims who was killed in daily shelling of the front line trenches and the back areas by the enemy.

GUARDSMAN GEORGE HULLEY No. 8698
2ND BATTALION GRENADIER GUARDS
DIED APRIL 10TH 1915 AGED 34

George was born at Beeley in 1880, the youngest of six children of Benjamin and Elizabeth Hulley. By 1891 the family was living close to the grocers and dyers shop, run by David Briggs, but by this stage the children's mother, Elizabeth, had died. She was a Baslow girl when she had married Benjamin, a native of Beeley, who was working as a general labourer on the Chatsworth Estate.

Some years before the war began, George left Beeley to live at Northwood, for he had married and settled with his wife, Mary Emily, in their new home, where they cared for their three young daughters. Sadly, Mary died and George was left to raise the young family with the help of relatives.

George Hulley of Beeley
Barbara Hawksworth

Earlier in his life, he had served in the Boer War as a regular soldier and used to say that the most thrilling experience was the cavalry charge on the enemy. On several occasions he had his horse shot from under him. At the conclusion of the South African War, the *High Peak News* reported that he was awarded the Queen's Medal with two bars.

For the following nine years he was a Reservist, and then signed on for another four years. He was summoned to join the Colours on the outbreak of the Great War and joined the Grenadier Guards. His time was spent in training recruits for Lord Kitchener's "New Army" of volunteers, but George was a born soldier and could not be satisfied till he was called to the Front.

On January 4th 1915 he crossed the English Channel with a draft of men for the 2nd Battalion Grenadier Guards and went into the line just north east of Bethune. George had a number of hair breadth escapes, including his hat strap on the top of his head being cut in two by a bullet, whilst he remained unscathed. Unfortunately, his good luck was not to last much longer.

93

At the Battle of Neuve Chapelle (March 10th to the 12th) the 2nd Battalion were only in support in a position of readiness, east of Gorre, and did not participate in the major action. On March 12th the Battalion relieved the Irish Guards at Givenchy, where the trenches were shallow and the parapet not bullet proof. The village was in complete ruins, the farms were burnt and farm wagons and implements were scattered on each side of the road. Shelling and sniping went on intermittently.

All throughout April the Battalion remained in the same trenches and were relieved by the Irish Guards every 48 hours, when they would go into billets at Preol.

Mining by the Germans had now become a regular and worrying practice, and everyone was always listening for any sound that might denote mining operations. The shelling continued regularly, and at times a battalion coming up to take its turn in the trenches would be subjected to unpleasant shelling, whilst the danger from German snipers was ever present. The Prince of Wales, who was a constant visitor during this period, even tried his hand at sniping back.

It was during this period of routine front line activity that Guardsman George Hulley was killed. News came to his father Benjamin that the end came on April 10th. He was buried in grave 1.F.18. In the Guards Cemetery, Windy Corner, Cuinchy, east of Bethune, France, and his name was later inscribed on the war memorials at Beeley and Darley Dale.

A week after his death, the vicar of Beeley, Reverend Hewetson, conducted a very impressive memorial service on Sunday evening. George had been a chorister in Beeley Parish Church, where for so many years his father had been clerk and sexton.

Sadly, George's death left three little girls orphaned and they were brought up in Darley Dale by George's sister, Mrs. Wall, and her husband Tom.

The Allied attack at Ypres never materialised because the plans were over-taken by a surprise German attack on April 22nd, preceded by a cloud of chlorine gas emitted from some 5000 cylinders. This was the first use of poison gas in the West. The Second Battle of Ypres had begun.

Gas had an insidious effect, similar to pneumonia, with its victims drowning as their lungs filled with fluid. Those who survived initial attacks could suffer from bronchial disease throughout their lives.

Two German Corps drove through two terrorised French Divisions and bit deeply into British and Canadian lines, creating a wide gap. The Germans, however, had made no preparations to exploit such a breakthrough, and had few reserves available because of their build up of forces in the east, as they attempted to defeat the Russian armies.

Local counter-attacks by the British Second Army, including Canadian forces, finally stemmed the German advance by May 25th, after bitter fighting. German losses were some 35,000 men; the British, Canadian and Indians lost 60,000 and the French 10,000 men.

Another man associated with the Chatsworth villages was included in these Allied losses.

LIEUTENANT ALWYN CHADWICK HOBSON
2ND LIFE GUARDS (HOUSEHOLD CAVALRY)
DIED MAY 13TH 1915 AGED 22

The Hobson family home was at Bromborough, Cheshire, on the Wirral Peninsula, between Ellesmere Port and Birkenhead. Alwyn was the youngest child of Richard and Mary Hobson, his father and mother being aged 56 years and 46 years respectively when he was born at Bromborough in 1892. By 1901, his father, Richard, was a retired cotton broker (agent), born in Manchester, who had married Mary, a native of Ashton-under-Lyne.

Lieutenant
Alwyn Chadwick Hobson
Chatsworth Photo Archive

Unfortunately, I have been unable to find any further information about Alwyn's education and what he did for a living. I have also failed to discover his connection with the Chatsworth Estate, for we know that his name is commemorated on the war memorial plaque in St. Peter's Church, Edensor. It is possible that he was working in some capacity for the estate or that he was living in rented property on the estate.

Whatever the connection, we know that Alwyn Hobson enlisted early in the war and joined 2nd Life Guards (Household Cavalry). By May 1915 he had risen to the rank of Lieutenant and the Regiment was stationed in the Ypres Salient and involved in the fighting during Second Ypres.

By May 1915, certain senior officers were suggesting that it would be wise to prepare for a withdrawal to a less acutely bent line nearer to Ypres. However, the French and members of the British High Command argued against a withdrawal and declared that lost ground could and should be retaken. Sir John French overruled the fighting commanders' wish to withdraw to the natural straight line of defence formed by the ramparts of Ypres and the canal.

So they stayed in the reduced Salient, "one huge artillery target", there to be pounded and gassed incessantly, with their scanty ammunition running out, until relief at last came, in the fourth week of May, through the Germans at last exhausting their surplus of shells. During this period, throughout May, men's lives were thrown away where there was no reasonable chance of advantage. One of these men who lost their lives was Alwyn Hobson.

During the second week of May the German 53rd Reserve Division attacked the 27th and 28th Divisions (including the 2nd Life Guards) in great strength along a ridge that runs west of Frezenberg, southwards from Wieltje, to merge into a higher ridge, covering the woods and lake at Bellewaarde, to the east of Hooge chateau on the Menin Road. Heavy bombardments and persistent infantry assaults caused many casualties. Eye witness accounts comment on the agonies of horses hit by shell splinters or by breaking their legs in pot-holes.

Four days later, on May 12th, The Cavalry Force, fighting as dismounted infantry, relieved the 27th Division. They had hardly reached the lines facing Frezenberg on that Thursday when the full fury of bombardment fell on them. The shellfire continued for eleven and a half hours, inflicting heavy casualties, particularly on the Life Guards, whose trenches were destroyed.

A counter-attack with bayonets was made later in the day but renewed shellfire checked two other counter-attacks by the re-grouped cavalry during the afternoon.

Lieutenant Alwyn Hobson was killed by shellfire on May 13th during this period of renewed fighting, and with his body never being recovered, he is commemorated on Panel 3 of the Menin Gate.

A month later, on June 16th, the Ypres Salient claimed another life when a man whose name is also commemorated on the Edensor memorial was killed in action at the charge at Hooge, undertaken in an attempt to retrieve from the Germans the high ground of the Bellewaerde Ridge, just to the east of Ypres.

The Germans had captured the Ridge during the Second Battle of Ypres and from the high ground their artillery could fire at will into the Allied positions. The Ridge was a trump card for the Germans and needed to be taken back from them.

Even Hooge Chateau was in the hands of the Germans – if it could still be called a chateau now that only two walls were left standing. No more than 50 yards away, the British held grimly on to the Chateau stables and to the pulverised rubble that was the ruins of Hooge village.

It was a nasty kink in the line and the task of the Third Division, including the 1st Battalion Northumberland Fusiliers, was to straighten the line and take the high ground of the Ridge. Unfortunately the slopes across which they would attack were entirely open, with little dead ground and no cover. Many were excited at the prospect of going over the top but sadly, our man with

Edensor connections, a Captain attached to the Northumberland Fusiliers, would not survive the day.

CAPTAIN LEONARD VALE BAGSHAWE
3ᴿᴰ BATTALION KING'S OWN SCOTTISH BORDERERS
(ATTACHED TO 1ˢᵀ BATTALION NORTHUMBERLAND FUSILIERS)
DIED JUNE 16ᵀᴴ 1915 AGED 37

Leonard Vale Bagshawe was born at Uppingham, in Rutland, on November 30ᵗʰ 1877, the son of Reverend William Vale Bagshawe, a cleric and schoolmaster, and Alice Bagshawe. His father had been Assistant Master at Repton School, before becoming the Master of the Uppingham Lower School (founded in 1584, a public school for boys). He resided at Baslow for some years, then became the Vicar of Isel and Rector of Pitchford (south of Shrewsbury), before settling at "Moorlands", Calver, near Baslow. William had been born at Wormhill, Derbyshire, whilst his wife (née Partridge), came from Bishopswood, Hertfordshire.

Leonard Vale Bagshawe
of Chatsworth and Edensor

Young Leonard was educated first in the Lower School, Uppingham, then at Shrewsbury, before entering Christ Church College, Oxford. He then entered the service of the Bombay Burma Trading Corporation and became one of their forest managers.

Whilst in England, he had been a keen and successful all-round sportsman. At college he rowed in the eight and represented Christ Church in the crew which competed for both Thames and Ladies in 1897 at Henley Regatta. They were beaten in the semi-final of the Ladies Plate by Emmanuel, and in the final of the Thames Cup by Kingston, after a thrilling race.

Leonard happened to be home on leave, at Calver, when war was declared, and he and three other members of the Company applied at once for a commission in the King's Own Scottish Borderers and was gazetted Second Lieutenant on August 30ᵗʰ 1914 and promoted to Lieutenant by November 9ᵗʰ. He trained at Portland and Sunderland and on December 4ᵗʰ 1914 he left for the Western Front in a draft of men and was attached to the 1ˢᵗ Battalion Northumberland Fusiliers in the vicinity of Ypres.

After acting as Captain for his Company for several months, whilst in training in Belgium and France, he was gazetted to that rank in May 1915. By this point, the Battalion had become part of the 3ʳᵈ Division which was destined to attack the Bellewaerde Ridge at Hooge on June 16th.

The first line trenches were easily taken in the early hours of Wednesday June 16th but mistakes were made when the 7th Brigade in reserve got carried away by the success and excitement and went charging forward before their time had come and got caught up in the British artillery barrage. When the barrage lifted, the survivors of the carnage advanced and took the second trench line, but it was the death-knell of the attack that might have won them back the Bellewaerde Ridge.

By 9-30a.m. the survivors were forced back to the first captured line of German trenches. They had been beaten by their blind enthusiasm, their own bravery and their own artillery. The total casualties on that day for the 3rd Division was 3,500 men, including the Commanding Officer of the 1st Battalion Northumberland Fusiliers and Captain Leonard Bagshawe.

Lieutenant Edward Partridge, a relative of Leonard's, wrote from Ypres:

"His example enabled his men to carry the position and retain it against counter-attacks, and they all speak so highly of his pluck and resource."

Private Pike, Northumberland Fusiliers, speaking from his hospital bed at Sheffield, said:

"I was with your son when he got killed in the great charge at Hooge on June 16th. I was very proud to be led by such a brave and noble man – for he led the Company as if he were in the streets of England.

"Captain Bagshawe and his men were in the fighting during the Second Battle of Ypres, at St. Eloi, St. Julien and Hill 60. One night he had 18 men in a trench which was shelled by the Germans in readiness for an attack. 16 men were killed or wounded. Captain Bagshawe mounted the parapet and fired into the attacking enemy. He and his two men held the trench through the night until daylight, causing the Germans to withdraw."

The Adjutant of his Battalion related:

"He was as popular with his men as with the officers. He was from the first in a responsible position, which he filled with great energy and tact.

"We were attacking, and I heard that he got into the first line of the enemy's trenches, and I think he was hit in the actual assault. He will have been buried close to where he fell, which is just south of the Ypres - Roulers railway, three miles east of Ypres."

Sadly, he was not buried close by where he fell. His body was not recovered and his name is honoured on Panel 22 of the Menin Gate. He is also commemorated on the war memorial plaque inside Edensor Church, Chatsworth. However, I have been unable to discover what his real connection was with the village and estate, although his father, Reverend Bagshawe, had lived for a time at Baslow and was only living a few miles away, at Calver, when Leonard died.

Our attention is now drawn many miles away from the Western Front, to a different theatre of war, the Gallipoli Campaign, fought against Turkish forces in 1915, which resulted in the deaths of those men from the Devonshire and villages, two of them serving in the same Battalion and losing their lives on the same day.

An amphibious operation led by General Ian Hamilton was planned on the little known peninsula called Gallipoli. The plan provided for two day-light assaults on April 25th, one at Cape Helles on the tip of the peninsula, the other by the Anzacs (Australian and New Zealand Army Corps) on the western side. At Cape Helles, the British landed on five beaches in a welter of mismanagement, incurring murderous losses. The Anzacs were beaten back by a vicious Turkish counter-attack, with a loss of 5000 men.

Both assaults had failed to capture the hill masses towering above the beaches and without these two critical heights the landings were doomed to failure. The Allied forces found themselves pinned down on their tiny beach-heads, involved in the same kind of trench warfare experienced on the Western Front.

Between August 6th and 8th, following months of the bitterest fighting on the rocky slopes of the Peninsula, General Hamilton attempted a co-ordinated assault. The Anzacs were to make the main effort with a night attack. The newly arrived British Divisions, including men from Rowsley, Edensor and Baslow, landing at Suvla Bay to the north, were to make a secondary attack, whilst from the Cape Helles position a holding attack was to pin down Turk-ish reserves.

The holding attack fulfilled its mission, but the Anzac attack bogged down in the darkness. Only the Suvla Bay landing, made without serious opposition, promised success. But the Corps Commander lacked vigour and drive. The advance lagged until Turkish reinforcements had time to come up, and again it was too late. The entire operation had failed.

PRIVATE FRANK HEMMING No. 13283
9TH BATTALION SHERWOOD FORESTERS
DIED AUGUST 9TH 1915 AGED 27

Frank was born in 1889, the sixth of the eight children of Thomas and Elizabeth Hemming, with all the children being born at Malvern Link, part of Great Malvern, in Worcestershire. Thomas came from nearby Madresfield and married Elizabeth, who originated from the town of Worcester. He was a coach wheeler by trade, whilst by 1901, Elizabeth was earning extra money for the family as a charwoman, taking in other people's clothes to wash.

At some stage before the start of the Great War, Frank had arrived in

Derbyshire to work on the Chatsworth Estate and like Joseph Barber, he travelled to enlist at Derby, joining the 9th Battalion.

PRIVATE (DRUMMER) FRANK VICK No. 13109
9TH BATTALION SHERWOOD FORESTERS
DIED AUGUST 9TH 1915 AGED 25

Frank Vick of Baslow
Derbyshire Times
and John Taylor

Born in 1890, Frank was the only son and second child of Frank Vick senior and Carrie Vick. Frank senior originated from Birmingham but came to Sheffield, where he met Carrie and by 1891 was earning his living as a bicycle manufacturer. It was in the Eccleshall and Bierlow area of Sheffield that Frank junior and his elder sister, Ethel, were born, but by 1901 they were living in Baslow, where their father was the proprietor for three years of the Royal Hotel, next to the Devonshire Arms Hotel. Eventually, he became proprietor of the latter inn and served as President of the local Licensed Victuallers Association.

Between 1902 and 1905 Frank junior was educated at Lady Manners School on Bath Street, Bakewell. After leaving school, Frank served his apprenticeship as a joiner with Robert Smith of Bakewell, after which he was employed at Hardwick Hall and other places under the "Association for the Restoration of Old Halls and Abbeys".

He was Sergeant drummer in the late Church Lads Brigade at Baslow, a fact which stood him in good stead in the Army, as he was quickly appointed a drummer in the 9th Battalion. He was a playing member of Baslow Football Club and at one time was a promising player. Unfortunately, knee trouble developed and he was kept out of the later teams. He was a member of the Church Lads Brigade when they won the Diocesan Shield, under the late Captain Harry Taylor, a unique performance for such a small place as Baslow. He enlisted at Derby and he too joined the 9th Battalion. Shortly before his death in 1915, Frank's father had retired from the hotel business, to a cottage in Baslow.

By April 1915 the 9th Battalion Sherwood Foresters were part of the 11th Division of Kitchener's New Army. They were now ready to take their place in the eight month campaign in Gallipoli. The landings on April 25th had not gone very well and progress was limited. Demands were made in Britain for some of Kitchener's New Army to be sent to Galliploi, and so it was that Frank Hemming and Frank Vick sailed from Bristol on the "Empress of Britain" on July 1st.

Stopping en route at Malta and Alexandria, there followed a pleasant crossing of the Aegean Sea to Mudros Bay, on Lemnos, a Greek island off the Gallipoli Peninsula, which was the Allied base for the whole operation.

They landed on July 20th at Cape Helles, to find the British Army in a state of complete exhaustion and they were withdrawn to Lemnos to prepare for a new attack on the Peninsula. The landings took place north of Suvla Bay on August 6th but little headway was made in the scorching heat and against fierce resistance by the Turkish soldiers.

At dawn on August 9th, orders were received to move forward. After advancing about 1000 yards the Battalion encountered heavy fire and suffered many casualties. Eventually the advance was held up on the right and in the centre near the orchard at Hetman Char. The majority of officers had been casualties by 7a.m. However, the Battalion held on to the line until 6p.m., when it withdrew 100 yards to the rear. At the end of the day there had been 19 officer casualties and about 300 men.

It was during this bloody day of battle that Joseph Barber, Frank Hemming and Frank Vick were killed, the latter being shot through the head whilst attacking "Chocolate Hill". Their bodies were never recovered from the battlefield and their names are now commemorated on Panel 150 to 152, Helles Memorial.

LANCE CORPORAL SYDNEY JOHN CHANDLER No. 6469
8TH BATTALION NORTHUMBERLAND FUSILIERS
DIED AUGUST 19TH 1915 AGED 22

Sydney was eight years old in 1901 and living in Trowbridge, Wiltshire, 13 miles east of Bath, with his father, George Chandler, a police constable, and his mother Jane. She had been born in Kensington, London, whilst George was a native of Collingbourne, Wiltshire.

At some stage before the First World War Sydney Chandler arrived at Chatsworth to be employed in the Kitchen gardens. We know that on March 1st 1910, Sydney's uncle, Alfred James Chandler, aged 37, a gardener living at Cheam, Surrey, married Emily Hutchinson, daughter of the Pilsley blacksmith, Robert Hutchinson, at Edensor Church and came to work at Chatsworth. It would seem that Sydney joined his uncle to work in the Chatsworth gardens.

Shortly after the war commenced he enlisted at Sheffield and eventually joined the 8th Battalion Northumberland Fusiliers and rose to the rank of Lance Corporal, although at the time of his death he was serving as an Acting Corporal.

By the beginning of August 1915 the 8th Battalion were part of the Mediterranean Force at the Dardanelles and between August 1st and 5th were in bivouac at Lemnos, waiting to take part in the attack at Suvla Bay.

At 4p.m. the Battalion embarked on two destroyers and left at 7-30p.m.for Suvla Bay, on the Gallipoli Peninsula, arriving about 11-30p.m. The enemy opened shrapnel and rifle fire as the men disembarked at 3-30a.m. under fire. The Battalion took part in the attack on Turkish trenches which was successful and fighting continued until 7a.m.

They remained on the beach during August 7th and then went into Divisional Reserve. By August 9th they were back in the firing line, receiving casualties, whilst consolidating their position. For the next 7 days they were in and out of the front line trenches, receiving casualties from sniper fire and shell fire. On August 17th they marched out at 8p.m. to occupy the trenches, relieving the 5th Dorsetshire Regiment and between August 17th and 18th they had casualties of 4 men killed and 11 wounded.

At 4a.m. on August 19th they were ordered to attack an entrenched position 700 yards in front of their line, with "X" and "Z" Companies attacking and "W" and "Y" Companies in support.

They advanced almost up to the enemy trenches but were unable to capture the position owing to the heavy fire from machine-guns and rifles. The men occupied a gulley and were caught in closed order at dawn by shrapnel. They had to retire to the reserve trenches with 2 officers killed, 5 wounded and 3 missing, whilst 23 other ranks were killed, 141 wounded and 88 men missing.

One of the 23 men killed was Sydney Chandler, whose body was never recovered and he is commemorated on Panel 33 to 35, Helles Memorial.

The year 1915 was now drawing to a conclusion. In the wider view of events on the world stage, Gallipoli was entering its final stages, with huge casualty lists posted but no success. Gallipoli was finally evacuated on January 19th 1916, with the eight and a half month campaign costing the Allies some 215,000 men, of whom 145,000 were due to sickness, 50,000 from dysentery.

Appalling losses had been suffered on the Western Front during 1915 on both sides. 612,000 Germans, 1,292,000 French and 279,000 British became casualties. The year ended with no appreciable shift in the hostile battle lines scarring the land from the North Sea to the Swiss Alps.

Both French and British had gained in experience, if not in wisdom, from the 1915 battles, but they had afforded the Germans still better experiences in the way to frustrate such attacks. In 1916, therefore, it was to be the Germans who profited heavily both by the offensive and the defensive lesson. Fifteen men from the Devonshire and Rutland villages had lost their lives during 1915 but the sacrifice made by these villages in 1916 would prove just as traumatic, with the loss of a further 14 men.

Chapter Four

1916 – THE YEAR OF THE SOMME

The year 1916 will always be remembered by the British and the French for its association with the names **SOMME** and **VERDUN**. The year was to witness a terrible escalation in the number of casualties for both the Allies and the Germans on the Western Front as a result of these two major battles.

The German offensive against the French at the Siege of Verdun (February to December 1916) and the British and French offensive against the German forces in the Battle of the Somme (July to November) resulted in the cost to the British and the French of upwards of one million casualties for very little gain, especially on the Somme.

The German attack on Verdun was intended to "bleed France white", for the Germans knew that the French would defend the city to the last man. By June 1916 the French situation was desperate and the French asked General Haig, British Commander-in-Chief, to hasten a relieving action on the Somme. This, despite the fact that the German defences were at their strongest on this sector of the Somme front. The offensive was set for July 1st. From that date, no fresh German divisions would be sent to the Verdun Front. The German attack there slowly stalled, then failed. The Somme battles therefore contributed to save Verdun but at a terrible cost to Britain's citizen army.

By the end of 1915 most people shared an optimistic view of how the war would progress, but this was shattered by the unfolding events of 1916. More Devonshire village men were to die in battle during the year, all on the Western Front, and ten lost their lives during the Battle of the Somme, two falling on the battlefield on the very first day of the offensive.

Voluntary enlistment was no longer an option for Britain and even before the Somme, casualties on the Western Front and at Gallipoli demanded replacements that could only be filled by conscription. In January 1916, by the Military Service Act, the voluntary system was abandoned and compulsory enlistment came into being.

As a result of these actions, all families were now deeply affected by the Great War. In addition, casualties were increasing from bombing raids from

Zeppelins, food stuffs were not so readily available and a movement of labour from the land and in domestic service into the munitions industry was steadily mounting.

A report in the *High Peak News* in March 1916 indicates that the villages in the locality were playing their part in contributing to the war effort on the Home Front. The newspaper reports that in addition to raising funds for the Belgian refugees and providing comforts for the servicemen, they were taking part enthusiastically in the National Egg Collecting Scheme, inaugurated locally in January 1915, for the supply of local eggs to hospitals and convalescent homes catering for wounded servicemen.

It appeared that Baslow had responded most handsomely. Out of 15 depots in the Bakewell district, Baslow had the honour and distinction of supplying the largest total so far (5844), with Alport and Youlgreave collecting 5307 and Bakewell 5010.

For the 9th Duke of Devonshire and his family, 1916 witnessed great changes to their lives as a consequence of the war.

Victor Cavendish (1868 - 1938) was the eldest nephew of the childless 8th Duke of Devonshire, and on his uncle's death in 1908, Victor inherited the title as 9th Duke. In the House of Lords before the Great War he had been Conservative Whip and later the Civil Lord of the Admiralty.

In the summer of 1916 the King summoned the Duke of Devonshire and asked him to become the new Governor General of Canada. The Duke, his wife Evelyn (daughter of the 5th Marquis of Lansdowne), his family and most of the Devonshire establishment – servants, furniture, pictures etc. – departed by the end of October 1916, and by mid November they were comfortably installed in Rideau Hall, the Governor General's official residence in Ottawa. The next few years proved to be the happiest and most successful years of Duke Victor's life. He performed his role as constitutional head of state impeccably throughout the turbulent years ahead and he and his family did not return to live at Chatsworth until 1920/1921.

PRIVATE HERBERT GRINDEY No. 178077 1ST BATTALION CANADIAN INFANTRY (WESTERN ONTARIO REGIMENT) DIED JULY 9TH 1916 AGED 44

Herbert's grandfather, William Grindey, was born at Beeley in 1812, and after leaving school he became an agricultural labourer on the Duke of Devonshire's Chatsworth Estate. He married Mary Brown, an Irish girl from Belfast, who was possibly working in service at Chatsworth and by 1871, 59 year old William was a shepherd on the ducal estate and still living at Beeley.

Living with them were his sons John, a 21 year old labourer and 25 year old

Isaac James Grindey, a stone mason. On February 9th 1870, Isaac had married Sarah Ann Hawksworth, aged 22, daughter of Samuel Hawksworth, a Beeley labourer. With Isaac and Sarah was their 10 month old son, William.

Their second son, Herbert Grindey, was born in late 1872 and younger brother Ernest in 1877, but sadly, in March 1878 their mother, Sarah,

Isaac Grindey
Barbara Hawksworth

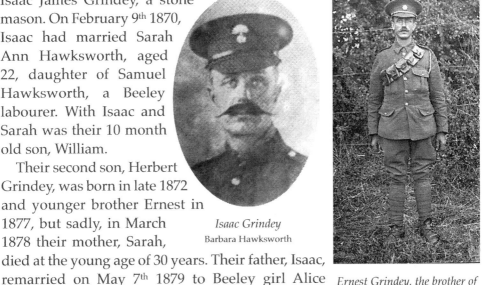

died at the young age of 30 years. Their father, Isaac, remarried on May 7th 1879 to Beeley girl Alice Hawksworth, 30 year old daughter of Beeley stone-cutter, Joseph Hawksworth.

Ernest Grindey, the brother of Herbert Grindey
Barbara Hawksworth

By 1891 we find that although Isaac and Alice were still living in Beeley, with their 14 year old son, Ernest, 19 year old Herbert Grindey had left England and emigrated to Canada. This was the period when there was a great deal of interest in the search for gold and other precious minerals and in fact, around 1896 the famous Klondike gold rush occurred in the Yukon territories, North West Territories of Canada. When Herbert enlisted for the Canadian Army on December 6th 1915, it is interesting that he gave his occupation as prospector.

He travelled to Montreal to enlist and I believe he gave a false age. Herbert told the Military Authorities that he was born on June 15th 1875, making him 40 years of age, when in actual fact he had been born earlier, in 1872. If it had been known that he was over 40 years of age, he would probably have been turned down at this stage of the war. His medical record stated that he was fair, with blue eyes, five feet eleven inches tall, with a tattoo of his own name on his body. At first he was drafted to the 87th Battalion, Canadian Grenadiers, but eventually joined the 1st Battalion Canadian Infantry (Western Ontario Regiment).

Herbert sailed with the Canadian Expeditionary Force in March 1916 and landed at Liverpool (with the Expeditioary Force was another Derbyshire emigrant, Edgar Fletcher from Edensor, who would die from wounds in 1919). Herbert was able to return to Derbyshire to see his brothers, Ernest and William. William was a gritstone quarry worker, married to Maud and living with their children, Edith and Mabel, at Beeley. Ernest was a blacksmith on the Chatsworth Estate, but later in life he would look after the Chatsworth Golf Course and resided at Edensor. However, in the Great War, he too had joined the Army, the British Army, but unlike his brother Herbert, he would survive the conflict.

By early 1916, Herbert travelled with his Canadian Regiment to be stationed in the Ypres Salient. The severest fighting in the Salient during the year came at the start of a very wet June, when an attempt was made by the Germans to relieve the Allies of the one remaining section of rising ground east of Ypres that they possessed. Known as Observatory Ridge, it ran eastwards from Zillebeke to Sanctuary Wood and Hill 62 and Mount Sorrel. It would also strengthen the German position at Hooge, astride the Menin Road.

Facing the Germans was the Canadian Corps, including Herbert Grindey, deployed to defend Mount Sorrel under a British Corps Commander, General Sir Julien Byng. The German assault was preceded by a bombardment, tunnelling and the planting of mines.

At 1p.m. on June 2nd the first mines exploded at Mount Sorrell and the Bavarian Infantry burst through the Canadian position, resulting in high casualties to the defenders. Torrential rain fell and General Byng was able to call upon 200 artillery guns. With this support, the Canadians were at last able to go forward on the night of 12th/13th June and recovered the lost trenches south of the Menin Road. Beyond the Menin Road, however, the fortnight's fighting left the German hold on Hooge strengthened and they looked down upon the Allied line, able to shell the defenders at will.

Herbert Grindey had survived the fortnight's severe fighting, but his luck ran out in early July, when he was caught by shell fire whilst serving in the front line trenches. His body was recovered and he was later buried in grave XV11.E.5. Hooge Crater Cemetery, 4 kilometres east of Ypres.

Well to the south of Ypres, the Battle of the Somme continued to be ground out during the months of August and September and with its insatiable appetite for lives, it claimed more victims from the Chatsworth villages during these months. The first casualty from the area came from Edensor and was the young son of the Duke of Devonshire's Agent.

SECOND LIEUTENANT ANDREW PEPYS COCKERELL
2ND BATTALION KING'S ROYAL RIFLE CORPS
DIED AUGUST 15TH 1916 AGED 19

In 1901 the Cockerell family was to be found at Compton Lodge, Eastbourne, part of the Duke of Devonshire's estates. 34 year old John Pepys

Cockerell, born in London, was the Land Agent to the Duke of Devonshire in this part of the Duke's domain, and was married to Florence. The rest of the household consisted of four year old Andrew, who was born at Horndean, just north of Portsmouth, and eight servants. In later years, further children were born to complete the family.

By 1913, however, John Pepys Cockerell was living at Edensor and was Agent for the Chatsworth Estate. Their eldest son, Andrew, was educated at Eton and had entered for Trinity College, Cambridge, in May 1915. When an appeal was made for officers, he responded to the call, entering Sandhurst.

Andrew Pepys Cockerell
of Edensor and Chatsworth

High Peak News, courtesy of
Potter and Company, Solicitors

He was granted a commission in November and underwent a course of musketry at Hythe. He showed exceptional ability as a marksman, particularly with the Lewis gun, gaining 5th position out of 500 in competition. Andrew was invited to join the Machine-Gun Corps on account of his proficiency but he declined to do so, and after acting as instructor in the 5th Battalion, a reserve Battalion based at Sheerness, he was posted to the 2nd Battalion King's Royal Rifle Corps and went to France on May 16th 1916. Three months later he would be dead.

The Battalion was involved in early actions in the Battle of the Somme and sustained high casualties. Again, on July 23rd, after an intense artillery barrage, the Battalion attacked the Switch Line near Pozieres. The Germans opened up a violent machine-gun fire from the left flank. "D" Company succeeded in penetrating the German line and portions of other Companies were successful. Unfortunately, the Royal Sussex Regiment, who were attacking another trench to the left, failed completely, as did the 10th Gloucesters on the right.

The Germans kept up a severe bombing attack on both flanks and the remains of the Battalion were forced to withdraw, with severe losses, the second time within a month. Since June 30th they had lost 22 officers and 52 men killed, 303 wounded, 150 missing and 64 gassed, a total of 591 men.

After a rest on the night of July 23rd they marched to billets in Albert, where they received a draft of 95 men. On July 26th they marched to Franvillers and welcomed another large draft, which made up for the losses on the 23rd.

For a fortnight they were in camp at Henencourt Wood, resting, but also involved with training until the evening of August 13th, when they marched to Becourt Wood and went into bivouac, before going into Divisional Reserve at Mametz Wood.

They remained in Mametz Wood until August 18th, furnishing working parties. This was not the simple bloodless work that it sounds, as the Germans heavily shelled the Wood daily and on August 15th the Battalion casualties for the day were Second Lieutenant Andrew Pepys Cockerell killed and two officers wounded, together with many NCO's and Riflemen. Andrew Cockerell was buried in grave V.O.10. Dantzig Alley British Cemetery, Mametz, 8 kilometres east of Albert.

A most impressive memorial service was held at St. Peter's Church,

LANCE CORPORAL GEORGE CHARLES RADFORD No. 17472
"3" COMPANY 1ST BATTALION GRENADIER GUARDS
DIED SEPTEMBER 10TH 1916 AGED 22

In 1901, seven year old George Radford was living with his family in the estate village of Old Warden entire, between Bedford and Biggleswade. His father, 45 year old Charles Radford, a cowkeeper, was born at Old Warden, whilst his mother Ann came from nearby Biggleswade. Twelve year old Maud, Arthur, eleven and William aged five, completed the family.

At some stage before the Great War, George left the estate village of Old Warden entire to work on another estate, that of Chatsworth, and lived in the village of Edensor.

He enlisted in the army at Derby early in the war, and, being a tall man, became a member of the Grenadier Guards and was drafted into No. "3" Company of the 1st Battalion.

The Battalion was not involved in the earlier actions of the Battle of the Somme, but through late August to September 7th they went through a period of training nearby. On September 8th they moved up into the line and took over the village of Ginchy, which had just been captured, and were in reserve.

Early on September 10th, it was learned that a gap had opened up between the Welsh Guards, who were digging in near the corner of Delville Wood, and the 4th Battalion Grenadier Guards.

It was decided to employ some companies from the Battalions in reserve to fill up the gap and one company of the 1st Battalion was sent to support the 4th Battalion Grenadiers and another company to the Welsh Guards.

Hardly had the Welsh Guards finished their relief, when they were attacked, and had to fight hard to maintain their position. Attacking in great force at 3a.m. on September 10th, the Germans began to press them back on the right. Every available man had been hurried to the front line, where the casualties were thinning out the ranks to an alarming extent, and even the

100 Grenadiers who had been sent up as ammunition carriers had to be put in as supports.

At that vital point, No. "3" Company 1st Battalion Grenadiers arrived, having passed through a barrage of 5·9 inch shells near Trones Wood, in artillery formation. They were sent to take over the line and relieve the Munster Fusiliers, who were very shaken after heavy fighting, achieving this by noon.

Two sections were placed in shell holes on the left and established a double block at that end of the trench with a strong bombing section, supported by a Lewis gun, with the other Lewis gun stationed on the right flank.

At 10p.m on September 10th the German attack began, coming on in four waves and succeeding in getting between No. "3" Company and the Welsh Guards. The Germans even entered the front trench. The Lewis gun did excellent work but the men in the bombing post were all knocked out. The front line was falling back somewhere to the centre of Ginchy and No. "3" Company was asked to fill the gap until reinforcements could arrive.

The Company's situation was now precarious. The enemy were at each end of a very long trench and were in front and behind. The men were short of bombs and practically out of ammunition, yet they refused to yield an inch and managed to kill the Germans in this advanced trench with their bayonets.

Two officers, many NCO's and 56 men of No. "3" Company were killed, but the rest fought on. When the ground was afterwards cleared, over 100 Germans were found dead in front of the trench. However, one of the many NCO's of the Company killed on September 10th was Lance Corporal George Charles Radford. He has no known grave but is commemorated on Pier and Face 8D Thiepval Memorial.

PRIVATE ROBERT BRATBY BATES No. 3499
4TH BATTALION (TERRITORIAL) NORTHUMBERLAND FUSILIERS
DIED SEPTEMBER 15TH 1916 AGED 27

We find that in 1901 the Bates family was living at Heath and Reach, a village in Bedfordshire, two miles north of Leighton Buzzard. The head of the household was 39 year old George Bates, a miller and farmer at Grange Mill, although ten years earlier, his occupation was bricklayer. He had been born at Edlesborough, 12 miles from Aylesbury in Buckinghamshire and had married Mary, a Bedfordshire girl. At Grange Mill they were raising a family of ten children, with Robert being the third eldest, at 11 years of age.

Before the start of the war, members of the family moved into Derbyshire.

His sister, Mrs. J. Windle, lived at Pilsley, on the Chatsworth estate. Robert lived at Baslow and was first employed in the building department at Chatsworth and later in the gasworks. This was situated below the kitchen gardens, near the present day caravan site. Pipes led off from the works to provide gas for Chatsworth House and for Edensor.

Robert enlisted in the Army at Bakewell and joined the 4th Battalion Northumberland Fusiliers, which was part of 149th Brigade, 50th Division. Whilst on leave, on March 4th 1916, he married Mrs. Fanny Horne (née Matthews), whose first husband had only lived nine months after their marriage. Sadly, she would lose her second husband just six months later.

Private Robert Bratby Bates
of Baslow and Edensor
Chatsworth Photo Archive

In September 1916, Robert and the 4th Battalion were preparing for another major "push" in the Battle of the Somme, planned for September 15th and aimed against the villages of Martinpuich, Flers and Courcelette, together with the much sought after High Wood. The use of a limited number of tanks formed part of the plan.

The 50th Division of 149 Brigade, including the 4th Battalion, was involved in the attack on High Wood and Martinpuich. The Germans defended High Wood in three lines of trenches at the rear of the wood (Hook Trench, Martin Trench and Starfish Line). The 50th Division front was about 1100 yards in extent, with the right flank exposed to fire from the enemy in High Wood, whilst the left flank was exposed to fire from trenches south of Martinpuich. Even so, it was decided that they would begin the advance on September 15th despite knowing that the casualties would be heavy.

At 6-20a.m. the 4th Battalion advanced in good order, with the support of two tanks, and quickly gained Hook Trench. On the high ground to the north-west corner of High Wood, the enemy had very strongly defended positions, containing a large number of machine-guns.

The advance to the second objective was timed for 7-20a.m. and until that hour the 4th and 7th Battalions Northumberland Fusiliers made every effort to take shelter from the devastating fire coming from their right.

It was apparent that the 47th Division on their right had not taken High Wood and were held up. It was therefore all the more urgent for 149th Brigade to push on and outflank the enemy in the wood, thus compelling him to evacuate his position.

At 7-20a.m. they advanced and captured part of Starfish Line and Martin

Trench but from both flanks the enemy's fire caused very heavy casualties amongst the attacking troops. The 4th Battalion, unsupported on their right by the 47th Division, were driven back to Hook Trench, which was strengthened and made secure.

Although both the 4th and 7th Battalions suffered heavy losses, their splendid dash and gallantry helped High Wood and Martinpuich to be subsequently occupied by the flank divisions.

The losses of the 4th Battalion between September 14th and 16th 1916 were 17 officers killed or wounded, 110 men killed, 229 wounded and 143 men missing.

One of those who was killed on September 15th was Robert Bratby Bates of Baslow, whose body was not recovered and whose name appears on Pier and Face 10B, 11B and 12B, Thiepval Memorial.

LANCE CORPORAL JOHN FORBES No. 13106
9TH BATTALION SHERWOOD FORESTERS
DIED SEPTEMBER 26TH 1916 AGED 23

Lance Corporal John Forbes of Chatsworth (Edensor)
Chatsworth Photo Archives

John was born at Castlepollard, County West-meath, Ireland, on October 26th 1892, his parents being Mr. and Mrs. Archibald Forbes. They moved to County Cork, to live at Ballymacar-berry and then Clonmel, both villages being a few miles from Lismore and the Irish estates of the Duke of Devonshire. It would appear that John worked on the Lismore estate, before coming to live at Edensor and working on the Chatsworth Estate as a woodsman.

John enlisted at Derby soon after war was declared and joined the 9th Battalion Sherwood Foresters, and by the middle of 1916 he was serving with the rank of Lance Corporal and about to take part in the Battle of the Somme.

Throughout mid to late July 1916, the Battalion was engaged in training at a camp between St. Pol and Arras, but on September 2nd they entrained at Frevent for the Somme area, moving into billets at Bouzincourt by the 5th and relieving the 13th Cheshire Regiment in the trenches at Ovillers, north of Albert, the following day.

Between September 7th and 23rd, the Battalion was in the front line, being

111

heavily shelled and receiving casualties each day. When a further big "push" was attempted on September 15th towards Combles, with the use of tanks, the 9th Battalion moved from reserve into support dug-outs and suffered a few casualties. By the end of the day the crest of the ridge had been gained except on the right, and with it the commanding observation which the Germans had so long enjoyed.

The following day also saw support being provided and during the next six days they received casualties of 13 men killed and 40 wounded, mainly by shell fire. At 12 midnight, on September 22nd, the Battalion was relieved and the men proceeded to camp in huts and tents at Mailly-Maillet, north of Albert. New clothing was issued and baths were taken by the men.

September 25th saw the Battalion moving at 3-30p.m. to Ovillers Post, teas were taken at Martinsart Wood at 5p.m. and at 8p.m. they moved off to Ovillers, where tools and bombs were issued, ready for the attack on the following day, September 26th.

At 10-15a.m. on September 26th, companies began moving into position and by 11-30a.m. the movement was complete. The three assaulting companies moved off by whistle signal at zero hour, 12-35p.m., and occupied the first objective. "B" Company pressed too close into the barrage and small parties had to come a short way back and casualties occurred through this. Two machine-guns were captured, being fired up to the last moment and the teams were killed to a man by "D" Company, whilst one trench mortar and 92 prisoners were also taken.

At 12-59p.m. the assaulting companies moved towards the second objective, Zollern Trench, and a specially chosen bombing party went forward. Companies again pressed too close to their own barrage and casualties occurred, but by 1-45p.m. Zollern Trench had been captured. Seeing that the assaulting companies had suffered many casualties, two platoons of reinforcements were sent forward from "C" Company.

200 prisoners had been taken in Zollern Trench and three machine-guns. The Germans in many dug-outs refused to come out and these were bombed.

By 2-40p.m. "B" and "D" Companies had gone forward to attack Hessian Trench and this was taken, with 45 men and an officer captured.

All companies of the Battalion had moved into Hessian Trench by 3-23p.m. During the night the enemy was very active in sniping and collected in some numbers in the right end of Hessian. The night passed without incident and bombs, flares and water was sent up to the trench.

It was during the severe fighting on September 26th that Lance Corporal John Forbes was killed in action. He became one of many casualties whose bodies were never found and his name is inscribed with others on Pier and Face 10C, 10D and 11A, Thiepval Memorial.

PRIVATE EDWARD THOMAS EDWARDS No. 43096
1ST BATTALION LINCOLNSHIRE REGIMENT
DIED SEPTEMBER 29TH 1916 AGED 24

The village of Pulford, five miles south of Chester, on the English side of the border between England and Wales, was the home of the Edwards family in 1901. Edward Thomas Edwards was nine years of age and lived with his three year old sister, Margaret, and Welsh parents, 34 year old Edward and 32 year old Annie.

Edward senior, an agricultural labourer, was born at Pennant in North Wales, whilst Annie was born at Guilsfield, near Welshpool. Their children, however, were born in England, Edward at Tattenhall, six miles south-east of Chester and Margaret at Pulford.

Some years before the start of the Great War we find that Edward junior was employed on the Chatsworth Estate and when war was declared he enlisted at Bakewell and joined the Sherwood Foresters (No. 3308). At some point in the war he was transferred to the 1st Battalion Lincolnshire Regiment and took part in the Battle of the Somme.

September 15th saw a major "push", with the object of breaking down German resistance and getting through to Bapaume and saw the use of tanks for the first time as they pushed beyond Flers and took High Wood, Martin-puich and Courcelette. Ten days later, on September 25th, another big attack compelled the Germans to evacuate Combles.

Early on September 16th the Lincolnshires marched to a position on the road between Mametz and Montauban and remained until night, when they went into the trenches south of Gueudecourt, between Flers and Les Boeufs, in Brigade Reserve, three miles from the front line.

Between September 17th and 22nd the Battalion was heavily engaged in the fighting and lost one officer and seven men killed and three officers and thirty three men wounded.

Bad weather set in during the close of the Battle of Flers-Courcelette and it was September 25th before the next attack could be undertaken, with a general attack on the whole front from the Somme to Martinpuich. The 1st Battalion was part of the attacking brigade, with their objective being a track south east of the village of Gueudecourt.

The Battalion moved from Fricourt Camp to arrive at Pommiers Redoubt at 1p.m. and after hot tea and rum were served around 10p.m., they marched to the assembly trenches.

Zero hour was 12-35p.m. on September 25th and "A" and "C" Companies advanced 50 yards when they came into the enemy's artillery barrage from the right and machine-gun fire from the right front. In spite of heavy casualties, there was no wavering until the brigade front was reached.

"A" Company advanced towards the first objective and assisted the Grenadier Guards to attack a strongpoint in "Gas Alley". The casualties by now were heavy and they were unable to reach it and so they began to consolidate.

Meanwhile, "B" and "D" Companies, supported by the Battalion bombers, left Switch Trent but were met with a terrific barrage falling on their advancing line, with shells bursting and tearing gaps in their line.

These two Companies advanced 1500 yards, with officers and men falling every minute. It was 1p.m. when "B" and "D" Companies arrived in the original front line trench, greatly depleted in numbers. At about 1-37p.m., the barrage lifted, but the enemy's machine-guns continued to pour a venomous fire and it was not possible to advance to the assistance of "A" Company, which had gone to assist the attack of the 4th Grenadiers.

The Lincolnshires were withdrawn to the Sunken Road east of Flers and reorganised. Their losses in the battle were three officers and twenty one men killed, eight officers and 127 men wounded and sixteen men missing. It was during these actions that Edward Thomas Edwards was severely wounded. Taken first to a Casualty Clearing Station near the front line, it was found necessary to evacuate Edward to one of the base hospitals grouped in the town of Rouen. Despite every care and attention, he succumbed to his wounds on September 29th and was buried in grave B.15.36., St. Sever Cemetery, Rouen.

September merged into October and the fighting on the Somme continued, as General Haig called for more futile efforts throughout October and into November.

A woodsman on the Chatsworth estate became the final victim of the fighting during 1916, killed by shellfire in the aftermath to the fighting on the Somme.

SERGEANT FRANK GEORGE CHAMBERLAIN No. S/43007
1ST BATTALION QUEEN'S OWN CAMERON HIGHLANDERS
DIED NOVEMBER 22ND 1916 AGED 25

Born in 1891, at Didling, Sussex, Frank was fourth eldest of the six children of John Thomas Chamberlain and his wife, Lydia. Didling was a small village near Midhurst, ten miles north of Chichester and in 1891 John Thomas Chamberlain was the village police constable. He had been born at Brampton in Hampshire, whilst Lydia was a native of Hertford, but most of his adult life he spent on the South Downs as a police constable, in a number of villages clustered around Midhurst.

By 1901, ten year old Frank Chamberlain was living with his family at nearby Iping, but before the Great War he arrived in Derbyshire to work on the Chatsworth Estate as a woodsman, living at Edensor in the home of a senior woodsman.

Frank enlisted at Bedford and joined the Army, being drafted to the 1st Battalion Queen's Own Cameron Highlanders.

Between November 1st and 4th 1916, the Battalion was in the Somme area, billeted in huts at Hennencourt Wood, just to the west of Albert. On November 5th they marched through Albert, to Becourt, on the eastern outskirts of the town. They supplied large working parties every day between November 6th to the 15th.

On November 16th Frank and his Battalion marched to huts just west of High Wood and the following day took over the front line trenches east of Eacourt from the 4th Battalion Yorkshire Regiment.

It was here on November 18th, a few kilometres south-west of Bapaume, that the enemy began a heavy barrage at 6a.m. on the Support Company and inflicted several casualties. Conditions in the trenches were bad as there was heavy artillery fire throughout the day and also on the following day.

Sergeant Frank George Chamberlain of Chatsworth (Edensor)
Chatsworth Photo Archive

It was during this period of bombardment that Frank Chamberlain was wounded.

Taken to a Casualty Clearing Station he succumbed to his wounds on November 22nd and was buried in grave V11.H.48. Warlencourt British Cemetery, five kilometres south-west of Bapaume.

In the atrociously wet days of late October and early November, the last major attack on the Somme in 1916, on November 13th, had succeeded in capturing the shattered village of Beaumont Hamel. The blood soaked disputed high ground had been won, but the October/November fighting condemned the British soldiers to spending the winter in cloying mud and flooded trenches, down in the valley.

Nothing of any strategic value had been attained by this latter effort. The "Big Push" was over and it had cost the lives of servicemen from the

Chatsworth villages who were killed during that terrible year. 1916 had shown the difficulties the British Army faced in standing up to machine-gun fire interlacing a defensive zone, stretching in depth for miles. They had only succeeded in advancing a little more than eight miles in four and a half months of almost continuous attack.

As a result of this, we find that the casualty figures for 1916 had been horrific, with those sustained on the first day of the battle alone, exceeding the battle casualties in the Crimean, Boer and Korean Wars combined.

On the German side, their defensive actions had been magnificent and extremely effective, but they had come at a cost. After 1916, and the Battle of the Somme, the German Army would never be quite the same force again. Repeated German counter-attacks had proved even more costly than Allied assaults.

CHAPTER FIVE

1917 – PASSCHENDAELE – THE DARKEST HOUR

Men connected to the Chatsworth villages had lost their lives in 1916. There was, however, to be no let up for other families within these villages during 1917. By the end of the year more servicemen would become fatalities in this dreadful war. By the end of the year more servicemen would become fatalities in this dreadful war, some of them as a result of the Third Battle of Ypres, more commonly known by the name "Passchendaele" (July 31st to November 10th). It achieved little except horrendous loss of life, whilst the seemingly inexhaustible powers of endurance and sacrifice shown by the soldiers in the hellish battlefield conditions was amazing and made even more poignant by the futility of the purpose and result.

Von Ludendorff, the German General, was fearful of over-extending German lines in the west and of Allied preparations for an offensive later in the year. He therefore deliberately chose a defensive attitude and between February 23rd and April 5th, the Germans withdrew to a specially prepared, much shorter, highly organised defensive zone – the Hindenburg Line, some twenty miles behind the over-extended line from Arras to Soissons.

As they withdrew, the Germans left a scene of utter devastation as they destroyed the crops, killed the animals, poisoned the wells, demolished the villages and blew up the bridges. The new defensive line they withdrew to lay behind a lightly held outpost line, heavily manned by machine-gun posts. Two heavily fortified, defensive positions came next and behind these again lay the German reserves, concentrated and prepared for counter-attack.

General Nivelle, the French hero of Verdun in 1916, now had command of Anglo-French forces and planned the Nivelle Offensive on the Aisne and in the Champagne region (April 16th to 20th). The British preliminary to this French offensive was the Battle of Arras, April 9th to 15th, a tactical victory, but without a breakthrough, and resulted in the death of a Pilsley man and one from Beeley.

For the French and the British, therefore, the newly established Hindenburg Line had proved too great a defensive barrier to break through. More significantly, the Nivelle Offensive had proved an expensive disaster, with elements of the French Army mutinying and large numbers of soldiers stating that, although willing to defend their positions, they would refuse any order to attack. Great pressure was therefore placed upon the British to take the fight to the enemy, and so draw German forces away from the French.

The British Commander, General Haig, wished to break out of the Ypres Salient on to the Flanders Plain and on to take the ports used by the German U-boats. The British Government, however, only gave him sanction for a limited offensive to ease the pressure on the French. It would come, though, at a terrible cost.

The first part of the operation, the attack on the Messines Ridge on June 7th 1917, was a complete success. After a seventeen day bombardment and the explosion of nineteen huge mines under enemy positions, the British 2nd Army swept the Germans off the ridge, in the southern section of the Salient, between June 7th and 14th.

Tragically, it was six weeks before the main assault was launched on the Passchendaele-Gheluvelt Ridge. This infamous battle began on July 31st, and the rains began immediately. Empire troops were expected to advance through swamp-like terrain in full view of the defending Germans on the higher ground. 80,000 British and Empire troops were killed and twice that number wounded before Passchendaele was taken and the battle halted on November 10th, with the Salient deepened by five miles.

But Haig, still determined to keep pressure on the Germans to permit the French armies to recover from the mutiny, played his final card of the year between November 20th and December 3rd, with a surprise attack on German positions in front of Cambrai. 381 metal monsters crashed into the German lines, as the world witnessed the first mass attack of tanks.

It was, however, in April 1917, during the Battle of Arras, that news came of the first casualty from this region, an employee on the Chatsworth Estate and a resident of Pilsley.

PRIVATE JOHN FEARNLEY No. 41137
13TH BATTALION ROYAL SCOTS (LOTHIAN REGIMENT)
DIED APRIL 11TH 1917 AGED 38

John Fearnley was born in 1880 at Astley, on the western side of Greater Manchester. His parents, John and Martha, were both natives of Astley and John senior worked in the local coalmine.

By 1901, John Fearnley senior had died and the family, consisting of widow Martha (57), Thomas (23), John (21), Annie (19) and Alice (17) were living at 222 Bolton Road, Worsley, Greater Manchester, west of Salford. Both John junior and his elder brother Thomas were working in the coalmine, as their father had done before them.

Some years before the Great War, John Fearnley changed his way of life drastically by finding employment on the Chatsworth Estate and making his home at Pilsley, with his wife, Elizabeth Ellen Fearnley and two young children. John had first worked in the Chatsworth gardens and subsequently became a member of the laundry staff. We find that their daughter, Doris Margaret Fearnley, was born on February 20th 1913 and was baptised at Baslow Church.

The war intervened and John Fearnley enlisted at Bakewell on August 9th 1916, joining first the Army Service Corps, then the Sherwood Foresters,

John Fearnley of Pilsley
Derbyshire Times and John Taylor

followed by the Royal Scots Fusiliers and finally being transferred to the 13th Battalion Royal Scots. By this stage, his mother Martha had also passed away. He left with his regiment on January 10th 1917.

In April 1917 the 13th Battalion took part in the Arras Offensive (April 9th to the 15th) in which John lost his life, and were positioned south of the River Scarpe, ready to attack the village of Blangy on April 9th. The village had to be cleared in order to protect the left flank of the division and the task fell to "A" and "C" Companies.

On the night of April 7th, "A" and "C" Companies moved up from the cellars in the Grande Place, Arras, by an underground passage, into the sewers of the town. On the night of the 8th they emerged into the open and quietly marched to their assembly positions, while the remainder of the Battalion sheltered in the sewer.

Machine-guns threatened to hold up the attack even before No Man's Land was bridged, but "A" Company swept through the village and reached its objective. "C" Company experienced very stubborn fighting before it succeeded in clearing Blangy. Lewis guns and Stokes mortars at last ended resistance and various village strongpoints were cleared, with 33 prisoners taken by 8-45p.m.

After the capture of the first objective, "B" and "D" Companies were called on to carry up supplies of ammunition, a task they had completed by late afternoon. Meanwhile "A" and "C" Companies moved forward beyond Railway Triangle and established themselves in trenches near Spider Corner, in the vicinity of the village of Feuchy. At this stage on April 9th, 26 men of the Battalion had been killed, 47 wounded and two were missing.

Definite tasks remained to be completed on April 10th. The 13th Battalion, lying near Spider Corner, were in the afternoon ordered to move up and consolidate the line, but the position was still in hostile hands and fighting was severe, with an attempt to stampede the Germans by a cavalry charge ending disatrously for the British.

The struggle south of the River Scarpe increased in stubborness on April 11th, the day of John Fearnley's death. On this day the 13th Battalion were engaged in supporting an attack by the 6th Camerons against Lone Copse and a ridge beyond it. The Battalion, advancing in artillery formation about 600 yards behind the Highlanders, came under intense machine-gun fire from the north of the Scarpe and suffered more heavily than on April 9th. Seven officers and 155 men became casualties.

Though no barrage supported the attack, the copse and the ridge were captured and the position taken up by the Royal Scots at the end of April 11th lay west of Lone Copse. As a result of the sustained pressure on this day, the village of Monchy came into Allied hands.

However, one of the casualties was John Fearnley, cut down on the battle-field and leaving a widow and two youngsters. There was to be no known grave reserved for John and therefore his name is to be found on Bays 1 and 2 of the Arras Memorial.

Elizabeth Ellen Fearnley first received news that her husband was reported wounded and missing, but two weeks later received official intimation of the news and a letter from the chaplain stated that there was little hope that he was alive. A letter from a comrade also added that he saw him fall but did not see him alive afterwards. John Fearnley was the first casualty from Pilsley.

Three days after John Fearnley's death, came news of the demise of a son of the proprietor of the Devonshire Arms Inn, Beeley, whilst in action on the Somme sector of the Western Front.

PRIVATE ERNEST REEVE No. 35574
"D" COMPANY 1ST BATTALION SHERWOOD FORESTERS
DIED APRIL 14TH 1917 AGED 25

In 1901, nine year old Ernest Reeve, the seventh of eight children of Lewis Reeve, was living with his family at Station Road, Pilsley, near Chesterfield, having been born at Eastwood, in Nottinghamshire.

His father, Lewis, was an Eastwood man and was employed as a wheel-wright and joiner. He had married Jane, and together they had six children whilst at Eastwood, but in 1890 she died in childbirth, when being delivered of her sixth child, Lewis Herbert Reeve (Bert). Soon afterwards, Lewis Reeve

Harry Reeve of Beeley is seated on the back row (first right) on board the 'Carpathia', as it returns from North America, to England, in 1912

Pauline Harrison

Ernest Reeve of Beeley

Derbyshire Times and John Taylor

Ernest Reeve on the left, with his father Lewis Reeve, landlord of the Devonshire Arms Inn, Beeley, in 1912, on the occasion of the Club Feast

Derek Neave

Lewis Reeve, senior, landlord of the Devonshire Arms, Beeley, from 1909. He would lose two of his sons, Ernest and Bert, during the First World War

Joyce Gowen

senior married Jane's sister, Catherine, and two more children were born, Ernest at Eastwood and Catherine junior, after they moved to Pilsley.

At Pilsley, Chesterfield, Ernest's older brothers, Thomas, John, Frank and Harry worked as a carter, butcher's assistant, shoeing smith and gas boiler colliery stoker, respectively.

Their father, Lewis, and his brother John decided to go into the car business in its infancy, but Lewis decided there was no future in the new-fangled motor car and pulled out of the venture. John persevered and joined in partnership with Mr. Kenning of Chesterfield.

Instead, Lewis changed direction by becoming a licensee, first at the Holly Bush, on Smedley Street, Matlock and then at the Holmesford Cottage Inn, near Cromford. However, he wished to run a farm as well as a pub and so it was that Lewis, Catherine and their family arrived at the Devonshire Arms at Beeley in 1909, rented from the Duke of Devonshire. When Lewis Herbert (Bert) left School, he began working on the farm with his father.

By this time, Jack (John), Fred and Harry Reeve had emigrated to Canada. Jack went first, panning for gold in the Toronto area, followed by Fred, who travelled to Vancouver, where he played the honkey-tonk piano in pubs, and eventually became a taxi-driver, whilst Harry emigrated in 1906, working in the mining camps and travelling to America, before returning to England on the "Carpathia" in 1912. It was on this return journey that the ship was able to help in plucking survivors from the "Titanic", out of the freezing waters of the Atlantic.

Soon after his return, Harry Reeve married Alice Burdekin, daughter of Thomas and Mary Burdekin, who ran the Post Office, village shop and refreshment room at Beeley. Thomas had died and Harry and Alice moved in with Mary Burdekin, with Alice helping her mother and Harry becoming the Post Master.

Whilst Bert Reeve helped on the farm, his brother, Ernest , was employed as a clerk on the Midland Railway, at their goods department at Mansfield. He lodged there during the week and returned to the Devonshire Arms at the weekend.

When war was declared, Bert joined up and became a member of the Machine-Gun Corps, before transferring to a Labour Company near the close of the war. When Ernest attempted to join the Derbyshire Imperial Yeomanry, he was rejected because of deficient eye-sight. However, he persevered and in August 1916 he enlisted at Bakewell and became a member of the 1st Battalion Sherwood Foresters. On December 12th 1916 he was sent to join his Battalion in France, part of a draft of 167 posted when the Battalion was camped at Selincourt, and by December 30th they went into camp near Combles.

Towards the end of January 1917, the Division came to the Somme area for a third tour of duty near Albert and experienced the hardest frost it had ever known (on several nights there were 23 degrees of frost. The Drums attempted to play the "Retreat" but were unable to do so owing to the flute key-pads becoming frozen as the men played).

February 10th saw the Battalion going back into a camp near Bray, between Albert and Corbie, on the Somme, where a very intensive training was entered upon, ready for an attack on March 4th, the objective being to capture a nearby ridge. Casualties were heavy early in the attack, as a German barrage hit them and as the Foresters entered the enemy lines there was much hand to hand fighting. Groups of Foresters cleared the dug-outs in the process of "mopping up". During the day the enemy made four local counter-attacks, but were unsuccessful (this action was part of the follow up to the withdrawal of the Germans to the Hindenburg Line and the Battalion continued the slow pursuit).

On April 4th the 25th Brigade attacked Gouzeaucourt, and during the afternoon a party of Germans crept up under cover to within fifteen yards of the left-hand Lewis gun post and a hand to hand fight ensued, the enemy being repulsed after a strong encounter. Positions were re-occupied by the Germans and retaken by "C" Company and it was not until April 12th that Gouzeaucourt was finally captured and then held.

At 8-30p.m. on April 12th the barrage lifted and the companies advanced with great dash, swept aside all opposition and consolidated their gains – the line of the sunken road from Metz to Gouzeaucourt.

April 13th saw the Battalion being sent forward again with orders to straighten matters out on the right flank; there was much opposition by machine-gun and rifle fire, the wire in front was thick and unbroken, and the Battalion was finally forced back to its original line by April 14th, having incurred many casualties. Ernest Reeve was one of those killed.

On April 13th/14th, Ernest had been part of an outpost group, holding ground in advance of the main Battalion, when the group was overpowered by a German counter-attack. He appears to have been hit on the head by shell shrapnel and the lower part of his right side. A soldier from another Battalion claimed to have buried him, even though under shellfire. Soil was placed over Ernest, then banked up with sods, whilst his bayonet was fixed at his head and his steel helmet placed on top of it. A small wooden cross was made with two bits of wood from a bomb box that was lying nearby, tied with a shoelace, and placed with his identification disc at the head of the grave. However, the British advanced again on the 14th and the shellfire destroyed the grave.

Ernest's body was never recovered and his name is commemorated on Pier and Face 10C, 10D and 11A of the Thiepval Memorial. Sadly, because the body was never found, it would be many months later before it was confirmed to the family that he was officially dead.

Ernest's brother, Bert Reeve, survived the war by a few days, only to succumb to Spanish flu, six days after the war had ended. Great sadness was felt by his father, but their mother, Catherine, was spared the extra grief, for she had died in 1917, some months after the death of Ernest. Certainly news of her youngest son's loss had contributed to her death.

A Beeley family was the recipient of bad news, when the blacksmith's son succumbed to his wounds after being involved in fighting during the aftermath to the Battle of Arras.

PRIVATE ARTHUR TOWNDROW No. 48203
22ND BATTALION ROYAL FUSILIERS (CITY OF LONDON REGIMENT)
DIED MAY 1ST 1917 AGED 26

Arthur's grandfather, Matthew Towndrow, was a quarryman, born in Beeley in 1837, who had married another Beeley resident, Martha Hibbert, in February 1863. Amongst their children were eight sons who all grew up to be over six feet tall.

Jacob, the eldest son, was apprenticed as a blacksmith and by 1901 he was 34 years of age and a senior blacksmith for the Duke of Devonshire, on the Chatsworth Estate. On January 22nd 1891 he had married 24 year old Clara Elliott, who originated from Worksop in Nottinghamshire and had come to Chatsworth with her father, Thomas Elliott, who was a coachman on the estate. Jacob and Clara were living at Church View, Pig Lane, Beeley.

Arthur Towndrow of Beeley
Derbyshire Times and John Taylor

They had begun married life, however, at Pilsley, where Arthur Towndrow was born in 1892 and Harry (Henry) in 1898, but by the end of 1899 they were setting up home at Church View, where their third son, Frederick, was born in 1900.

After attending Beeley and Edensor schools, Arthur left the family home in 1907, at the age of 15, entering the service of Lady Egerton, the Duke of Devonshire's sister and remained in that establishment for five years. Afterwards he was butler to several well known families and immediately before the outbreak of war was in the service of Lord Meux at Admiralty House, Portsmouth.

Arthur enlisted in the Army in London during 1915 and joined the Royal Fusiliers. He was involved in the Battle of the Somme in 1916, in which he was wounded, but recovered, and by this stage his younger brother Harry had joined up, serving with the Highland Light Infantry.

Arthur had been promoted to sergeant in his Battalion, but wishing to

Left, and above: *Harry Towndrow of Beeley, brother of Arthur Towndrow*
Harry Towndrow

Right: *Clara Towndrow holding grandson Harry Towndrow, with Arthur Towndrow, c1932*
Harry Towndrow

proceed to the front again without delay, he gave his sergeant's stripes up and was drafted to the 22nd Battalion. Despite his wish to be involved in action once more, he was realistic about his chances of survival and on one of his periods of leave at Beeley, he related to his brother that he did not believe he would see the family home at Beeley again.

Back once again in France, he and his new Battalion were involved in the Battle of Arras (April 9th to 15th)

Jacob Towndrow, blacksmith for the Duke of Devonshire, stands on the left. His son, Arthur, died from wounds during the Great War
Harry Towndrow

and Arthur survived the conflict. However, as the French Army mutinied in other sections of the Western Front, the British continued to push against the German line on smaller scale raids, in order to contain the German forces in the Arras area.

Zero hour for just such an attack was 4a.m. on May 1st, but unfortunately it was found that the supply of bombs at the assembly point dump was inadequate and this would contribute to the failure of the mission. It would also be discovered that the artillery had failed to cut much of the German wire.

By the time gaps had been made, the men were exposed to rifle and machine-gun fire. "B" Company found the second row of wire to be impenetrable and the whole of one platoon was shot down. The fighting undertaken by other platoons was desperate, with no quarter asked or given.

The right platoon of "D" Company also found the wire uncut and so were all shot, the only survivor being Second Lieutenant Palmer, VC, whilst Platoons 14 and 15 suffered similar fates as No Man's Land was raked with machine-gun fire from Oppy Wood. The men only carried three bombs each and these soon ran out. The fight in the trenches needed to be a bombing fight and rifle fire and bayonets were useless. Had more time been given to properly organise the dumps and carrying parties, the operation would most likely have succeeded, but it ended in failure.

On Saturday May 5th 1917 Jacob and Clara received information that Arthur, aged 26, had died in hospital having been severely wounded and badly gassed whilst taking part in the attack on the German line south of Oppy Wood. He had died on May 1st, the day on which he was admitted to the Casualty Clearing Station. The Chaplain wrote that if he had survived he would have been severely disfigured.

Arthur Towndrow was buried in grave 11.J.70. Aubigny Communal Cemetery Extension, 12 kilometres west of Arras. His brother, Harry, survived the war, despite receiving a slight wound to the head and all his life he was to suffer with very bad feet as a consequence of having "Trench Feet" during the war and wearing badly fitted army boots. After the war he worked on the Chatsworth estate, around the House and in the House Gardens.

William Lovell, a Chatsworth employee working in the kitchen gardens, died from wounds received when his Battalion was involved in a local attack on enemy positions in the French colliery district of Lens.

PRIVATE WILLIAM THOMAS LOVELL No. 241010
6TH BATTALION SHERWOOD FORESTERS
DIED MAY 20TH 1917 AGED 36

William was born at Tewin, Hertfordshire, on June 10th 1880, the eldest of the three children of Henry and Jane Lovell. Henry had been born at Tewin, a small estate village four miles west of Hertford and married Jane Jackson from the nearby village of Ayot St. Peter, three miles away. He was employed as a gardener on the estate and he and Jane raised their children, William, Agnes and Joseph.

The family was still at Tewin in 1901, with 20 year old William employed like his father, as a gardener on the estate. However, a few years before the war began, William left Tewin to work in the kitchen gardens at Chatsworth and by 1914 had been promoted to foreman gardener, working under head gardener, Mr. F. Jennings.

Soon after war began, William enlisted in the Army at Bakewell and became a member of the 6th Battalion Sherwood Foresters, and after a period of training, he landed in France on June 29th 1915.

As the Germans withdrew to the Hindenburg Line through March and April 1917, the 6th Battalion was involved in fighting the enemy's rearguard actions in the follow up.

By April 13th the Foresters were taking part in severe training and then marched to billets at Noeux-les-Mines, near Bethune, where three days were spent in billets, constantly bombarded by a high-velocity gun, 15 miles away.

Private William Thomas Lovell of Chatsworth (Edensor)
Chatsworth Photo Archive

On April 19th they moved into the front line at the colliery village of Lievin, near Lens, which the enemy had recently vacated. It was decided that the 6th Battalion should be involved in the attempted capture of the colliery village of Riaumont, behind which rose the slag heaps and pit-shaft buildings of Fosse 3, strongly fortified by the enemy. This night attack on April 21st/22nd was to be the preliminary to an attack on the remainder of the enemy position. This night time attack was completely successful, with few casualties being sustained.

On April 23rd the main attack was carried out, with the 6th Battalion attacking the position known as Fosse 3, incorrectly thought to be only moderately defended.

The enemy put down a heavy barrage as the companies advanced, with machine-guns commanding and firing down all approaches. "C" Company, No. 9 Platoon, was heavily fired upon and could not go forward. No. 10 Platoon encountered a wall five feet high, with uncut wire on the other side. The men had to lay in shell holes until dark, with others falling back.

No. 12 Platoon came at the outset under heavy machine-gun fire and was sniped at from houses occupied by the enemy. They took cover in gun pits and brought a Lewis gun into action, helping to knock out some German machine-gun positions. No further progress could be made and they took cover until dark, when the Battalion was relieved. The attack had failed, with the 6th Battalion alone sustaining over 100 casualties.

It was during this attack on Fosse 3, near Lievin, that William Lovell was severely wounded, being first removed to a Casualty Clearing Station and then to a large base hospital at St. Omer. It was at St. Omer that William succumbed to his wounds on May 20th and was buried in grave 1V.C.3.

Longuenesse (St. Omer) Souvenir Cemetery.

Another gardener from the Chatsworth kitchen gardens died in mid May as he too took part with his Battalion in attacks on enemy positions south-east of Arras, in order to keep German forces occupied, whilst the French recovered from the effects of the mutiny in their ranks.

RIFLEMAN JOHN JAMES WOOTTON No. R/18632
16TH BATTALION KING'S ROYAL RIFLE CORPS
DIED MAY 20TH 1917 AGED 25

John was born in 1892 at Newton Solney, a village three miles north-east of Burton on Trent, Derbyshire, at the confluence of the Rivers Trent and Dove. Aged 9 in 1901, he was the fourth of seven children of John and Phoebe Wootton. John senior, who was born at Melbourne, Derbyshire, and was a bricklayer by trade, had married Phoebe, a girl from Newton Solney and all seven children were born in the village.

By the time of the Great War, John Wootton junior was living at Baslow and at one time had been employed in the Chatsworth gardens.

However, he returned to Burton on Trent to enlist and eventually joined the 16th Battalion King's Royal Rifle Corps. At Baslow Church on Saturday April 22nd 1916, whilst home on leave, he married 21 year old Louisa Gertrude Sheldon, the daughter of Baslow builder, David Sheldon. Soon he was back at the front and Louisa received news from her husband at the end of July that he had received two shell wounds in the shoulder, but that they were not too serious. He was in hospital in France but made a good recovery.

In April 1917 the 16th Battalion had been involved in the Battle of Arras, resulting in 270 casualties. The remainder of the month was spent at Berles-au-Bois, refitting.

On May 2nd they moved to Moyenneville, south of Arras, receiving considerable drafts of men and continued training until May 19th. Through late April to May 20th the French Army had mutinied and to help their situation by keeping German forces occupied in the British sector, British attacks were planned during this period. One such attack on the Hindenburg Line, south-east of Arras, took place on May 20th, involving the 16th Battalion and John Wootton.

The Battalion arrived at its assembly position without casualties at 11-40 p.m. on the 19th, its objective being from the Fontaine – Croisilles road to a point 400 yards south-east of that road.

At 4-15a.m. on May 20th the Battalion moved into position and formed up with the two leading companies in four waves. At 5-05a.m. the first objective was gained with practically no resistance. The morning was very misty, and to effect a surprise, no barrage was put down.

The first objective being reached, the British artillery opened on the support line. This line was strongly held and "D" and "A" Companies, who attacked, were thrown back on "C" and "B" Companies, which were holding the front German line. Only one officer was left with the two former companies, the others having become casualties.

Under a heavy artillery fire the Battalion held the German front line and established posts further in front. At 10a.m. orders came to prepare for a further advance. The Battalion now consisted of eight officers and 260 men. Though depleted, the companies reorganised and prepared to follow the orders, but this was cancelled at 3.25p.m. and instead, an advance was made at 7-30p.m. by two other Battalions, but was unsuccessful. Between May 20th and May 22nd, the 16th Battalion received 218 casualties and one of these was John James Wootton.

He was killed by shellfire during the advance, but due to the forced withdrawal back to the German first line, his body was never recovered. John Wootton's name is inscribed on Bay 7 of the Arras Memorial. As we have already seen, Louisa Wootton's father, David Sheldon, was a Baslow builder and in 1923, six years after John Wootton's death, 28 year old Louisa married another builder, 21 year old Robert Hancock Fletcher, at Baslow Church.

On the same day as the death of John Wootton on the Western Front, the death occurred much nearer to home, of a Scottish officer who was based on the Chatsworth estate with a Canadian contingent and who died as the result of a tragic accident.

MAJOR LAWRENCE JOHNSTONE
50TH BATTALION CANADIAN INFANTRY (ALBERTA REGIMENT)
DIED MAY 20TH 1917 AGED 45

Major Lawrence Johnstone was the son of William and Margaret Johnstone of Edinburgh and husband of Grace Johnstone of Hillfoot, Dollar, situated between Stirling and Kinross in Scotland.

Lawrence Johnstone was on the reserve list of Canadian officers and was serving with the 50th Canadian Infantry, having arrived from Winnipeg. He had been billeted at the Grand Hotel and Hydro, Baslow, for some time and used the Rifle Range in Chatsworth Park whilst studying and improving a new kind of gun upon which he was working.

On Sunday May 20th a dummy bomb inserted into the gun became jammed and in order to release it he used a hammer. He allowed himself to be in line with the gun, with the dire result that it unexpectedly fired and blew part of his head away.

Major Johnstone's funeral was held at St. Peter's Church, Edensor, on Thursday May 24th. The funeral cortege started from the Royal Naval Convalescent Hospital, at Edensor Institute, where the Union flag floated at half mast.

First came the firing party, with weapons reversed, being a squad of Marines from the Hospital in charge of Sergeant Yates, followed by the coffin upon a wheeled bier, covered with a Union flag. Next came petty officers carrying wreaths, then patients from the Hospital and the Royal Navy and VAD nurses, in charge of Sister Skinner, plus soldiers from the Red Cross Hospital in Bakewell.

Major Johnstone's widow, Grace, rode in a carriage to the church, which was crowded, with people also grouped outside.

After the service, Major Lawrence Johnstone's body was buried in Edensor churchyard.

June 7th 1917 had seen the start of the successful attempt to gain the high ground of the Messines Ridge, a preliminary to the main assault on the Passchendaele Ridge, and six weeks later, on July 31st, the Battle of Passchendaele began. The ordeal for the British and Empire troops would last for the next four and a half months.

Before returning to the battlefield, however, we find that on the Home Front during this period, Beeley Church Sunday School Treat was held on Tuesday August 21st, in beautiful sunny weather. Horse drawn conveyances were provided and the children, accompanied by their teachers, in charge of Miss Leah Ratcliff, enjoyed a drive to Baslow, Bakewell and on to Haddon Hall, where a short stay was made to see the historic mansion. The children were accompanied by the Reverend Howard Chadwick. On returning to Beeley they sat down to a tea, after which the evening was spent in playing games in a meadow lent by Mr. Fearn.

On August 23rd the grounds of Chatsworth House were open to the public for a garden fete given by the staff and patients of the Chatsworth Royal Naval Convalescent Hospital, the object being to augment the entertainments fund of the hospital.

The establishment was doing a splendid job in restoring to health again those boys in blue who were "nerve shattered and in some cases, bodily wrecked" and had come to Chatsworth for a complete rest.

The programme of the day's events was in the capable hands of Sergeant A.E. Yates. Amongst the large crowd were invalid soldiers from convalescent

The Pierrot troupe of the Chatsworth Royal Naval Convalescent Hospital.
They raised by concerts over £100 on behalf of the Red Cross Fund.
BACK ROW: *A. B. Welch, Nurse Barnes, Nurse Robinson, Sergeant Gardner (Royal Marines Light*
Infantry). MIDDLE ROW: *Chief Petty Officer Wright, Sergeant R. A Yates (RMLI), Ord sc Baxendale.*
FRONT ROW: *Stoker Cole, H. Goodwin (SBR)*
High Peak News, courtesy of Potter and Company, Solicitors

hospitals at Hathersage, Darley Dale, Ashgate, Derby and Matlock, who were provided with a free tea and cigarettes.

Side shows made up an excellent pleasure fair with coconut shies, a "Kaiser" shy, billiards, Aunt Sally, darts, donkey rides and hoopla. Sports were also held on the South Lawn.

A war ration tea was served in the Orangery by the Pilsley baker, Mr. G. Siddons, to a large crowd of people. One of the great attractions was the Band of the West Riding Volunteers and a concert was performed by a troop of Pierrots called the "Merrie Frolics". Dancing in the evening concluded a very pleasant day at Chatsworth.

One week after the happy event of the fete on the lawns of Chatsworth House, the estate and the village of Edensor witnessed the sad sight of a military style funeral at St. Peter's Church, as a patient at the Chatsworth Royal Navy Convalescent Hospital died a few weeks after his arrival. Although his name does not appear on the Edensor Memorial, I have included details of his story because of his wartime connection with the estate village.

CHIEF STOKER WILLIAM EDMUND SEFTON No. 293447
HMS "PEMBROKE" ROYAL NAVY
DIED AUGUST 30TH 1917 AGED 42

Born in Belfast on August 9th 1873, William became a sailor in the Royal Navy well before the Great War and rose to the rank of Chief Stoker. In 1915, the ship he was serving on at the time was part of the naval section of the Mesopotamia Expeditionary Force, based in the Persian Gulf and helping to fight against the Turkish forces.

It was there that he contracted a disease, which meant that he was returned to England and spent time in hospital receiving treatment in a Royal Naval Hospital at HMS "Pembroke", the Royal Naval Barracks at Chatham in Kent.

In early July 1917 he was discharged from the Chatham hospital and was brought to the Royal Naval Convalescent Hospital at Edensor, Chatsworth. However, after only six weeks stay, the condition worsened and he died from pernicious anaemia on Thursday August 30th.

Full military honours were accorded the Chief Stoker at his funeral and internment on Saturday September 1st. The funeral cortege left the hospital and wended its way to Edensor Church, the body placed upon a wheeled bier, on which were a Union flag and his cap, and the bier drawn by nine sailors from the hospital. Sixty sailors walked behind.

The coffin was of pitch pine, from wood grown on the estate and made by the patients at the hospital. A firing party fired three volleys over the grave, which was situated next to that of Major Lawrence Johnstone in Edensor Churchyard. Sadly, despite his burial in the church yard, William Sefton's name was not included on the Edensor Memorial.

By October 1917 the bloody Battle of Passchendaele, that began on July 31st, was now into its third month and resulted in horrendous casualties as British and Empire troops fought across the quagmire that represented the battlefield. Torrential rain had fallen during much of this period and the constant shelling by both sides resulted in the drainage ditches being destroyed and the streams overflowing. In the glutinous swampland of the Passchendaele landscape, many of the men and animals struggled to push forward as "push" followed "push", and were simply swallowed up in the cloying mud.

Beeley was not to be neglected by Passchendaele, when, a villager who worked on the Chatsworth estate lost his life whilst fighting with the Sherwood Foresters.

PRIVATE EDWARD HAYNES No. 14487
10TH BATTALION SHERWOOD FORESTERS
DIED OCTOBER 12TH 1917 AGED 24

Edward, who was born in 1893, was the ninth of the ten children (7 sons and 3 daughters) of William Alsop Haynes and Rebecca Haynes of Hawthorn Cottage (later called Church View), Beeley.

William Haynes had been born at Oker, South Darley, into a farming family and was farming at Oker around 1883 when all his animals were drowned during the flooding of his farm land by the River Derwent. By this time he was married to Rebecca Bown, a farmer's daughter from near Ashover, and they already had a number of children.

Edward Haynes of Beeley
Vera Russell

The Haynes family of Beeley outside Hawthorn Cottage
STANDING, LEFT TO RIGHT: *Thomas Haynes, William Haynes, Hannah Haynes, Kate Haynes,
Martha Haynes, John Haynes, Frank Haynes, Stanley Haynes*
SEATED: *Edward Haynes, William Alsop Haynes, Leonard Haynes, Rebecca Haynes (née Bown)*
Vera Russell

133

William took a job as farm bailiff at Flash, near Ashover, but eventually the family moved to a farm at Gladwin Mark, on Darley Moor. Around 1888, William decided to get a job on the Midland Railway as a labourer in the railway engine shed at Rowsley marshalling yard. Their new home was at Hawthorn Cottage, close to the Church at Beeley and it was here that Edward was born in 1893.

Frank Haynes,
who served at Gallipoli and
Salonika and survived
Vera Russell

William Haynes served in
England and survived the
Great War
Vera Russell

Rebecca, his mother, was quite a character in Beeley and was the person people sent for if there was a birth in the family or if a person needed to be "laid out" after death.

In 1901, eight year old Edward was attending Beeley School, whilst, of his older brothers, John was working as a butcher, 16 year old William was a carter for a stone merchant at Rowsley Station Yard and 15 year old Stanley was beginning his first job as an errand boy at the Beeley Post Office, run by Thomas and Mary Burdekin.

After leaving Beeley and Edensor Schools, Edward Haynes eventually began working as a domain labourer on the estate and, by 1912, was working for the Duke's Agent, Mr. Cockerell, who lived at Edensor House. One of his jobs was to work as the odd job man for the vicar of Edensor, both at the Vicarage and in the gardens.

Edward volunteered for service in the Great War in early September 1914, one month after war was declared, and joined the 10th Battalion Sherwood Foresters. He had been in several engagements and was wounded by shrapnel in the leg and after being in hospital for a short time he returned to duty again. He paid a visit to his parents at Beeley at Christmas 1916, but had not been home since. By the time of his death in October 1917, three of his other brothers were also serving their country. Frank was in Salonika, Stanley in France, whilst William was in training in England. The youngest son, Leonard, had been given exemption by the local Military Tribunal.

By the end of September 1917, Edward and the 10th Battalion were in France, but rumours hinted that they would shortly be travelling north into Belgium and playing their part in the Battle of Passchendaele.

*Edward and Sydney Haynes' sister,
Kate Haynes, eventually found service in the Royal Household.
During the Great War she became head of the Still Room at
Buckingham Palace, dealing with the provision of cakes,
confectionary, etc. She travelled with the Royal Family and met
Charles Ward, who was a regular soldier in the Life Guards and
was on duty at Windsor Castle.
He had joined the Life Guards in 1907 and served on the
Western Front during the Great War. Although his brother was
killed whilst serving in the Army, Charles was very forunate to
survive the conflict and in October 1919
Kate Haynes and Charles Ward were married.
Eventually, Kate arrived back in Beeley to settle down with her
family*
Vera Russell

On October 4th the Battalion entrained at 2p.m. and journeyed for some six hours to Pezelhock. By October 10th they were in the Front Line.

The whole area had been pounded until it was made up of nothing but mud and rubble. The 10th Battalion moved into the support area on the eastern side of Langemarck village, moving into what remained of the old German trenches. Orders were received on October 11th to attack the German positions on the 12th and during the night the Battalion moved to the assembly point.

At zero hour, 5-25a.m. on October 12th, the Battalion lay waiting, but as the barrage came down the Sherwoods moved forward and by 6-40a.m. the first objective had been reached without any opposition. Prisoners were taken, as were several pill-boxes.

"A" and "C" Companies now moved forward through the leading companies and began the advance to the final objective. Nine German officers and 250 men were captured. During the remainder of the day the ground was held, in spite of three counter-attacks, all of which were broken up. The mud made movement across the ground terribly difficult and everyone was heavily coated with it.

Casualties had been relatively light, with two officers and 15 other ranks killed, four officers and 150 men wounded, but one of the men who was killed in action was Edward Haynes. His body was never recovered and his name is commemorated on Panel 99 to 102 and 162 to 162A Tyne Cot Memorial, Beeley War Memorial and Edensor War Memorial.

Thankfully, brothers Frank and William would survive the war, but we shall see that Stanley Haynes died in hospital in France, just nineteen days after the war ended.

The horrendous conditions of water, mud and slime, which were the living conditions of the soldiers at Passchendaele, for much of the time

As the year 1917 came towards its close, General Haig made one last effort to take the pressure off the French by assaulting the German lines at Cambrai, in the first massed tank attack of the war. During this battle, an estate worker who was formerly employed in the kitchen gardens died from wounds received in the aftermath of the fighting at Cambrai.

PRIVATE CHARLES WILLIAM FROUDE No. 37445
7TH BATTALION SOUTH LANCASHIRE REGIMENT
DIED DECEMBER 30TH 1917 AGED 29

Charles's parents, Charles Froude senior and Martha Jane Froude, were born in neighbouring villages in North Somerset, to the south and south west of Bristol. Charles Froude senior was a gamekeeper and whilst in North Somerset, two daughters were born to the family. By 1884 the Froude family had moved to Park Hill, near Horningsham, in Wiltshire, an estate near Longleat, on which Charles was employed as the gamekeeper. After the addition of two more daughters, Charles Froude junior was born in 1887.

At some point between 1893 and 1900, Charles Froude senior died and Martha Jane went with her family to live at Tompkins Road, Horningsham, where she earned money as a sick nurse. I believe that whilst working in Wiltshire in the years prior to the Great War, Charles junior served in a Territorial Battalion of the Wiltshire Yeomanry.

With his father's connection of having worked on various country estates, we find that by the year 1913, Charles Froude junior had left Wiltshire to find employment in Derbyshire and was working on the Chatsworth Estate, in the kitchen gardens, and living nearby with his wife Emily.

26 year old Charles married 23 year old Emily Rydout from Chatsworth Gardens at Edensor Church on December 19th 1914. Emily's father, George Rydout, was employed as a Chatsworth gardener, like Charles, and at their wartime wedding, Charles was stated to be a sergeant in the Wiltshire Yeomanry in the marriage register. Having served in this Territorial force before he came to Chatsworth, he had enlisted as soon as war began.

At some point during the war, Charles served for a period as a sapper in the Royal Engineers, but when his daughter, Joyce Adeline, was baptised at Edensor Church on February 25th 1917, Charles was still registered as a sergeant in the Wiltshire Yeomanry.

It was during 1917 that Charles Froude was transferred to the 7th Battalion South Lancashire Regiment, surprisingly only with the rank of private.

Throughout September and October, the 7th Battalion was in the Ypres Salient during the Battle of Passchendaele and although not involved in any actual fighting, the incessant shell fire exacted a daily toll of casualties. Between September 21st and 29th they had lost 36 men killed and 114 men wounded or missing. They had helped to carry the wounded in the Kemmel area, followed by weeks of gruelling action in the front line.

During the whole of October they continued to hold a section of the front line in the neighbourhood of the Ypres-Comines Canal, but were not called to take any active part in the fighting.

At the beginning of November 1917 they withdrew to a training area near Hazebrouck. But at the end of the first week of December they were sent to the Cambrai sector, where the Germans had just counter-attacked, regaining considerable ground they had lost in late November.

The Battalion moved by train and route march and became established by December 12th in the reserve trench at Ribecourt, just to the south-west of Cambrai. The new sector was in a salient and there was every expectation of a further attack by the Germans and all units were specially warned to be on their guard. On December 14th the Battalion entered the front line after an inspection and "foot rubbing" parades were held during the morning.

The situation necessitated constant patrolling, although no actual fighting took place, beyond patrol encounters. On December 17th a patrol of an officer and six men from "A" Company found a dug-out 600 yards from their lines occupied by 25 Germans and promptly bombed them, causing them to flee, but only a few escaped. Two days later an offensive patrol of 25 men and an officer successfully "cut-out" a German machine-gun post and the gun and six prisoners were brought back.

On the afternoon of December 25th the enemy shelled the support trench and also obtained direct hits on the front line trench. Similar shelling took place the following day, just before the 7th Battalion was about to be relieved. Unfortunately, it was during the period of shelling on December 25th that Charles Froude was severely wounded and taken to a Casualty Clearing Station behind the lines. It was there that he succumbed to his wounds on December 30th and was buried in grave V11.D.11. Rocquigny-Equancourt Road British Cemetery, Manancourt, 13 kilometres north of Peronne.

Charles left a young widow and a baby daughter on the Chatsworth estate. They settled down to peacetime life at Baslow and it is interesting to note that on September 19th 1942, Joyce Adeline Froude, aged 25, married 29 year old Flight Lieutenant Norman Dudley Greenaway, RAF, at Baslow Church. Unlike her father's wartime marriage, however, hers proved to have a happier result because Norman survived the war.

As the last serviceman from the Devonshire and Rutland villages to die in 1917, Charles Froude's death brought the total of local servicemen who had been killed in action or died during the year to seven. Their loved ones suffered almost unbearable pain and heartache but there would be no noticeable "let up" during 1918, as eleven men from these villages perished during that year and into 1919.

CHAPTER SIX

1918 – WILL IT NEVER END?

It was mentioned in the *High Peak News* that by the first week of January 1918 there was annoyance in Baslow at the failure of the local Gas Company to supply the village with light. Three times in Christmas week the village had been plunged into darkness early in the evenings, sadly interfering with Christmas entertainments being held at the Hydro and the Schools. On Sunday night, the evening service in the church had to be brought to an abrupt close owing to a failure of light.

On Saturday January 5th there was a football match at Baslow between Baslow and a team from the Royal Naval Hospital, Chatsworth, with Baslow winning by three goals to two.

In the school room at Rowsley on Saturday January 12th, a concert was held in aid of servicemen serving their country. An impromptu stage was erected with curtains and flags and the Reverend Bullock presided over the event.

At Baslow, in January 1918, the village collection for Christmas gifts to the Soldiers and Sailors had realised £21 18sh 1d, the Whist Drive £7 2sh. 6d. and an organ recital £5 4sh. 9d. As a result of this, 82 gifts of 8 shillings each had been made, with the rest of the money providing comforts.

At Edensor, Augustaus De Vadda, a Belgian refugee, whilst employed with a sawing machine, unfortunately sustained a bad injury, his hand coming in contact with the saw. Dr. Edleston of Baslow was in attendance and it was necessary to amputate the thumb.

During early February the Reverend W.H. Foster-Pegg was appointed vicar of Edensor and Chatsworth, having arrived from South Essex. Educated at Malvern and University College, Oxford, he was ordained in 1908 at St. Clement's, Leeds, and was Chaplain to the Forces at Aldershot in 1909 and Hong Kong and China 1910-1914. He was ministering at Warley in Essex in 1914, but proceeded to France with the BEF in 1914, being at Mons and the Aisne and was mentioned in despatches. Invalided home, he became senior chaplain to the South Essex and Hertfordshire Regiment 1914-1917 and was invalided from the Army on account of ill-health at the start of 1918.

It was into the third week of March 1918 before Edensor and its two neighbouring villages received news of the first casualties of the year, with the deaths of men from Beeley and Pilsley. They were all victims of the Ludendorff Offensive that began on March 21st.

On April 6th 1917 America had declared war against Germany, but with her small army of 210,000 men, it would take some while before her manpower resources could become a decisive factor. During the winter of 1917/1918 General Ludendorff realised that Germany's only hope of winning the war lay in a decisive victory in the West in 1918 before the weight of American manpower began to tell. The Bolshevik Revolution of 1917 in Russia had resulted in that country being knocked out of the war.

General Ludendorff therefore shifted most German forces from the East and prepared for an all out offensive in the West, to be launched as early as possible in the Spring, using "shock troops" as spearheads for the assault. It was planned to smash the Allied Armies in a series of hammer blows, driving a wedge between the British and French forces, and then destroy the British in subsequent assaults. Preparations were made for this massive attack in the Somme area to begin on March 21st between St. Quentin and Arras, towards the goal of capturing Amiens.

Servicemen from the Chatsworth villages would die during the "Kaiser's Battle" and its immediate aftermath, when overwhelming German forces would roll forward and swallow them up in the desperate weeks of late March and early April.

Liddell Hart, the military historian, wrote:

"At 04-30 hours on March 21st the sudden crash of some 6000 German guns heralded the breaking of a storm which, in grandeur of scale, of awe and destruction, surpassed any other in the World War. By nightfall a German flood had inundated forty miles of the British front; a week later it had reached a depth of nearly forty miles and was almost lapping the outskirts of Amiens, and in the ensuing weeks the Allied cause itself was almost submerged. Germany came desperately near to regaining that lost chance of victory which she had forfeited in early September 1914."

On the third day of this titanic battle, a soldier from Baslow would be the first man from the villages to be "swallowed up" in the German tidal wave.

PRIVATE WILLIAM FRANCIS HEATHCOTE No. 46868
1ST BATTALION BEDFORDSHIRE REGIMENT,
BUT ATTACHED TO 1ST BATTALION HERTFORDSHIRE REGIMENT
DIED MARCH 23RD 1918 AGED 19

William was born at Leeds in 1898, the son of George Henry and Florence Heathcote. George was a native of Leeds, whilst Florence originated from Doncaster. By 1901 the family had recently settled in Derbyshire, where two year old William was living at Baslow with his 26 year old mother, Florence. George Henry, however, was to be found living away from his family because of his employment. He was a boarder at the Star and Garter Inn, Chesterfield, where he was working as a postal mail driver.

William Heathcote of Edensor and Baslow, as a schoolboy at Edensor in 1912
Derek Neave

By 1910/1912 William Heathcote was attending Edensor School for boys, situated on the village green and run by headmaster, Mr. Wragg. George Henry Heathcote was no longer working as a mail driver but instead, he and his wife were involved in running the newly established Institute at Edensor, in part of the former Chatsworth Hotel. It is for these reasons, we find that William's name is commemorated on both the Edensor and Baslow war memorials.

It would seem that William was employed in London after his school days, for in 1917, William enlisted at Chiswick, joining first the Army Service Corps as a driver/mechanic, and then was transferred to the 1st Battalion Bedford-shire Regiment, before finally joining its sister regiment, 1st Battalion Hertfordshires, in a draft of men making up the numbers after the Battalion had been severely mauled at Passchendaele, during September 1917.

At the end of January 1918 the Hertfordshires left the Ypres Salient and moved south to the area immediately east of Amiens. When the German Offensive began on March 21st they were in reserve, but due to the early pressure of the attack, they went into the line on the evening of March 21st, between Epehy and Ste. Emilie, north-west of St. Quentin. During the 16th Division's withdrawal on March 22nd the 1st Battalion, as rearguard battalion, was heavily engaged throughout the day and suffered considerable casualties. One Company was cut off in the hamlet of Ste. Emilie and held up the enemy advance for a further valuable two hours before being overcome.

During the night of March 22nd/23rd, the 1st Battalion withdrew five miles to help prepare a further defensive line at Bussu. Enemy pressure was such that a further retirement was ordered in the early afternoon of March 23rd and the Battalion made a fighting withdrawal through the area of Mont St Quentin to establish a defensive perimeter in front of Clery-sur-Somme, an important crossing point on the river.

It was during the intense fighting of the afternoon of March 23rd that William Francis Heathcote was killed in action, most likely by shell fire. His body was never recovered and his name is therefore commemorated on Panel 28 and 29 of the Pozieres Memorial.

LANCE CORPORAL JESSE HARRISON No. 89138
35TH BATTALION MACHINE-GUN CORPS (INFANTRY)
DIED MARCH 26TH 1918 AGED 32

Jesse was born on March 29th 1884 at Church View, Beeley, the son of a single woman, 28 year old Emma Rebecca Harrison. Jesse's grandfather, Thomas Harrison, was a stone mason and farm labourer who was born in the village of Sheldon, near Ashford in the Water, and married Emma Grafton, a Beeley girl. Emma Grafton's father, Samuel Grafton, was a farmer who was also involved in quarrying.

Emma Rebecca Harrison, who was born in 1856, was one of eleven children, and these included elder brother, Samuel and younger sister Charity, who were both sadly born deaf and dumb.

By 1881, Emma had left home at Church View to work as a domestic servant, and in that year, the 25 year old was to be found at Upper End, Baslow, at the home of 28 year old Arthur Geeson, his wife,

Jesse Harrison of Beeley
Barbara Hawksworth

Jane, and their two young children. Arthur Geeson was an innkeeper in Baslow. Three years later we find that Emma, a single woman, had become pregnant and gave birth to Jesse in 1884. She and the baby returned to live with her family at Beeley.

By 1891, her father, Thomas, had died and at some point before 1901 she and Jesse moved with her widowed mother and siblings, Samuel and Charity, to live for a period at Beeley Moor, in a property belonging to the Grafton family. By 1901, 17 year old Jesse was employed as a carter on a farm.

The Harrison and Grafton families had a long history of involvement with horses and therefore it is not surprsing that when Jesse enlisted at Chesterfield, he joined the Army Service Corps, which was mainly employed in the transportation of supplies, equipment and ammunition to the front line soldiers, using horse-drawn vehicles as well as motorised transport.

It was dangerous work but Jesse wished to be involved in front line fighting and was transferred to the Machine-Gun Corps, supporting the infantry in defence and attack. By this stage of his service he had risen to the rank of Lance Corporal.

In March 1918 he was stationed with his Battalion on the Somme and they found themselves overwhelmed by the superior forces of the German Army in the first few days of the Ludendorff offensive. Throughout the following days they attempted to stem the German advance, rallying then retreating, rallying again and then continuing their withdrawal until, on March 26th, just three days after his thirty third birthday, Jesse Harrison was killed by shell fire. His body was never recovered and he is commemorated on Panel 90 to 93 Pozieres Memorial, six kilometres north east of Albert.

PRIVATE ALLAN BOWERING No. 50396
15TH BATTALION SHERWOOD FORESTERS
DIED MARCH 28TH 1918 AGED 31

Allan Bowering during the First World War
Gordon Bowering

The Bowering family originated from Pilsley, but Allan's grandfather, Arundel John Bowering, had two farms in the Darley Dale area, one at Mortledge Farm, Hackney Lane, where Allan's father, Arundel George Bowering was born, and the other at Two Dales.

The Bowering family sold the Hackney Lane farm and went to live on a farm at Milltown, Ashover. In 1881 Arundel George Bowering married Elizabeth Holmes, the daughter of the landlord of the Devonshire Arms, Beeley. The Devonshire Arms, also run as a farmstead in those days, had been in the Holmes family for generations.

At the Devonshire Arms, Arundel and Elizabeth had five children (William, who died young, Ellis, Florrie, Allan, born April 15th 1886, and Maude). Sadly, Elizabeth Bowering, their mother, died in 1888, when Allan was just two years old.

Soon afterwards, Arundel left the inn, together with three of his children, to work as a coalminer at Shirland, leaving young Allan to live at Beeley with Hannah Hutchinson and her family.

After leaving school in 1899, Allan began work on the Chatsworth domain (ploughing, cutting grass etc.). On May 6th 1907 he married Ruth Beebe from

Youlgreave and they settled down to married life at Number 5, Duck Row, Pilsley. It was here that children Ellis, Elizabeth, Thomas Allan, Winifred, Roy, Gordon and Eric were born.

When war broke out, Allan continued working on the Chatsworth Estate, but after conscription was brought in, he joined up in September 1916, enlisting at Bakewell, and was posted eventually to the 15th Battalion Sherwood Foresters.

Allan was home on leave for the last time in January 1918. By late February 1918 the Battalion was in the front line at Langemarck, in the Ypres Salient. At 3a.m. on February 23rd, the enemy attempted to raid the Right Company outposts but retired after a few shots were fired by the Sherwoods. The Company area was heavily bombarded between 3 and 3-20a.m., resulting in two dead and one wounded. A patrol followed up the retiring raiders, estimated at from 12 to 20, but no trace was found. On February 26th the Battalion was relieved and moved into support.

March 9th saw the Battalion moving south by rail and road into Reserve at Chauny Farm Camp, close to the Somme area. There they trained between March 10th and the 22nd and were ready to move to any part of the line at twelve hours notice. On March 21st the great German offensive began and on the 23rd/24th the Battalion moved by train from Rouse-

Allan Bowering as a member of Chatsworth Football Club 1912

Gordon Bowering

brugge at 9p.m. to Mericourt, arriving there at 9-30p.m. and then marched through the night, reaching Maricourt at 6a.m. A halt was made there until 8-30a.m., when they pushed on to Curlu Wood. At 12 noon, orders were received to counter-attack. "Y" and"X" Companies at once moved forward and held the advancing enemy. Towards 4-30p.m. the enemy began out-flanking the two front companies who had very few survivors. At 5p.m. orders were received to withdraw, which was successfully carried out and a fresh position occupied on the Curlu-Maurepas road.

At 10-30a.m. on March 25th, owing to heavy enemy shelling from the rear, the troops on either flank retired, and to avoid being isolated, the Battalion withdrew to a defensive line in front of Maricourt, where it with-held the enemy, who again were round the left flank. The Battalion was then relieved and marched by parties to a position east of the Bray-Albert road and put forward outposts.

A warning was received at 10a.m. on March 26th that the enemy were approaching. The outpost line was manned and touch was quickly gained with the 15th Cheshires on the right, but no British troops could be seen on the left. The enemy were heavily engaged during the day, particularly on the left flank, which was exposed, except for some valuable assistance rendered by tanks.

At 3-30p.m. orders were received to retire and a withdrawal having been effected, a position was occupied west of the River Ancre, in front of the village of Buire.

The 27th March passed at Buire without incident and at 4p.m. the Battalion was relieved and removed to a support position in the quarry behind Buire. At 10p.m. on March 28th the Battalion relieved the 19th Battalion Durham Light Infantry in the right section of the front and all was quiet during this period. Total casualties for the period March 24th to 28th were 12 officers and 458 other ranks.

The Commonwealth War Graves Commission give March 28th as the date of Allan Bowering's death. However, very little action was taking place on either the 27th or 28th March and no casualties are reported. I believe that Allan died during the desperate fighting between March 24th and March 26th inclusive. His body was never recovered and his name is commemorated on the Pozieres Memorial (he can also be found on the war memorials at Beeley, Edensor and Pilsley).

Allan left a grieving widow and family at Duck Row, Pilsley, and sadly we shall find that during the Second World War, his son, Gordon Bowering, would be killed whilst serving in the Royal Air Force.

CORPORAL WILLIAM HAWKSWORTH No. G/62219
4TH BATTALION ROYAL FUSILIERS (CITY OF LONDON REGIMENT)
DIED APRIL 9TH 1918 AGED 22

William was born at Beeley on February 26th 1896, the eldest of the four surviving children of William and Louisa Hawksworth (a 3 year old daughter, Sarah, had died of pneumonia in 1897, with William's surviving siblings being Lucy, Mary and Rollinson).

William senior was a carpenter and joiner at Chatsworth House, as was his father John before him. He had married Louisa Rollinson from Froggatt, near Curbar, in 1892 and they were living at the Hawksworth family home on Church Lane, Beeley, next to the Vicarage. By this time, his father John had died and his 75 year old widowed mother, Rebecca, was living with them.

William Hawksworth junior went to Beeley School until he was eight and then transferred to Edensor Boys School, where he was taught by the strict headmaster, Mr. Wragg (the girls stayed on at Beeley School until they were 14). William was also a member of Beeley Sunday School and the parish church choir.

After leaving school, he went into service as a stable lad in the main stable block at Chatsworth House, eventually becoming a groom and living in accommodation above the premises. On special occasions they wore splendid livery. However, as the Duke of Devonshire obtained a fleet of motor vehicles in the early years of the 20th century, William's role accommodated this change in transportation.

William Hawksworth of Beeley
Barbara Hawksworth

Some years before the start of the Great War, William went to work as footman for Miss Egerton, the Duke of Devonshire's relative, at St. George's Hill, Byfleet, Weybridge, and it was from there that he

William Hawksworth, dressed in livery, stands second from the right
Barbara Hawksworth

William Hawksworth is riding the lead horse, in front of the Chatsworth House stables. His accommodation is marked with a cross
Barbara Hawksworth

William Hawksworth is the third rider from the front. They are taking part on the Mayor's Sunday Procession, Chesterfield on November 12th 1911
Barbara Hawksworth

William Hawksworth stands on the left
Barbara Hawksworth

William Hawksworth as a stable boy at Chatsworth House.
He is the lad standing on the left on the front row.
The stable block is behind them
Barbara Hawksworth

William Hawksworth as
footman for Miss Egerton
Barbara Hawksworth

went to enlist in the army at Chelsea, in November 1915. His cousin, George Hawksworth, also enlisted during the war but thankfully survived the conflict.

With his previous experience of working with horses, we find that William was first of all drafted into the County of London Yeomanry, but shortly afterwards he became a member of the 4th Battalion Royal Fusiliers.

At the time of the Easter Rising in 1916, the Battalion was sent across to Ireland to help suppress the rebellion in Dublin.

By December 1916, they were stationed on the Western Front, with Willam serving as a Lewis gunner and being fortunate to survive the actions throughout 1917. The Fusiliers were heavily engaged in the Ludendorff Offensive in March 1918, between the 21st and 28th, and it was during the early stages of this battle that William's left calf was badly shattered, severing a number of blood vessels.

He was transferred from the Casualty Clearing Station to the 53rd General Hospital, on the Channel coast at Boulogne, being admitted on March 31st. Gas gangrene set in, necessitating the amputation of his leg, but he sadly passed away at 8-30p.m. on Tuesday April 9th.

William was buried in grave X.B.7. Wimereux Communal Cemetery, a few miles north of Boulogne.

The Germans, finding that their advance was being brought to a standstill in the direction of Amiens, turned their attention further north and determined to threaten the Channel ports. On April 9th they began a concentrated attack along the River Lys, on the British and Portuguese front between Armentieres and La Bassee, and the fighting spread to Messines in Belgium. Battalions were once again decimated as they struggled desperately to halt the fresh advance.

LANCE CORPORAL HARRY BRUMBY No. 241493
6TH BATTALION SHERWOOD FORESTERS
DIED MAY 18TH 1918 AGED 24

Jarvis Brumby, younger brother of Harry Brumby, as a schoolboy at Edensor School, 1912
Derek Neave

In 1901 Harry was the second of four children of William and Emma Brumby, with the family living next to the Vicarage at Edensor, on the Chatsworth Estate. William Brumby had been born at Belchford, a village 20 miles east of Lincoln and had married Emma, who was born in the Lincolnshire village of Scamblesby, three miles away.

William was a coachman and he and his wife eventually came to Edensor around 1892, where William worked on the estate in that capacity, very likely being employed by the vicar, at times. It was at Edensor that Ellen was born in 1893, Harry 1895, Edith 1897 and Jarvis Brumby in 1900.

When Harry left Edensor School, where he had been taught by A.E. Wragg and Miss K. Hutchinson, he began working on the Chatsworth Estate. The family by this stage was living on Duck Row, Pilsley, in the house with the bay window.

Eventually, Harry enlisted in the Army at Chesterfield and became a member of the 6th Battalion Sherwood Foresters. His younger brother, Jarvis, joined the Royal Navy and thankfully survived the war, becoming an engine driver at Rowsley.

The German offensive of March 21st to the middle of April 1918 created a sharp salient some 15 miles deep in the British line. From April to August the 6th Battalion were involved in holding the southern flank of this salient, close to the La Bassee Canal and the bridging point at the little village of Gorre, which was always heavily shelled, especially by gas shells. There were often a thousand or more such shells in one small area and gas casualties were frequent, with the men often sleeping in their gas masks.

This new front was continuously active, the Germans wishing to enlarge their salient, the British to hold them and prepare for an attack on the flanks.

British raids were frequent, involving the 6th Battalion.

The Foresters were in and out of this sector for three months, the usual routine being six days in the line, six days in support on the Canal at Gorre and six days in reserve, resting in the woods at Vaudricourt or Fouquieres.

The gas shelling was so bad that cooking, food and ammunition supply and weapons training were carried out in a gas mask and on one evening, "C" Company had to sleep with their masks on when they were bombarded by mustard gas. The casualties from such attacks were heavy. The days spent in support at Gorre were also uncomfortable for the place was frequently shelled, there was little shelter and training and working parties were continuous.

It was on one of these occasions when the Battalion was in the front line near Gorre, between May 6th and 10th, that Harry was wounded. He was taken to the Casualty Clearing Station and then for urgent attention

Jarvis Brumby,
brother of Harry Brumby
Fred Fearn

behind the lines, but just over a week later he succumbed to his wounds and was buried in grave 1.E.40. Pernes British Cemetery, on the main road from St. Pol to Lillers.

On May 27th 1918 Ludendorff launched his next major offensive, this time in the Champagne countryside, the very area to which a number of British Battalions had been sent to in order to recuperate from the terrible mauling they had received during March and April. A serviceman from the Devonshire villages would die in the early days of this major offensive.

PRIVATE ARTHUR SHELDON No. 82486
"B" COMPANY 15TH BATTALION DURHAM LIGHT INFANTRY
DIED MAY 29TH 1918 AGED 18

In 1901, one year old Arthur was living close to Baslow Vicarage with his father, 34 year old James William Sheldon, a Baslow born stone mason and his mother, 34 year old Alice (née Wall), who originated from Edensor. Arthur's four year old elder brother, James Edward (Teddy) and younger brother, three month old David, completed the family. Their mother Alice had been working in service at Chatsworth House when she met her future husband, James William Sheldon.

By the start of the Great War the Sheldons were living at The Green, Baslow. Young Arthur received his education at Baslow School before beginning work on the Chatsworth Estate, but his older brother, Teddy, had been sent off to a school in Blackburn to receive a higher standard of education, paid for by an aunt of the family.

Before the war, Teddy began work in the Chatsworth Estate Office as a clerk, joining up in 1917 as a gunner in the Royal Field Artillery, although much of his time was spent in dealing with the horses that pulled the guns.

Private Arthur Sheldon of Baslow
Martin Brightmore
and St Anne's Church

He left for the Western Front in October 1917, but in May 1918 he was wounded on the arm by shrapnel, resulting in long term treatment lasting into 1919 at English hospitals. Teddy Sheldon returned to work in the estate office and eventually became the well-respected Private Secretary to Edward Cavendish, 10th Duke of Devonshire.

Arthur Sheldon enlisted in 1917 when he reached the age of 18 and joined the 15th Battalion of the Durham Light Infantry. The Battalion had received heavy losses during the offensive of March 21st to April 14th 1918 and the law of the land was changed to allow 18 year olds to fight overseas, so that the

Alice Sheldon (née Wall), mother of Arthur Sheldon
Margaret Sheldon

Alice Sheldon and James William Sheldon, parents of Arthur Sheldon
Margaret Sheldon

Teddy Sheldon, brother of Arthur Sheldon
Margaret Sheldon

numbers could be "made up". Young, inexperienced soldiers such as Arthur found themselves being sent out in drafts to the Western Front in April 1918 and the Baslow lad found himself a member of "B" Company, 15th Battalion. In mid March 1918 he had spent his last leave with his family at Baslow.

A number of the battle-weary British battalions were sent in late April, early May to rest and recuperate in a French sector of the line, to the north east of Paris, in the Champagne area, between Soissons and Rheims, where it was thought they would be "safe". As we have already seen, sadly for them this sector between the Rivers Aisne and Marne had been chosen by Ludendorff as the scene of his next massive offensive.

On May 12th, the 15th Battalion went by light railway to Savigny and marched across the River Vesle to Hermonville, where they relieved a French battalion. On May 21st they were relieved and withdrew to a support position near the main road to Rheims and then into reserve. Training was done here and a church parade was held on the evening of May 26th.

However, at 1a.m. on May 27th a heavy bombardment of mustard gas shells came down upon the camp. The 15th Battalion moved off in gas respirators through the dense fumes and reached Cauroy by way of woodland tracks. At 10a.m. "B" Company, including Arthur Sheldon, pushed out on the left to hold the Boyau de la Somme. The Germans came on in determined fashion, supported by a fierce bombardment and pushed "B" Company back to Avancee de Cauroy. The Durhams counter-attacked with bombs and a bloody struggle was waged in these trenches on the outskirts of the village until the German numbers prevailed.

Despite their desperate resistance, "B" and "C" Companies were forced back to the sunken road. Two hours later, at 7-30p.m., came another onslaught in overwhelming strength and the British line drew back to the road behind the village. An ordered withdrawal took place in the hours of darkness.

By 4-30a.m. on May 28th they were in brigade reserve but the Germans made rapid progress and three hours later the Durhams were under machine-gun fire at the eastern end of the ridge. Though the fight was stoutly maintained, the line withdrew 500 yards, but again had to retreat in order to escape annihilation. Not all members of the Battalion arrived safely back because of the disjointed nature of the desperate fighting.

The tired troops, consisting of only six officers and forty men, were assailed with heavy shell fire and German patrols were active on the 28th but no fresh infantry attack developed that day. The line was now on the River Vesle. The Durhams first held the south bank but after a fierce enemy bombardment that lasted until 2-30p.m., the 15th Battalion were relieved by French troops and moved back to Rosnay, where they rested for the night, south of the village.

However, Arthur Sheldon was not with the few survivors. The young

Baslow lad of 18 years of age had been killed by shell fire on the morning of May 29th. His body was never recovered from the battlefield and after the war his name was commemorated on the Soissons Memorial. In the heavy fighting of May 27th to 29th, the 15th Battalion had lost 456 men in killed, wounded and missing, the heaviest casualties in the brigade. They had fought a splendid rearguard action on May 28th, helping to check the German advance.

*** *As an interesting side note, the vicar of Baslow, Reverend James Smith, wrote letters to servicemen at the front, including Gunner Teddy Sheldon, the brother of Arthur. The following are extracts from a number of these letters:*

July 12th 1917. "My dear Sheldon, Miss A. Wright let me see your letter to her. It seems rather silly to put a man with your qualifications to be with horses. It would be different if no clerks were wanted, but, as I heard last Monday, there is a real dearth of clerks in the Army Pay Department. But of course, you are an "A" man and I suppose all in your class have to go for general service.

"I am sorry that you have no opportunity of going to church. This is a great drawback throughout the Army and the result is that many who have been churchgoers in old days lose all interest in church services when they return. In the early days of the war, when many of our lads came home on leave, they felt they must at least come to the old church once. Now they come and go and hardly one of them thinks of putting his nose into the church.

"I was in Sheffield today and Mr. Ferranti ran me as far as the Grindleford Station. His eldest son (Basil) was badly wounded a week ago last Sunday in France. He was in a tent with two other officers and a Corporal when a shell hit them. The three other men were killed outright and Basil Ferranti's legs were badly hit. One thigh had a big hole made in it, the other was also wounded, one foot was crushed and a toe had to be taken off and he had four other wounds in his body. It is hoped he will recover, but he will be no more good in the Army.

"I hope you will get leave some of these days. I want to see how you walk along with those mighty spurs you RFA men wear. I expect by then you will be an expert."

October 30th 1917. "My dear Sheldon, You seem to be well and I see from your letter you could tell a thing or two if you were only allowed to do so. You were certainly a long time on the water when you crossed the Channel.

"Yes, you are undoubtedly soldiering now. Your travelling in the cattle truck in France would be quite an introduction to the trials of life on active service. You and your colleagues have much to go through. May God be with you!

"On such a subject as this, it is not good for other people to talk much. If they express their real thoughts they lay themselves open to the charge that they are talking humbug. But I must say this and it is really true. The thought of all you young men fighting for us fills many of us with keen regret. Here am I, a man approaching fifty one, and my life inevitably running out and my best days done, and then all you young men, so many cut off on the threshhold of life. Believe me, it is true when I say many of us older folk would gladly take your places and die if we could. This is so sad that the young and useful should go, and we the useless ones, comparatively speaking, should be left to go on living."

November 12th 1917. "My Dear Sheldon, We shall send another recruit into the Army tomorrow. Frank Thorpe is called up (* the son of the Baslow Gas Company's manager, who would be killed in 1918). I do not know who will go next. I quite expect that there will be another good old search for men before long. Men must be got more than ever now, and there are still some young ones in "funk holes", and I should not be surprised if the age was raised and older men taken for Home Service.

"I spent last week in Liverpool and had an interesting time. The ships always have a fascination for me. I saw as much as I could of the docks, and it was striking the way the ships are now painted so that the enemy cannot easily spot them.

"As there is nothing going on in Baslow, there is nothing to write about. But I was anxious to send you a line so that you may know that I, like so many others, have not forgotten you and to express the fervent hope that you will go through this frightful hell all right. Keep a good heart. Whatever happens, you are safe in the Lord's keeping and He will watch over you."

April 14th 1918. "Dear Sheldon, This is Sunday evening and my day's work is done. Sundays are more full than usual for me now, for I am a Volunteer (Home Guard member)!. We drill for two hours on Sundays from 2-30p.m. to 4-30p.m. Also one hour on Tuesdays and Thursdays. There are 23 of us and there ought to be more. The Doctor is one of us, and he is as busy as anyone. Some men say they have no time to drill, or too tired after their day's work. Well, Dr. Edlestone has to turn out to confinements in the night and lose his rest, as well as work all day. But I do not think he has missed a drill once. Coates, Hodgkiss (senior and junior), J. Holmes, R. Hibbert, Woodhouse, Spooner, Wigfull, Dent, F. Taylor, A. Burgess, H. Beswick, A. Downes, W. Sheldon, Stones (from the Ford), W. Hulley, W.H. Hearnshaw, George Hearnshaw, W. Hearnshaw and myself are among those who form the "Baslow Army". At present we are very much the "Awkward Squad", but we are doing our best and are getting on well.

"We have two very good sergeants from Bakewell. Hudson, who used to keep the Castle Hotel, and Stewart of the Bakewell Clothing Hall. Of course, we make horrid mistakes, and we generally have a group of little boy spectators to laugh at us and this they do heartily if the Vicar or Doctor makes an ass of himself. But this is part of the discipline of the thing.

"Mr. Cockerell (the Duke's agent at Chatsworth) was asked to raise a Stretcher Unit, consisting of 87 men. He could not do this without the help of Baslow, as Edensor, Pilsley and Beeley could not of themselves raise so many. He accordingly asked us to join. But we were not having any, as we did not wish to be non-combatants and we did not want to have to go down to Edensor every time for drill. The chief thing was we preferred to fight if need be, desiring rather to kill Germans than have to carry any of them on stretchers.

"I saw your mother yesterday and she looked well. Of course she is anxious, but she is very brave and sensible, or I should say self-controlled. This reminds me that I have not said a word about your being wounded. You know how sorry I was to hear this and I only wish it had been a "Blighty" one to bring you home.

"Mr. Cockerell has given the Sports Club notice to quit the Recreation Field in March 1919. I am convinced he is making a great mistake and doing the Duke no good, nor any good either to the Landowner Class. It means that when the men come home there will be no field where the men can play cricket or football. This will cause great resentment in the place. This is not the only thing. Wages are still poor at Chatsworth. The agricultural labourer has to have his 25 shillings but I believe the gardeners still get only 23 shillings. This won't do. When the war is over the leaders of Labour will have time to think of the Land Question as well as that of the Town Industries, and they will make a dead set against the Landowners, unless the latter act justly and with reason now. You know how hard it is for any one to get hold of a piece of land here for himself.

"From your experience in an estate office, you know that the ground rents are quite ridiculous. Well, Master Edward, this sort of thing will have to cease. There is no reason under the sun why good land should be monopolised by a few big owners and this rotten system will be changed.

"Well, my good lad, I must go to bed and stop my chatter. May the Almighty Father have you in His keeping and may you come home to us safe and sound."

Although the next casualty, from the village of Beeley died on August 10th, he had been wounded and taken prisoner by the Germans on March 23rd 1918, during the Ludendorff Offensive of March 21st. He was to die behind the German lines.

PRIVATE RICHARD MORTON No. 59447
16TH BATTALION SHERWOOD FORESTERS (CHATSWORTH RIFLES)
DIED AUGUST 10TH 1918 AGED 34.

Richard was the eighth of nine children of Elias and Emma Morton and was born in 1884 at a cottage next to Brook House, in Beeley. His father, a Beeley man, was a farm worker on one of the Chatsworth estate farms and had married Emma, a Yorkshire girl from Wakefield. In fact, their first child had been born in Halifax but the other children were all born at Beeley.

By 1901, sixteen year old Richard Morton was living at home in Beeley with his parents and siblings Minnie (21), Elias (19 and a carter on a farm), and Olive (11) and was employed as a farm worker like his father. However, in the years before the Great War, he began working both as a

LEFT: *Richard Morton of Beeley and Edensor, in uniform, after joining the Sherwood Foresters*
Davina Askey

RIGHT: *Richard Morton as a member of Chatsworth Football Club*
Gordon Bowering

Barbrook House, built for Sir Joseph Paxton. It was situated next to the Kitchen Garden (today, the site for caravans). It was demolished in the 1950s
Derek Neave

groom and in the Chatsworth kitchen gardens (now the site of the caravan park) and the gardens of Gerry Hartopp, Land Agent for the Duke, who lived at nearby Barbrook House. A keen footballer, he was a member of the Chatsworth football team and also played for Beeley on the Meadows.

Annie Septamay Walters, a native of Pentrich, near Ripley, who was working in service at Barbrook House for the Hartopps, met Richard and they were married, setting up home at Edensor, in the house attached to the old post office. It was there that their three children were born; Leslie (October 28th 1909), Eric (February 18th 1912) and Nancy.

However, as with so many families, war intruded on their lives and Richard eventually enlisted at Bakewell, joining the 16th Battalion

Richard Morton and family at Edensor, c1917
LEFT TO RIGHT: *Leslie Morton, Annie Morton holding Nancy, Eric Morton, Richard Morton*
Davina Askey

Sherwood Foresters, known as the Chatsworth Rifles. The flag hanging in front of the war memorial in the north aisle of St. Peter's Church, Edensor, is the King's Colour of the Chatsworth Rifles, 16th Battalion, Sherwood Foresters. The Colour hangs here because the unit was raised in 1915 by the Duke of Devonshire in his capacity as Lord Lieutenant of Derbyshire and when the Battalion was disbanded in 1922 the Colours were presented for safe-keeping to Edensor Church when the Duke unveiled the memorial to those locals killed during the Great War.

The Chatsworth Rifles first saw action on the Western Front in March 1916. Over the next two and a half years, 29 officers and 600 men of the Battalion were killed. Of the officers who were with the unit when it first went to France, over two thirds were killed or wounded. The Battalion won one VC, six DSO's, 28 Military Crosses, 14 DCM's and 63 Military Medals. The name "Chatsworth Rifles" derives from a local militia, raised in 1859 and disbanded in 1881.

It was in the middle of 1916, whilst he was in the Army, that his third child, Nancy, was born. Thankfully Richard survived the fighting of 1917, including the Battle of Bulgar Wood on September 20th, during the Battle of

Passchendaele, in which the Battalion lost many men.

The first three months of 1918 found the Battalion on the Somme, and by March they were in Dessaet Wood Camp, Sorel, to the east of Bapaume, resting, training and playing sports. However, everyone knew the great German attack was coming on March 21st.

At 4-30a.m. on that day, a heavy gas and high explosive bombardment opened on the front and the men struggled to their assembly point wearing gas masks, yet suffered 20 gas casualties. Throughout the next few days they were forced back by overwhelming enemy force towards the bridges over the Somme River, staging many gallant efforts to hold up the German advance and having to leave the wounded behind on the battle ground. Many casualties had been sustained.

By 2-30p.m. on March 23rd they were in position on high ground on the Peronne - Haut Allaines road. They could see Peronne in flames, undergoing a heavy bombardment. The enemy were swarming down the road and along the Somme Canal. Behind, the Chatsworth Rifles could see a great army in retreat – lorries, limbers, guns and transport of all types, retiring towards Clery, the main crossing point over the River Somme. The enemy were shelling the roads at intervals.

About 4p.m. the Germans massed and suddenly launched an attack against the Sherwoods in enormous numbers, driving in the flank and turning the position. The enemy was only 30 yards away in places and they only extracted themselves from the pincer movement just in time. They fell back, fighting a rearguard action to cover the withdrawal. They struggled, scattered, formless and exhausted, into Clery, whilst 60 men remained be-hind to form a defensive flank.

The difficulty of evacuating the wounded was increased and many had been left to fend for themselves on the battlefield. By this time, the effective fighting men of the Battalion numbered just five officers and 168 other ranks.

I believe that it is almost certain that on this day of intensive, desperate fighting, Richard Morton was wounded and became a prisoner of war of the Germans. He was taken back behind the German lines, first to a Casualty Clearing Station and later a Stationary Hospital, where he began to recover.

It is known that many prisoners of war were held back, close to the front, in order to carry out work of various types in an effort to keep the German advance moving forward. They were used to move supplies (even ammunition under threat of force, against Geneva Conventions) and repair and maintan roads and light railways which were vital to the German supply lines. After recovering, it is likely that Richard was used in this way, instead of being taken to Germany as a POW. The conditions would be hard and onerous in the summer heat and it may be that he drank contaminated water.

*War Grave headstone for
Richard Morton at
Valenciennes Communal
Cemetery*
Davina Askey

*Valenciennes Communal Cemetery,
showing Richard Morton's headstone*
Davina Askey

We certainly know that he contracted diphtheria (an acute infectious disease causing a membrane to form in the throat, preventing breathing, with toxins causing heart attacks).

Richard was taken to a German military hospital at Valenciennes, France, and it was here that he died from diphtheria and cardiac weakness on August 10th 1918, aged just 34. He was buried in grave V.E.19. Valenciennes (St. Roch) Communal Cemetery.

His death left a widow and three young children back in the house attached to Edensor Post Office. The family remained in the house but times were hard for Annie and she made ends meet to provide for her family by taking in and ironing the Hartopp's family washing, cleaning the estate offices every night (in those days they were sited in the Old Stable Block, nowadays the Cavendish Flats) and serving afternoon teas from her bay window, to visitors to Edensor and the Park.

The German offensive of May 27th in the Champagne area of France ground to a halt on the River Marne and as they withdrew from the Marne front, the French and Americans, with British contingents, began an offensive on the Marne and Aisne between July 18th and August 5th.

Meanwhile, on the Somme front, General Haig launched his Amiens Offensive between August 8th and September 4th, which caught the Germans off guard by a well mounted assault, secretly prepared. Troops advanced without preliminary bombardment, preceded by tanks, and bit deep into the German positions. General Ludendorff stated that August 8th had been the "Black Day" of the German Army.

PRIVATE GEORGE EDWARD SIDDALL (MM) No. 58660
"B" COMPANY 10TH BATTALION SHERWOOD FORESTERS
DIED OCTOBER 13TH 1918 AGED 40

George was born at Bubnell, Baslow, in January 1878, the son of Henry and Charlotte Siddall. In 1881, two year old George was living at Baslow in the home of his grandfather, Henry Siddall, a labourer, born at Curbar and grandmother Ann, a Baslow woman, together with his aunty, Ann, a dressmaker. I have been unable to trace his parents, Henry and Charlotte.

Twenty years later, George is to be found living near Heathy Lea and the Cupola, on the northern fringes of Baslow, with his wife Eliza Emily Siddall (née Heath), who came from a farming family at Brampton, near Chesterfield. Their family eventually consisted of Percy, Eliza (Leila), Josephine and Charlotte. They had been

George Edward Siddall
of Baslow and Pilsley
Chatsworth Photo Archive

Baslow Football Team 1898/1899. George Edward Siddall, who would be killed in action in 1918,
aged 40, sits first from left. The clergyman is the Reverend Alfred Edward Drew, who was in Baslow
from 1898 to 1900. Later, in 1928, he returned to be Baslow's vicar until 1947 and would lose his
only son, Basil, during the Second World War
Eileen Bradley and Leonard Broome

159

Personnel from the Royal Naval Convalescent Hospital at Edensor Institute, Chatsworth, early 1915. George Edward Siddall stands third from the left, in civilian clothes, before he joined up. He would be killed on active service, later in the War
Eileen Bradley and Leonard Broome

RIGHT: *George Edward Siddall is shown sitting on the table*
Eileen Bradley and Leonard Broome

George Edward Siddall and family, c1916, at Pilsley.
BACK ROW: *Josephine Siddall, Lila Siddall, Percy Siddall*
SEATED: *Eliza Emily Siddall, Charlotte Mary Siddall, George Edward Siddall*
Eileen Bradley and Leonard Broome

married at Baslow Church on September 18th 1898.

A few years later, the Siddall family moved to Pilsley, where George was working on the Chatsworth estate as an agricultural labourer, and they lived in a cottage on High Street, above the Devonshire Arms.

Some years before the war, he came to work as a servant at Chatsworth House and one of his jobs was to direct visitors to the House from the entrance at "Sandy's Turn", near Edensor. Dressed in livery on these occasions, he stood in a hut, known by some as "Siddall's Cabin" (this cabin stood at Sandy's Turn until the 1950's).

By 1912, though, George had become the Institute caretaker at Edensor. When war was declared in 1914, the Institute at Edensor, formerly the Chatsworth Hotel, became a Royal Naval Convalescent Hospital and George Siddall continued to help the steward of the Institute in his work.

Eventually, George enlisted at Bakewell and joined the 10th Battalion of the Sherwood Foresters, with one of his duties being to act as a stretcher bearer. By September 17th 1918 the Battalion was in the vicinity of Heudecourt and Gouzeaucourt, with the objective of the Divisional attack being Gauche Wood. It was in this action that George won the Military Medal.

As a stretcher bearer he risked his life in bringing back a wounded young man under heavy shell and machine-gun fire and got him back to the line. When asked by his officer why he had risked his life, he said it was because the man was about the same age as his 18 year old son, Percy, who was beginning his training as a soldier back in England. On September 25th they were relieved and marched back to a rest camp at Mannancourt, where, for the next nine days the Battalion rested.

On October 8th they moved across the Canal de l'Escaut and to the north, Cambrai could be seen, parts of which were aflame. The 10th Battalion was in support and the attack pressed forward only to find that the enemy had evacuated his positions.

As an approach was made upon the outskirts of Montigny a strong resistance was met. There were many civilians to be found in both Montigny and Caullery and all were overcome to at last see the British come into their villages. They remained at Montigny until October 12th, when they moved to Inchy and at 6p.m. the Battalion moved forward and took over the front line near Selle.

Great difficulty was experienced in taking over as it was a wet and dark night, the bridges over the River Selle had been smashed and there was very heavy machine-gun fire. The front companies pushed forward and got as close as they could to the enemy, then dug themselves in, in the area of an old quarry.

The morning of the 13th revealed that many sections had established themselves in positions, which, in the light of day, were within full view of the enemy. They lay as still as possible, avoiding any movement, for the enemy was very active with both machine-guns and snipers firing from the windows and other high buildings in the village of Neuvilly, causing numerous casualties amongst both officers and men. Eventually the artillery strafed the village and quietened the snipers down, but sadly George Siddall had been killed that day.

In volunteering to rescue another wounded comrade George was shot by a German sniper. His body was never recovered and his name was eventually commemorated on Panel 7 of the Vis-en-Artois Memorial, between Arras and Cambrai.

Inspired by the Communists and sparked by a mutiny of the German High Seas Fleet, disorders, revolts and mutinies flared inside Germany between October 29th and November 10th. A new Socialist government took power and proclaimed a republic on November 9th, whilst the Kaiser fled to Holland on the 10th. A German delegation negotiated an armistice at Compiegne, France, at 5a.m. on November 11th and hostilities ceased at 11a.m. After nearly four and a half years of fighting the war had come to an end.

However, in the weeks and months after this welcome news was received in the Chatsworth villages, some families continued to receive less happy news about their loved ones. Between the Armistice and the end of 1919, more servicemen from these villages would die from wounds received during the war or from the effects of the flu pandemic, and their names would be added to the list of men commemorated on the village war memorials. News of the deaths of loved ones as a result of the flu virus must have been very hard for their families to accept. They had survived against the odds on the battlefield, only to succumb to the killer virus. For the First World War generation there was no protection. For them, this epidemic was a cruel epilogue to the suffering they had endured in the years of conflict. It was, as one historian has written, the gleaner of the war's harvest.

On the Home Front too, there were many victims struck down in the local villages between November and December, 1918. On November 13th, Rowsley School was closed for a fortnight and closed again between November 25th and December 7th, as the epidemic raged. Four mothers in the village, Mrs. Percival, Mrs. J. Percival, Mrs. Osborne and Mrs. Cannon, had died in the week leading up to November 25th.

PRIVATE LEWIS HERBERT (BERT) REEVE No. 577713
154TH LABOUR COMPANY, LABOUR CORPS
DIED NOVEMBER 18TH 1918 AGED 28

Bert Reeve of Beeley
Barbara Hawksworth

Lewis Herbert Reeve, known as Bert to family and friends, was the second youngest son of Lewis and Jane Reeve, and was born at East-wood, Nottinghamshire, in 1890. His father earned his living as a joiner and wheelwright.

His mother Jane died as a result of complications at his birth, and shortly after-wards, Jane's sister Catherine married Lewis Reeve. The family moved to Pilsley, near Chester-field, but later, Lewis Reeve senior became land-lord of the Holly Bush Inn on Smedley Street, Matlock and then the Holmestead Cottage Inn, near Cromford, before finally renting the Devonshire Arms at Beeley from the Duke of

The funeral of Thomas Burdekin of Beeley, 1902.
BACK ROW: *Samuel Burdekin, Alice Burdekin (m. Harry Reeve), Thomas Burdekin, Melissa Burdekin, Joseph Burdekin, Nellie Burdekin, George William Burdekin*
FRONT ROW: *Polly Burdekin (m. Hulley), Emily Burdekin (m. Speller), Mary Burdekin (widow of Thomas), Annie Burdekin, Sarah Ann Burdekin*
Pauline Harrison

Devonshire in 1909. As with so many such establishments, a smallholding was attached to the pub and when he left school, Bert helped his father run the farm.

Meanwhile, in 1906, his brother Harry had joined their brothers Jack and Fred in Canada, until Harry returned to Beeley in 1912. Having married a Beeley girl, Alice Burdekin, the couple helped to run the Beeley Post Office and refreshment rooms.

Bert Reeve volunteered for service early in the war and joined the army, serving eventually in the Machine-Gun Corps (Infantry), a branch of the service that brought much danger to its members and received the epithet of "Suicide Club". By mid 1918 we find that Bert had been transferred to the 154th Labour Company, mainly employed in digging trenches, providing gun emplacements and constructing roads and rail lines to the front. Although mainly serving just behind the front line, the work was dangerous, for they were often targeted by enemy shell fire. They would also be brought into the front line at night to dig and repair the trench systems.

In April 1917 we have seen that Bert's brother, Ernest Reeve, was killed by shell fire near Gouzeaucourt, on the Somme, whilst later in the year, his step mother, Catherine, died and Bert was allowed leave to attend the funeral.

In early October 1917 Bert's brother, Harry Reeve, the Beeley postmaster, enlisted after a refusal of further exemption from the District Military Tribunal. He joined the Army Service Corps but it proved to be a very brief spell of military life. After the third day he was sent to hospital and for seven weeks had been treated for complications to the legs. In November 1917 he returned home to Beeley with his discharge papers as no longer fit for military service.

Returning to the front after his mother's funeral, Bert survived through-out the rest of the war, living to see the signing of the Armistice, on November 11th. His family back home in Beeley were relieved that he had survived and looked forward to his homecoming in the near future.

Grave news arrived at the Devonshire Arms, Beeley, however, on November 17th, with the delivery of a letter from Sister M. Jennings of the 62nd Casualty Clearing Station at Courtrai (Kortrijk) in Belgium, 28 kilometres east of Ypres. She wrote:

"I am very sorry to tell you that your son, Private Reeve No. 577713 154th Labour Company is very ill in this hospital with influenza and we are feeling most anxious about him. I trust, however, that there will be better news for you soon and in the meantime I hope it will comfort you a little to know that he is getting every care and attention here." (Courtrai had been in German hands throughout the war, but the British had captured it on October 16th 1918 and Number 62 Casualty Clearing Station was set up).

There followed a second letter from Sister Jennings on the 18th November:

"I am very sorry to tell you that your son died in this hospital today at 12-55p.m. As I told you in my letter of yesterday he was very ill indeed with influenza and although we did everything possible for him, he gradually got weaker and passed away very peacefully at the time stated above. I am sorry to be the sender of such sad news to you. He will be buried in the cemetery near Courtrai with other British soldiers and any small personal belongings he may have brought with him into hospital will be forwarded to you through the War Office."

It was recounted that Bert was unconscious for some time before he died and left no message. Lewis Herbert Reeve was buried in grave A.22. Kortrijk (Courtrai) St. Jan Communal Cemetery.

Of the three Reeve brothers who went into the Army, only Harry survived, continuing his work at Beeley Post Office. His wife Alice and mother in law, Mary Burdekin, were mainly responsible for the shop and Post Office and during the 1920's Harry ran a taxi from the premises, meeting tourists and guests at Rowsley Station and taking them around the Peak District sights. When the Derwent Valley water pipeline was being laid in the early 1930's, many navvies (construction workers) arrived in the neighbourhood. Attached to Beeley Post Office was a refreshment room, where Mary Burdekin often put on choir suppers etc. Harry Reeve, who was a joiner by trade, constructed bunks in the refreshments room, where the navvies could sleep for a price, and some were even put up in the wash house.

GUNNER HARRY BERTRAM BOND No. 175530
153RD SIEGE BATTERY ROYAL GARRISON ARTILLERY
DIED NOVEMBER 30TH 1918 AGED 20

Harry Bond was born at Beeley in 1898, the youngest of three sons and a daughter, the children of Jacob and Ellen Bond. 27 year old Jacob had married 25 year old Ellen Brown on July 1st 1886, both being Beeley born and bred. She was a dressmaker and he a woodsman on the estate. Later he made a living as an agricultural labourer. Harry's other siblings were Winifred, Lewis and Fred.

Harry worked on the land for the Chatsworth Estate, but during the war he enlisted at Bakewell, joining the Royal Garrison Artillery and training as a Gunner, eventually joining the 153rd Siege Battery. There were usually four howitzers to a battery, with the normal rate of fire one shell every two minutes. The weight of ammunition was great, with twenty-two six inch shells weighing one ton and they all had to be man-handled.

As the war drew towards its close, it must have seemed to everyone that

Harry would survive the conflict, but as the war entered its final few months, he was wounded in the back by enemy shell fire and was gassed. After emergency treatment, he was brought to a Base Hospital in France and then across the Channel. On arrival he was taken to the Military Annexe of a hospital in Milton, on the southern outskirts of Portsmouth. His condition worsened and he died at the hospital on November 30th, nineteen days after the Armistice, from emphysema exhaustion, enlargement of the air vehicles of the lungs and a swelling caused by the presence of air.

Harry's body was brought back by rail to Rowsley and Jacob and Ellen, from Devonshire Square, Beeley, were able to attend the burial of their youngest child in the South West part of St. Anne's churchyard, on December 5th 1918.

The gravestone of Harry Bertram Bond, in Beeley churchyard. He died in England, from wounds received in France
Keith Taylor

PRIVATE STANLEY HAYNES No. M2/034995 XV CORPS TROOPS MOTOR TRANSPORT COMPANY ARMY SERVICE CORPS DIED NOVEMBER 30TH 1918 AGED 33

Stanley was the seventh of the ten children of William and Rebecca Haynes. He was born at Flash, near Ashover, where his father was a farm bailiff, having arrived there after he lost his living when his animals were drowned in a bad flooding of the River Derwent, in his native South Darley.

Stanley Haynes of Beeley
Vera Russell

The original cross on the grave of Stanley Haynes
Vera Russell

Having next moved to a farm at Gladwin Mark, in Darley parish, his father, William, eventually began work as a labourer at the Rowsley engine sheds, with the family moving to live in the village of Beeley in 1888, at Hawthorn Cottage (Church View), across from Beeley Church.

Stanley began work as an errand boy for Thomas and Elizabeth Burdekin at Beeley Post Office, then worked on the Chatsworth Estate as a carpenter.

Brothers Frank, William, Edward and Stanley enlisted in the Army, with Stanley joining the Motor Transport Company of the Army Service Corps. He had been a member of the Territorials (Sherwood Foresters) before the war and had been at their annual camp at Hunmanby the week before the war began.

There was a great deal of danger to be faced whilst serving in the Motor Transport Corps as they transported supplies, munitions and construction materials to the front and supply lines, often under conditions of severe shell fire.

It was with sadness that Stanley learned of the death of his younger brother Edward in October 1917 at the Battle of Passchendaele, but by early November his family in Beeley must have been happy in believing that surely now, after nearly four years' service in the Army, much of that time spent on the Western Front, Stanley would soon be returning to Chatsworth and entering civilian life once again.

It was not to be. We find that as the war came to a close with the Armistice signed on November 11th, Stanley was admitted to a military hospital at Tourcoing, a town in the Lille district of Northern France. He was suffering from peritonitis and the effects of influenza.

Lille and the district around had been in German hands for the whole war and Tourcoing had been used as a hospital complex by them. In November 1918, the 10th Stationary Hospital and the 8th and 10th Casualty Clearing Stations were posted at Tourcoing.

On November 30th 1918 Stanley Haynes succumbed to his illness and was buried in grave G.1. Tourcoing (Pont-Neuville) Communal Cemetery.

PRIVATE EDGAR FLETCHER No. 163825 MACHINE-GUN CORPS 36TH BATTALION CANADIAN 1ST DIVISION (INFANTRY) DIED SEPTEMBER 2ND 1919 AGED 43

Edgar's grandfather, Edgar Fletcher senior, was living at Edensor in 1881, where the 71 year old widower was still working as a painter on the Chatsworth estate. He had been born in Barnsley but came to Edensor as a young man.

Living with Edgar senior, in 1881, was his 37 year old son Michael, who was also a painter and decorator on the estate. Michael had married Elizabeth, a girl from Colston Bassett, a village just to the south east of Nottingham, who had been working in service at Chatsworth, and with them at Edensor were their six children, including Edgar Fletcher junior, born in 1875. Edgar junior was educated at Edensor Boys School, under A.E. Wragg, and from an early age showed an interest and aptitude in working with mechanical items and machinery.

By 1901, 25 year old Edgar Fletcher junior was living at Ecclesfield, a coal mining area four miles to the north of Sheffield, where by trade he was involved in working with colliery machinery. He was married to Mary Ann, 22 years of age and from Bakewell, and with them was their young daughter, two month old Ella.

Partly due to his association with Chatsworth, Edgar spent three years training with the Derbyshire Imperial Yeomanry in his spare time and at their annual camp. However, at some point before the Great War, the family made use of one of the emigration schemes favoured at this time and began a new life at 12 Poucher Street, Toronto, Canada, where he was involved in the working of machinery.

War intervened, however, and on August 11th 1915, aged 39, he volunteered for service in the Canadian Army and sailed from Halifax with the Canadian Expeditionary Force in March 1916, together with Herbert Grindey, a native of Beeley, who we have seen was killed in September 1916. They landed at Liverpool and began further training in England, allowing Edgar to visit his relations at Edensor.

Eventually, Edgar became a member of the Canadian Machine-Gun Corps, but in 1918 he was seriously wounded and was brought back to Canada for treatment. He survived for many months but on September 2nd 1919 he died and was buried in grave G.W.V.A. 337 Toromto (Prospect) Cemetery.

Edgar Fletcher's death brings to an end the account of those servicemen from the Chatsworth villages who perished as a result of serving their country during the Great War and whose names are to be found on the village war memorials.

There has probably never been a more prolonged and appalling experience for ordinary soldiers in all the history of the British Army than the four years of trench warfare 1914 - 1918. And now, after living through such nightmare conditions, the survivors could look forward to returning to the beautiful surroundings of the Derbyshire Dales, set amid the estates of Chatsworth.

Though victory had been achieved, the cost was enormous in both man-power and material, with 900,000 British and Empire troops killed and a further two million wounded. Those who survived came back to a land "fit for heroes" and were promised that the Great War had been "the war to end all wars". The sentiments seemed appropriate at the time but history would make a mockery of them.

As a silence fell over the battlefields, the village families back home counted the loss of so many men, but those who arrived back safely gave thanks that they had survived the horror of war. They were grateful for the war's end and wished to see the survivors take up their civilian lives again.

Each of the villages of Edensor, Pilsley and Beeley had been planning how they could welcome their "lads" back from the war, even before the Armistice had been signed. They also began to think how they could commemorate the names of the men from their community who had lost their lives and would not be returning.

During May and early June, the various parish councils and village organisations were planning "Welcome Home" parties for their returning servicemen, some planned for June and others in August.

Reverend Howard Chadwick
of Beeley 1917-1925
Vernon Mather

Beeley's "Welcome Home" took place on Friday June 20th 1919. Every household contributed something in money or kind to provide a substantial meat tea for 120, after which there was a dance. £12 - 9sh - 6d had been raised from contributions and the schoolrooms were decorated. Mr. J.E. Sutton, the church organist, played the piano.

During the evening the Reverend Howard Chadwick (vicar 1917 - 1925), on behalf of the parishioners, thanked the men for all that they had done for their country, the hardships they had suffered and the dangers they had faced. He said Beeley was proud of them, deeply grateful to them and most warmly welcomed them home. Mrs. Chadwick, on behalf of the women, spoke a few words of welcome and read the following verses, which she had composed for the occasion:

> There is no land like England,
> So valiant, fair and free;
> There are no lads like English lads,
> In that we all agree.

> There is no place like Beeley,
> The village on the hill,
> For here's our home, God keep it
> From every kind of ill.

The Beeley lads in old days,
'Neath God's Almighty hand,
From foreign foe and tyrant,
Went forth to save our land.

And theyr'e the same in these days,
As brave, as strong and true,
They've done their share, God bless them!
They've earned the praise that's due.
In years to come their doings
Will be the village pride;
The memory of all who went,
Cling to the countryside.

So let us bid them welcome
With heart, and hand, and voice;
With three times three and now, once more,
For gallant Beeley boys.

Samuel Burdekin returned thanks on behalf of the soldiers. On that same Friday, the children of the village, under the care of headteacher and staff, Miss Leah Ratcliff, Miss Evans and Miss Brown, had tea and buns in the Duke's Barn Yard, kindly lent by Mr. E. Fearn.

On the following Sunday, special prayers of thanksgiving were offered for the return of the men.

Meanwhile the whole country was planning for a day of "Peace Celebrations", on July 19th 1919 and the Chatsworth villages celebrated in style.

BEELEY

During the morning a copper beech tree, sent from Chatsworth, was planted on the open space outside the eastern boundary of the churchyard, to commemorate the occasion.

At 1p.m. the pageant of school children started from the Vicarage. On a dray decorated with flags and evergreens, was seated "Britannia", with "Peace" and "Victory" standing on

The Peace Tree, a copper beech, was planted on the day of Beeley's Peace Celebrations in July 1919. The sapling is surrounded by a wooden fence, and today is a sturdy, mature tree
Barbara Hawksworth

SERVICEMEN FROM BEELEY WHO SURVIVED THE GREAT WAR

Victor Palfreyman of Beeley
Barbara Hawksworth

?
Barbara Hawksworth

?
Barbara Hawksworth

William Hutchinson of Beeley
Barbara Hawksworth

?
Barbara Hawksworth

SERVICEMEN FROM BEELEY WHO SURVIVED THE GREAT WAR

*Joseph Burdekin of Beeley and Chatsworth. Born at Beeley around 1878, he worked on an Ashover farm aged 10 years to 14 years, before becoming a 'grease lad' in the carriage and wagon department at Rowsley sidings. He then spent some time on the Chatsworth estate and in Edensor Stables before working for 10 years in the loco department at Rowsley and Buxton. Returning to Chatsworth, he was employed as a steam tractor driver.
He mobilised as a Territorial with the Chatsworth Army Service Corps, reaching the rank of corporal by 1918, as a steam lorry driver. On demob, he drove a petrol lorry on the Chatsworth estate until he became the Duke's chauffeur in 1927*
Pauline Harrison

Harry Briggs of Beeley
Barbara Hawksworth

?
Barbara Hawksworth

George Hawksworth of Beeley
Barbara Hawksworth

Tom Fearn of Beeley
Barbara Hawksworth

SERVICEMEN FROM BEELEY WHO SURVIVED THE GREAT WAR

Sam Wall of Beeley
Barbara Hawksworth

Samuel Burdekin of Beeley
Barbara Hawksworth

Harry Downes of Beeley
Barbara Hawksworth

Reginald Roose of Beeley
Barbara Hawksworth

William Hodkin of Beeley
Barbara Hawksworth

SERVICEMEN FROM BEELEY WHO SURVIVED THE GREAT WAR

Charles Fearn of Beeley
Barbara Hawksworth

James Fearn of Beeley
Barbara Hawksworth

Lewis Bond of Beeley
Barbara Hawksworth

Alfred Grafton of Beeley
Barbara Hawksworth

Arnold Holmes of Beeley
Barbara Hawksworth

*Joseph William Hutchinson
of Beeley*
Barbara Hawksworth

SERVICEMEN FROM BEELEY WHO SURVIVED THE GREAT WAR

Wilfred Hulley of Beeley
Barbara Hawksworth

William Twelves of Beeley
Barbara Hawksworth

Jack Stone of Beeley
Barbara Hawksworth

Thomas Stone of Beeley
Barbara Hawksworth

*Sidney Bond of Beeley. His
father was Thomas Bond of
Moor End, who was a clerk in
the Chatsworth Estate Office.
Sidney became a Chesterfield
police constable in February
1915, but the following June he
joined the Army, serving in
France, Italy and Germany. He
escaped after being taken
prisonor*
Barbara Hawksworth

George Roose of Beeley
Barbara Hawksworth

175

SERVICEMEN FROM BEELEY WHO SURVIVED THE GREAT WAR

Emily Speller (née Burdekin) of Beeley, in 1918. She enlisted into the Women's Auxilliary Army Corps, established in March 1917. By early 1918, some 6,000 WAAC's were serving in France, including Emily Speller. The women were employed on such tasks as cooking, clerical work, telephony, printing and motor vehicle maintenanace
Pauline Harrison

Len Fearn of Beeley
Barbara Hawksworth

George Buckley of Beeley
Barbara Hawksworth

either side. The corners of the dray were filled with little children crowned with flowers. The dray was drawn by two fine horses driven by Mr. G.H. Hodkin, the leader being ridden by a boy postilian dressed in the Chatsworth livery; two other boys in livery sat with the driver. The dray was followed by the children and elder girls of the village, dressed in white, wearing wreaths of roses, accompanied by Miss Ratcliff, Miss Evans, Miss Brown, Miss Chadwick and the vicar.

During the circuit of the village, four halts were made, where patriotic songs were sung. At the first halt, at the church gate, "Peace" descended from the dray

The war memorial window in Beeley Church
Keith Taylor

during the singing of the hymn *Blest are the pure in heart* and placed a large wreath of roses and evergreen, bearing the inscription "In grateful memory of all our brave men who gave their lives that we might have peace" on the grave of Harry Bertram Bond, the only soldier whose body had been brought back to Beeley. "Britannia", "Peace" and "Victory" were represented respectively by Eileen Hulley, Marjory Holmes and Lois Bond.

During the afternoon the children played games and enjoyed themselves on swings erected for the occasion and at the same time a cricket match was played between single and married in Mr. Carline's field. The single were victorious.

The children had tea at 4p.m. in the Duke's Barn, and the adults had theirs at 5p.m. in the schoolroom (140 adults and 80 children had tea). Children's sports continued until 8p.m. and then there was dancing in the school until 11-50p.m. A bonfire was lit on Whiteacre and two flares were discharged.

EDENSOR

Celebrations commenced at 2-30p.m. with sports for the children, under the direction of Gerry Hartopp and the Sports Committee. At 4-15p.m. the children adjourned to the Edensor Institute for tea, followed by a meal for the adults. A number of women, under the supervision of Mrs. Hartopp, provided a substantial meal.

After tea, sports were resumed until 7p.m., when a ceremony took place – the planting of an oak tree on the village green by Mrs. Harrison, formerly of the Chatsworth Hotel and the oldest inhabitant, assisted by Joan Maltby, the youngest.

A move was made to the Institute, as it had commenced to rain, and here music, dancing and games took place, whilst at 9p.m. there was supper. A bonfire had been made on the hill opposite the village and this was lit at 10pm after rockets had been sent up and three Admiralty flares set off. Despite the heavy rain, it was successfully lit and the National Anthem sung at midnight. On the following Monday evening a whist drive was held, followed by a dance, open to the surrounding parishes.

As these joyful, yet poignant events unfolded during the summer months of 1919, it is interesting to see another sign of peace time activity developing, after years of wartime deprivation. This came with the decision by the Duke of Devonshire, still residing in Canada as Governor General, for Chatsworth House and gardens to be made open to the public between June 10th and August 21st 1919, a charge of one shilling per person to be applied.

Throughout 1919, however, minds were constantly drawn back to the war and its consequences, when village committees had to decide upon how the community would honour those servicemen who had died in the service of their country. Most men lay far away from home, on a "foreign field that is forever England" and it was important to their families that there should be a permanent memorial established "back home".

At Beeley, the Committee of the War Memorial Fund had decided upon a subject for a stained glass window, to be executed by Messrs. Heaton, Butler and Bayne of London and had decided also that the Roll of Honour should be inscribed on an illuminated sheet of vellum, framed and hung in the church.

The window, provided as a thanksgiving for all who safely returned from the Great War included Christ with a golden ball standing between two soldiers. Beeley Church stood in the background, with British flags in the upper lights. The Roll of Honour, both for the dead and those who survived, was illuminated by Theodora Chadwick, daughter of the vicar of Beeley and the frame was made by Advent Hunstone, woodcarver of Tideswell.

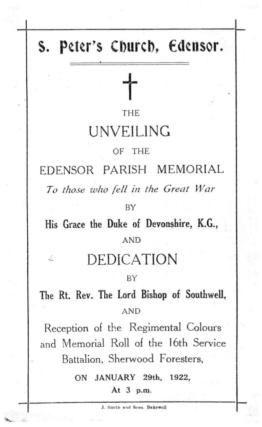

The unveiling and dedication of the war memorial in St Peter's Church, Edensor, January 29th 1922

Margaret Sheldon

On Armistice Day 1919, at Beeley, a short service of intercession and thanksgiving was held in church at 11a.m. At 4p.m. a tea was prepared for the children and every child of school age and under received a mug as a momento of the declaration of peace. The mugs had on them portraits of Admiral Beatty and Field Marshal Haig and dates of the commencement of war, the signing of the Armistice and the Peace Treaty. The money to purchase them was collected by Frank Grafton and the mugs were presented by Mrs. Chadwick. In the evening, a bonfire was lit.

At 3p.m. on January 29th 1922, the unveiling and dedication of the Edensor Parish Memorial took place in St. Peter's Church, Edensor.

The Memorial, on the north wall of the church, took the form of an alabaster tablet measuring seven feet by five feet and had been decided upon by the War Memorial Committee, the Chairman being the Reverend W.H. Foster-Pegg and the Honorary Treasurer, Gerry Hartopp.

In the frame were carved and painted the crests of the regiments to which the men belonged and on a ribbon running from each crest was carved the place at which each man fell.

Edensor war memorial
Dick Richardson

Previous to the unveiling and dedication, there was another ceremony. It witnessed the placing in the church of the regimental colours and memorial roll of the 16th Battalion, Sherwood Foresters (Chatsworth Rifles), whose formation came about through the good offices of His Grace, The Duke of Devonshire.

(In April 1915, His Grace was asked by the War Office to raise a service battalion in Derbyshire. The battalion was raised at Buxton and recruitment started on April 29th 1915. In six weeks they were 1500 strong).

The congregation on January 29th was large and the Chatsworth House Party consisted of the Duke and Duchess of Devonshire and Captain, the Marquis of Hartington.

The Memorial was covered by the Union flag and was unveiled by the Duke of Devonshire, who was in uniform. The Bishop of Southwell then dedicated the Memorial. Afterwards, the officers and men of the 16th Sherwoods were paraded outside the church and addressed by the Duke of Devonshire.

Sad though these occasions were, especially for the families who came to lay wreaths for their lost loved ones on these new memorials, it was possibly some comfort for them to know that their deaths had been recognised and their names honoured. Everyone could surely now begin to think of a new beginning and hopefully, a happy one.

However, within the space of nineteen years they would once again find themselves confronting the prospects of conflict with Germany and the possibility of world wide conflagration.

CHAPTER SEVEN

THE SECOND WORLD WAR 1939 – 1945

The early years of the 1930's had been the "Depression Years". The bottom had fallen out of the Wall Street stock market of 1929, resulting in a faltering in investment, less money for people to spend, factories closing due to a lack of markets, with demand reduced still further as men were thrown out of work. Whilst people "tightened their belts", farmers found that no one could afford the food they had grown. As Great Britain abandoned her policy of free trade, international trade virtually collapsed and more men were thrown out of work as more factories, shipbuilding yards and industries were closed down.

The inhabitants of the Chatsworth villages could not avoid being affected by these national and international ramifications in the business and industrial world, but the availability of jobs in the various quarries, on the estates and at the railway marshalling yard helped to ward off some of the worst ravages of the "Depression" for many in the area.

What could not be avoided in these villages, or elsewhere, were the repercussions from the growing tensions on the international diplomatic scene. The political climate in Europe was changing and "war clouds" loomed on the horizon. The strains imposed by economic collapse and the bitterness caused by the outcome of the Versailles Peace Treaty, imposed in 1920, had found certain countries' democratic institutions wanting. Fascist and Nazi regimes had won favour, determined to push their aggressive foreign policies in the belief that the remaining democracies were ill-prepared to defend their rights.

The likely victory of Fascism on the Iberian Peninsula during the Spanish Civil War of 1936 - 1939, only emboldened the aggressive plans of Adolph Hitler's Germany. In 1938 a German ultimatum led to the appointment of several Nazi representatives in the Austrian cabinet. On March 11th 1938 German troops entered Austria and the Anschluss, or forbidden union of Austria with Germany, was established.

Tension increased in Czechoslovakia, where Hitler demanded the handing over of areas of Bohemia to Germany, particularly those occupied by Sudetan Germans. Czechoslovakia agreed to this demand, under pressure from France and Britain, but Hitler demanded further considerable concessions by October 1st 1938, in default of which Germany would "march". The Czech Army mobilised on September 23rd, France on the next day, whilst on the 28th the British Fleet was mobilised, after Territorial AA and coastal defence units, the Observer Corps and Auxiliary Airforce were called up on the 26th.

Prime Minister, Neville Chamberlain, visited Hitler at Bad Godesberg and Berchtesgaden, without result, and on September 28th Hitler invited the British and French premiers to meet with Mussolini at Munich the next day. At this meeting, to which no Czech representative was admitted, it was agreed that German occupation of the areas demanded should proceed in stages between October 1st and the 10th. Chamberlain was able to return to London, claiming "Peace in our time" and most of Britain breathed a collective sigh of relief.

Relief turned to concern, when, in March 1939, Hitler ignored certain conditions of the Munich Agreement and occupied Bohemia and Moravia without British or French government intervention. Sensing a weakness of resolve throughout the European democracies, Hitler turned his attention to Poland during the summer months of 1939. War clouds were looming once again over Europe, for at last, Chamberlain spelt out clearly in Parliament British condemnation of Hitler's latest aggression and made it clear that an attack on Poland would not be tolerated. On April 26th Britain reintroduced conscription and quite a few young men from the Chatsworth villages found themselves serving in the Armed Forces.

The weakness displayed by Britain and France at Munich was Hitler's most powerful incentive to plan the attack on Poland, first for August, then for September 1939. He believed that Poland could be defeated in isolation, as Czechoslovakia and Austria had been before, especially when, on August 23rd, Germany and Soviet Russia signed a Non-Aggression Pact. Hitler's way to Poland seemed open, but on August 25th the signing of the Anglo-Polish Alliance was announced in London and Hitler realised that his attempt to isolate Poland had failed.

On Sunday August 13th two Buxton Platoons of "B" Company 2nd/5th Sherwood Foresters marched from the Drill Hall, Buxton, to the station, en-route for their first camp. Many of those who saw them go found it difficult to realise that it was only a few weeks ago that these young men enlisted in the service of their country. Their smart and soldierly manner greatly impressed those who saw them. The Platoon who went to Holyhead, were joined on the train at Chapel by the Chapel-en-le-Frith Platoon. Similar scenes were being repeated in many villages and towns within Derbyshire.

During the same week, Beeley Church Sunday School Treat was held on Friday August 11th, when a party of scholars and adults, numbering 46, went for a motor coach tour by way of Buxton and Castleton to Hathersage, where they had tea. Afterwards they played games in the playing field and returned home after a very enjoyable day.

Yet just three weeks later, at 11-15a.m. on Sunday September 3rd, Neville Chamberlain announced to a hushed nation that Britain was at war with Germany. It was the beginning of the greatest conflict the world has yet seen.

THE ARRIVAL OF THE EVACUEES

As the might of Germany's Armed Forces swept across the Polish frontier on September 1st and Britain still remained at peace, the reality of the situation was brought home to the inhabitants of the Chatsworth villages with the arrival of a special train at both Hassop and Rowsley Stations, Train Number M203 from Manchester. The evacuees had arrived, and with them the realisation that this time there was no turning back.

Manchester's plans were to evacuate as many as possible of the 190,000 children from the city to places of safety and 70% agreed to be evacuated in the event of war. Allowance had been made for the housing of teachers and the billeting of helpers. The first contingent to leave Manchester, when the

Manchester evacuee schoolchildren getting onto buses to take them to the railway station, and their journey into the Derbyshire countryside
Manchester Evening News

Manchester evacuee schoolchildren boarding the train for Derbyshire.
They each have a gas mask, supplies and a label
Manchester Evening News

emergency was declared, should be school children travelling with their teachers, one adult to each group of ten children. Helpers would also travel with the children and then return home.

Schools had ensured that each child was given a small, turquoise canvas rucksack for carrying clothes, whilst gas masks in boxes had been issued and food for 24 hours was to be carried. Parents were also told to put their children in their warmest clothes. As they arrived at school, a label was tied to each child's coat with their name on it. To help out financially, the Government paid an allowance to the host family for unaccompanied children. For board and lodgings they received ten shillings and sixpence for one child under ten years of age, with a rising scale for older children.

Two of the Manchester schools that arrived in the district on the special train were Ladybarn Boys School and Ladybarn Girls School of Parrswood Road, Withington. From Monday to Thursday of that last week in August the pupils had been practising the evacuation, with the assembly hall marked out as a railway station platform and each class split up into small groups and were made to assemble in a designated area. Each day, after completion of the exercise, the children were sent home and the exercises became routine and monotonous. A relaxed, unsuspecting atmosphere prevailed which made Friday's events more dramatic.

On Friday September 1st the children were told they were going away for the weekend and filed outside to a road full of red Corporation double decker buses. Many parents were only to find out later that day that this time their children really had gone away. The buses delivered them to Central Station and at 10-30a.m. the train departed. Later that day, at 3-10p.m., a second train, M209, would depart, carrying the remaining children from the schools.

Most children remember how hot they were, dressed in their warmest clothes on a warm September morning. For many of these evacuees it was the first time they had been away from home, their first journey on a train and most had never been separated from their parents. Tense with anxiety as to where they were going, the children were hot and tired as they arrived at their unknown destination, for all the signs had been removed from the stations.

The organisation of the civilian defence forces in the Bakewell district had reached a high state of efficiency and for over a week, hundreds of people had been helping the billeting officers. The Chief Billeting Officer for the Bakewell Rural District Council was B.G. Cadge, assisted by reception officers at Millers Dale, Hassop and Rowsley Stations. On Friday September 1st, buses and cars were waiting at Rowsley Station to transport 18 evacuee pupils to Beeley, 75 to Baslow, 8 to Chatsworth (Pilsley), 106 to Winster, 2 to Aldwark, 1 to Grange Mill and 28 to Elton, whilst 22 pupils remained at Rowsley, to be billeted in the village.

A major difficulty for most schools, with the increase in numbers, was the lack of space to accommodate these extra children. During the first few weeks, this problem was overcome by having part time education. The local children received lessons in the morning, whilst the evacuees had their education during the afternoon, with the times being reversed the following week. The incorporation of the shift system was not completely satisfactory to anyone.

Chatsworth House was vacated by the Duke of Devonshire and his family, who moved to Churchdale Hall, near Ashford, when a girls' boarding school arrived for the duration of the war. It was perhaps felt by the Duke that a few hundred girls would not do as much damage as servicemen and their vehicles.

Penrhos College, founded in 1880, was situated on the sea front at Colwyn Bay and in 1939 housed 320 female boarders, 250 of them being Senior and Middle School pupils. When Penrhos College buildings were requisitioned by the War Department as a food store for the Ministry of Food, the 250 Senior and Middle School pupils, ranging in age from 11 to 18 years, together with 36 members of staff and their headmistress Miss Constance Smith, arrived at Chatsworth House on September 26th 1939 and the school remained on site

Penrhos College pupils and staff in front of Chatsworth House in July 1941
Derek Neave

until March 21st 1946.

On the first day of the new term, September 26th 1939, the girls arrived from all over the country, mainly by coaches which had met the trains and also by car, with parents who had petrol coupons.

The previous two weeks had seen a difficult logistical operation undertaken by senior members of staff, as school equipment from Colwyn Bay arrived at Chatsworth. This included 26 pianos, for Penrhos College placed a high priority on music.

The Painted Hall, Chatsworth House, during the War years, 1939 to 1945. It was here that Penrhos College pupils assembled for morning and evening prayers and church services during their stay at Chatsworth House as evacuees, when their school in Colwyn Bay was requisitioned by the Army. The school's senior girls' choir sat on the stairs, on the cushions shown in the photograph
Courtesy of Derbyshire County Council

Just about every part of the House was used for classrooms and dormitories, with freedom given for the use of the gardens, woods and park. Only the world famous library was placed out of bounds. There were a few rules implemented to prevent too much damage being perpetrated. Dustless chalk was used, sand was sprinkled on the floor before sweeping and all written work had to be done in pencil. Only senior pupils could use fountain pens and ink wells were banned.

The magnificent Painted Hall was the centre and heart of the school. Morning and evening chapel (the College had a Methodist background) was held there and it became the school assembly hall. The choir sat on cushions on the grand staircase, with an organ sited at the foot. The most popular use of the hall was as a picture house, when a projector was provided (*** *to one side of the top of the*

Penrhos College pupils dined in the Servants' Hall, Chatsworth House, during the War years
Courtesy of Derbyshure County Council

Girls from Penrhos College skating on the Canal Pond at
Chatsworth in the winter of 1940
Pamela Halliwell

Penrhos College pupils learning to skate on the Long Lake,
Chatsworth, during their evacuation from Colwyn Bay,
between September 26th 1939 and March 21st 1946.
The pupils wore olive green uniforms
Courtesy of Derbyshire County Council

ABOVE: *Penrhos College girls set off from Chatsworth House, for matins at Edensor Church in the winter of 1940*
G. Scott

LEFT: *Three Penrhos College pupils at Chatsworth. Pamela Halliwell is seated on the extreme left*
Pamela Halliwell

BELOW: *Penrhos College girls leave Edensor Church after matins*
G. Scott

Sports on the cricket pitch at Chatsworth, with the pavilion in the far right hand corner.
Penrhos College girls are playing lacrosse
Pamela Halliwell

Sports being held for Penrhos College girls on the South Lawn, Chatsworth.
The high jump is in progress
G. Scott

189

staircase was where the girls' suitcases were stored. Pam Halliwell, a pupil at the school, relates that on one occasion she "blotted her copy book" when she forgot to remove a cheese from her suitcase, after returning from her home in Bury. An unpleasant smell lingered at the top of the stairs for some time before the errant cheese was discovered).

All three state rooms on both floors were used as dormitories (Drawing Room – 21 beds, Music Room – 15, Dining Room – 25, with numerous smaller dormitories). There were 13 bathrooms at Chatsworth and there was a strict rota for each girl to have two baths per week.

The squash court became the gym, whilst domestic science was studied in the area previously used for under-taking the Chatsworth laundry and ironing. The kitchen areas were used, with the Physics Laboratory being in the Butler's Pantry and Biology in the former stillroom, whilst the Chemistry Lab was situated in the Stables Block. The Devonshire Chapel was even used for piano lessons, whilst the Orangery (later the Chatsworth Shop) was used for art lessons, with games equipment stored there.

The Cavendish family at Edensor House, Edensor, 1943/1944. This was the wartime home of the Dowager Duchess of Devonshire, whilst the Duke and Duchess lived at Churchdale House.

BACK ROW:
*Lady Anne Hunloke,
Lady Anne Cavendish,
Lady Elizabeth Cavendish,
The Duchess of Devonshire*

FRONT ROW:
*Nicholas Hunloke,
Lady Andrew Cavendish
with daughter Lady Emma
Cavendish*

DOGS: *Benjy, Studley and Bootle*

Courtesy of the
Dowager Duchess of Devonshire

The severe winters, especially that of 1939/1940, proved difficult with regards to keeping warm at night. Chilblains flourished and many girls slept in their dressing gowns and some were known to wear Balaclava helmets, whilst the hot water bottle proved to be essential.

WOMEN'S LAND ARMY

DUCHESS OF DEVONSHIRE'S APPEAL

The Duchess of Devonshire on the extreme right, encouraging recruitment of women into the Land Army, at the Bakewell Show, August 1939, just days before the start of the Second World War

Games were held on the cricket field, but these were cancelled if it rained and instead they had to walk up to the Hunting Tower and back. Sporting success was keenly competed for between the four Houses: Shackleton, Scott, Raleigh and Drake.

The villages of Edensor and Baslow were out of bounds, unless pupils were accompanied by visiting parents or relatives. Edensor was only ever visited when attending Edensor Church for matins on Sunday. Outings with parents to Baslow and especially Bakewell, were a real treat, for the latter had numerous shops and there was the feeling of being let out into the world.

At Baslow, the girls loved to visit Strutts Cafe (Ivy House), run by Liz Rowarth and her daughter Mary, and were especially fond of the ham and egg teas.

The girls were encouraged to bring their bicycles from home, in the early days, and stored them in the Stables. However, they were only able to use them inside the Park and they could only roam in the woods in groups of four or more girls.

Overseas fruit, such as the banana, was unavailable during the war years and it was certainly a treat for the girls to save up their money in the summer months so that they could afford to buy a peach or a bunch of grapes from Bert Link, the head gardener, from one of his greenhouses

Throughout the school year, the Sheffield High School girls evacuated to Cliff College would also play games of cricket, hockey, rounders and netball against their near-neighbours at Chatsworth, Penrhos College.

During the period of the "Phoney War", between September 1939 and April 1940, when little activity was taking place on the military front, a considerable number of evacuee children at the village schools were taken back home by their parents. This was especially the case at Christmas 1939, when many pupils simply did not return to the schools, but remained in Manchester.

This eased the accommodation problem in these schools. However, after the defeat of British and French forces in May/June 1940 and the Dunkirk evacuation, the threat of war from the air returned and there was a fresh influx of evacuee children in July 1940.

Following the first raid on Sheffield, on December 12th, all the local builders from Baslow and surrounding villages were taken to the city to repair the damaged buildings and infrastructure. Some of the Baslow builders went to Sheffield after the Sunday raid to repair the roof on the Effingham steel works. We have seen that a number of families moved from Sheffield as evacuees to avoid the bombing. The adults travelled back each day to work in the city and a special 7-45a.m. Corporation bus was organised to take them.

AIR RAID PREVENTION
AND THE VILLAGE AUXILIARY FIRE SERVICE

Throughout 1938 and 1939, the nation had prepared for the possibility of war, with special emphasis placed on the probability of enemy air attacks and the need to combat this threat. Air raid prevention measures had been taken, with a nationwide call for ARP wardens in each town and village, and the provision of gas masks at the first sign of an emergency. Combined with a call for volunteers to join and form village Auxiliary Fire Brigades, these two organisations formed the backbone of the defence against the threat of fire and devastation in rural villages.

Members of the ARP and the Auxiliary Fire Service were trained to respond to possible gas attacks. Rudimentary de-contamination techniques were practised and a mobile gas van or hut was taken around the villages. Smoke cannisters were tossed inside and members of these organisations practised crawling through the smoke-filled room, with their gas masks on.

The fire service at Beeley was led by the vicar, the Reverend Williams, with the mobile pump stored in the stoke hole of the Methodist Chapel. It consisted of a red painted two wheeled cart with long shafts and hose attached, with sand buckets slung on either side. Fire practise at Beeley was sometimes spent hosing down the church windows. A fireman would switch on the hydrant and walk down the churchyard to where the nozzle of the hose was, but on occasions, lads being lads, it was known for certain village boys to turn up the pressure and stand around, innocently watching the men receive a drenching.

At the end of July 1939 an ARP exercise had taken place in the whole district to test the blackout. Wardens and special constables were called out at midnight on Thursday July 20th and patrolled the areas. At 3-30a.m. on Monday September 4th, the day after war was declared, air raid sirens went off in the district and the Air Raid Warden system was tested in action. It was a false alarm but it revealed the need for a more adequate siren warning in this hilly and scattered area.

From early days, wardens were issued with helmets and uniforms, stirrup pumps, stretchers and partially shaded torches to prevent the upward glare of light. Some members who were keen gardeners made extra use of their stirrup pumps when tending their allotments or gardens. On Monday evening, June 16th 1940, there was a good attendance of ARP workers from Edensor and villages around at a demonstration of fire fighting with a stirrup pump, near the Edensor Institute. Mr. G.A. Banks, area organiser, was in charge.

The main headquarters was at the County Council Depot yard at Calver and it was here that a gas de-contamination unit was built. A large concrete hut was constructed, which contained a number of showers. The men, dressed in oilskins, were showered, using a special detergent.

Whenever the air raid siren was sounded, the Penrhos College girl boarders sheltered in the Chatsworth beer cellar, especially on the occasions of the Blitz on Sheffield. Cream crackers and bovril were passed down the rows of girls sitting on forms, until the "all clear" was given.

It was to the beer cellar that the girls retreated in the summer term of 1942 when two German planes attacked Chatsworth House as they flew by. When the attack began, the girls were in the Painted Hall for evening prayers, after having supper. The north side of the House received a few machine-gun bullet marks and it was believed that the two planes were shot down later in Lincolnshire. The girls were fortunate that the attack did not take place a short while later, for many of them would have been outside on the lawns, enjoying free time, or playing tennis. On this occasion, evening prayers had been fortunately delayed. Not all the girls were able to seek the safety of the Beer Cellar. Two girls, Pam Halliwell and her colleague, Alison, were suffering from conjunctivitis and were being kept in isolation in the sick bay by the matron, Miss Martin. When the German planes appeared to be flying straight towards their room, they dived under their beds and a bullet that shattered their window embedded itself in the middle of the far door. Local villagers were also fortunate, for a cricket match was taking place at Chatsworth and children from Beeley were playing in Beeley Meadows at the time of the raid.

To guard against the possibility of aerial attack, the maintenance of the "Blackout" was essential. Fortunately at Chatsworh, most of the windows

*The beer cellars at Chatsworth House. It was here that Penrhos College girls came,
in order to shelter from the air raids*
Chris Heathcote

had large solid shutters that could quickly be closed. The Senior Girls went out on a rota basis at night to walk around the House and check for any chink of light. The younger members of staff and prefects also shared in a fire-watching role. Each night, one staff member and one prefect slept in a hut on the roof of Chatsworth House, while another pair slept in an alcove on Bachelor's Corridor. Each pair had a telephone at hand.

Air activity of a different kind occurred when, on a number of occasions, Allied aircraft crashed in the vicinity of the villages. On February 12th 1941, Wellington bomber L7811 of 149 Squadron, based at Mildenhall, was returning from a raid on the German port of Bremen. On a cloudy night, the pilot, Sergeant Turner and his crew found themselves hopelessly lost over full cloud. At 2a.m., whilst over Bakewell, the decision was made to abandon the aircraft and all the crew baled out. The plane impacted at river level just a few yards upstream from Conksbury Bridge, Lathkill Dale. One crew member landed in a tree at Swiss Cottage, on the Chatsworth estate, one near Sheldon, one by Beeley Bridge and another in Park Lane, Rowsley.

Sergeant McKnight landed just outside Over Haddon and knocked on the door of Manor Farm Cottage. The lady took him to Over Haddon Post Office where the Home Guard was stationed. There he was arrested by Special

Members of Baslow Observer Corps, c1942.
Back row: *Francis Thompson (Librarian at Chatsworth), X, Fred Stone (Electrician at Chatsworth), Charles Watson (Gardener at Chatsworth), X, ? Alsop, Billy Hulley, Joe Fletcher (local garage), ? Jackson (Clerk of Works)*
Front row: *James Fearn, Mr Roebuck, Alan Johnstone, Clem Watson (Plumber at Chatsworth), Bill Weir, Billy Horsborough (Gamekeeper at Chatsworth)*
Gill Watson

Constable Bill Bibby on suspicion of being a German spy because of his accent. It was only when another crewman was brought in that it was discovered that he was in fact a Scotsman.

On June 11th 1943 Wellington bomber DV678 of No. 14 Operational Training Unit, based at RAF Cottesmore, developed engine trouble over the district, one and a half hours into a night time training exercise. At 6,500 feet, both engines spluttered and Flying Officer Patkin, the pilot of the three man crew, found a gap in the cloud and saw a large expanse of grassland in Chatsworth Park. Flying low over Beeley he "belly flopped" the aircraft, with its wheels raised, on Lindup Top, on the Chatsworth estate. The only injury was to one airman's face. Sadly, Flying Officer Patkin would be killed on January 1st 1944 when his Lancaster was shot down over Celle, whilst taking part in a raid against Berlin.

We have already seen that fear of attack from the air had resulted in the imposition of the "blackout" and with this came changes to daily life in the villages from an early period of the war.

THE HOME GUARD

On May 14th 1940, four days after the Phoney War came to an end with the German invasion of France, Belgium and Holland, Anthony Eden broadcast to the nation that volunteers were required for a new force called the Local Defence Volunteers (with the nickname of "Look, Duck and Vanish"), later to be known as the Home Guard.

Rowsley, Darley Dale and Beeley Platoons often co-operated on manoeuvres. Beeley Home Guard members such as Arthur Hulley, Sam Bond, Isaac Broomhead, William Harrison, Albert Burdekin and Jesse Grafton had the village hall as their headquarters and met near the churchyard to drill. Training was undertaken in Horse Pasture, a field opposite the Vicarage, and straw men were used as targets for bayonet practice. Home Guard members spent their evenings on guard duty in a hut on Beeley Warren and Beeley Moor, and it was well known that some of the time was spent in poaching rabbits, and occasional pheasants. As with so many Home Guard units in the early stages of the war, Beeley did not have any rifles to begin with and were often to be seen drilling and parading with wooden replica guns. Two such guns are nowadays displayed in the village hall.

One Sunday, the Rowsley, Darley and Beeley Platoons went on training manoeuvres to defend Rowsley marshalling yard against supposed German paratroops dropping over Beeley Moor. The men marched up the Rowsley Bar Road to where it levelled out and lined up with bayonets fixed, whilst regular army soldiers acted as the German paratroopers. The regulars began throwing smoke bombs and the Home Guard members retreated down the hillside, through the East Lodge grounds, before their officers ordered them to stop and attempt to drive the enemy back. The "Germans" came off the better on that particular day.

RASC vehicles and troops were always to be seen in Pilsley, reversing up the alleys and drives and causing a great deal of damage to the village green. One piece of major damage was the destruction of the blacksmith's trough on Pilsley village green, caused by a reversing army lorry. RASC personnel held manoeuvres of their own in the fields and woodland by the side of Baslow Lane, Pilsley. Soldiers defended the wood whilst others attacked it with mortars and smoke bombs. Pilsley lads would attend the scene afterwards in order to collect munitions, receiving a good "telling off" by the head teacher at school the next day, which had little effect. The Pilsley lads wished to collect these items so that they could have their own war with the Chatsworth and Edensor children.

In early January 1940, circumstances prevented the annual treat given by the Duke and Duchess of Devonshire to the day and Sunday School children of Edensor, Pilsley, Chatsworth, Beeley and Baslow taking place at Chatsworth that year but their Graces decided that the children should not be deprived of this very popular gathering. It was held at the Edensor Institute on a Friday afternoon, with 200 guests attending.

They were accompanied by a number of their teachers and included some evacuated children. Hulley's buses and estate motor vehicles brought the children to the Institute and on arrival there was a sumptious tea provided. In the Institute Hall there was a large Christmas tree. Tea was followed by an entertainment provided by Mr. J. Wakefield of Derby (conjuring and ventriloquism). Each child received a handsome present, distributed by the Duke and Duchess and two daughters, Ladies Elizabeth and Anne Cavendish and their three cousins, the Misses Carol, Catherine and Sarah Macmillan. Lady Dorothy Macmillan and the Dowager Duchess were also present.

As wartime conditions worsened as the months went on, it was found that travelling and catering became difficult when the annual Beeley Chapel Sunday School Treat was due in 1941. The Morton family of Beeley Hill Top kindly invited the children to hold their outing at Hill Top Farm. The children gathered in the Chapel Yard and walked up the fields to the farm. They played "Tag" and other games in the croft and courtyard. They then gathered in the orchard for a picnic tea, with homemade bread and jam, lemonade and tea, with the milk coming straight from one of the cows.

With rationing having been introduced in 1939 and gradually being increased as the German U-boat campaign gained in strength, the villages all contributed in their efforts to increase the amount of home grown food. The Women's Institute played a vital role, as many of them established bottling and canning factories in their villages, using local ingredients from the garden and the hedgerow. Beeley Women's Institute met at their village hall, where they bottled fruit and then sealed the containers with candle fat when they ran out of kilner jars.

Gardening, poultry-keeping, pig-keeping and bee-keeping were all discussed at a conference held at the Chatsworth Institute, Edensor, on Saturday August 1st 1942, under the auspices of the Derbyshire Home Produce Council. It was the third conference of its kind to be held in the county that year. Chairmen of the urban, rural and parish councils, presidents of the WI, and representatives of Allotments Associations had all been invited.

The Duchess of Devonshire, Chairman of the Derbyshire Home Produce Council, presided. She reported that people had been able to buy seeds, fertilisers etc., at a considerable reduction on the usual prices. With the severe shipping losses, it was essential that as much food was grown locally as possible. There were now 68 producer clubs in the county. It was hoped

Slaughtering the pig. This photograph was taken at Tansley, Derbyshire,
but similar scenes were witnessed in all villages
Derbyshire Libraries and Heritage

that villages could become self-supporting all the year round, saving a great deal of transport in the process.

One method of killing the pig and processing the carcass was as follows: water would be boiled in either the copper boiler or in the boiler on the range, whilst a bucket was placed in the oven to warm. The pig, with its snout tied round with rope, had its throat cut so that the blood could be caught in the hot bucket and used later to be made into black pudding.

Boiling water was used to scald the pig's skin so that the hair could easily be scraped off with the pig scraper, which also had a hook attached that could be used for pulling out the pig's hooves. After scraping, a slit was cut out above the hock in each back leg to fit a piece of wood with notches in it (called a cambriol). A rope was attached and the pig hoisted up to hang from the roof beam. Its innards were removed and it was then cleaned with cold water and left for twenty four hours.

On the following day the body was cut up. The head was cut off, the carcass cut into two halves and the pork was taken out. Part of the leaf fat was used to help make the black puddings, whilst the rest was rendered into lard. The pork was cut into joints to be shared, whilst each half of the carcass was cut into a side of bacon and a ham, and was left in the pantry to drain.

Some days later, salt was sprinkled on the rind side of the bacon and hams to make them sweat and any brine was ladled back over the bacon and hams, and then the meat was left for four weeks. They were washed and hung on hooks to dry, with muslin bags wrapped around them to keep off the flies and allow them to finish curing.

For those who were keen to make even more use of the body, the head and tail could be used to make brawn, the feet for jelly for pork pies, sausages were made and the liver and heart could be eaten.

Women were taking more and more responsibility in a variety of jobs as they replaced the men who had gone to fight the war. Some went into munitions factories, others worked on the land as Land Army girls, as loco cleaners at the railway marshalling yards at Rowsley and as workers at the wartime shadow factory of Firth Derihon (nowadays Firth Rixson), when it was built in 1942.

*Land Army girl,
Marion Ward, of Beeley*
Vera Russell

The headquarters for the Derbyshire branch of the Land Army was at Compton Chambers on Dale Road, Matlock. Joyce Reeve of Beeley was directed to a job in the office as part of the war effort. From there, the office staff sent out girls from Derbyshire and Sheffield as Land Army girls, with most of them being directed to farms well outside Derbyshire.

Beeley girl Marian Ward was sent out of county, whilst her fellow Beeley villagers, Barbara, Doreen and Josephine Fearn were sent to farms as far away as Norfolk.

The organisation had a few lady volunteers, often from "well-to-do" families who had their own cars and petrol coupons (often with their own chauffeurs) and who went around vetting the farms and checking every so often to see that the girls were settling in well and were being well treated. As part of their job, Joyce Reeve and the other office staff would organise the distribution of bicycles by rail to the Land Army girls.

Some Land Army girls went to work in the kitchen gardens at Chatsworth (the site nowadays of the caravan park). These gardens provided for the needs of the House and were split into sections, with walls dividing off the sections and splendid glass houses were to be found on the site. The intersecting walls of the gardens even had heating mechanisms built into them so that fruit trees could be grown against them (Penrhos College girls also came across from the House to help hoe the soil).

Samuel and Jane Furness had taken over the tenancy of Bubnell Farm, on the Chatsworth Estate, in 1895. They had originally farmed Taddington Fields Farm until 1871, when they took over a farm at Stoney Middleton, driving their entire stock through the Dale to their new home, before eventually arriving at Bubnell. The 170 acre farm contained a mixed stock of dairy cows, pigs, chickens and a few sheep.

Their son, Gladstone, continued to run Bubnell Farm after Sam's death in 1908, but when Gladstone moved to Southport to run a milk delivery service, his nephew, James Furness and wife, Doris, took over the tenancy (when James died in 1969, his son James junior became the fifth generation of the family at Bubnell).

As the war drew to a conclusion, teams of 16 German POW's, together with a guard, arrived in autumn to pick the potatoes, as did Italian POW's. A number of these prisoners were still working on the farms in 1947, two years after the war had ended.

If we leave the Home Front and return to the Autumn of 1939 we find that the British Expeditionary Force had embarked for France, together with men from the Chatsworth villages. No hostile action was pursued, however, as the two opposing sides faced each other across the Siegfried and Maginot defensive lines during the bitter, freezing winter of 1939/1940, one of the coldest on record, in the period known as the "Phoney War".

The "Phoney War" came to an end with the German invasion of Denmark and Norway, and especially the invasion of the Low Countries on May 10th. Their plan was to defeat France and eliminate the British Expeditionary Force as the remorseless might of the Wehrmacht and Luftwaffe drove the British back on their retreat to the Channel coast and Dunkirk.

By June 4th 1940 the evacuation of Dunkirk was completed and 338,000 men had been lifted from the beaches. On June 5th Hitler had decided on the invasion of Britain and Operation "Sea Lion" was begun. Having no adequate surface force to oppose British naval strength, the Luftwaffe's task was first to defeat the RAF and then to neutralise the Royal Navy.

In the first phase of the Battle of Britain, August 8th to 18th, the Germans planned to coax the British into combat by attacking sea ports and fighter bases. Aided by radar, Fighter Command still dominated the air space over Britain. Phase two, August 24th to September 5th, saw the German attack shift to concentrate against the main inland RAF bases and by sheer weight of numbers came close to cracking Fighter Command. The British were partly saved by a change of plan by the Germans. London now became the target for incessant aerial bombardment and Fighter Command was able to concentrate its dwindling forces. By mid October the Battle of Britain had been won and Hitler cancelled Operation "Sea Lion" on October 12th.

Until the end of 1940, the Devonshire villages thankfully escaped the grim news of the loss of local men in the conflict on land, sea and in the air.

THE YEAR 1941

In January and February 1941 General Wavell's Western Desert Force in North Africa advanced 500 miles, taking Tobruk, destroying nine Italian divisions and capturing 130,000 prisoners, 400 tanks and 1290 guns. British casualties amounted to 500 killed and 1373 wounded. However, by March, the Luftwaffe had sent an Air Corps to nearby Sicily, General Erwin Rommel had landed in North Afica with the Afrika Korps, whilst Wavell's best combat troops were sent to fight in Greece and Crete. The British position was considerably weakened as Rommel launched his first offensive, March to May 1941.

1941 thankfully passed without further Devonshire village servicemen's deaths occurring, despite the fight being taken to the German and Italian forces in North Africa.

THE YEAR 1942

We have seen that in just over two years of warfare, no one from the Chatsworth villages had lost their lives, but during 1942, as the spheres of conflict widened, three servicemen would die in this year alone.

TROOPER WILLIAM STONE No. 7903879
50TH ROYAL TANK REGIMENT ROYAL ARMOURED CORPS
DIED AUGUST 26TH 1942 AGED 34

William's father, Percy Stone, was born at Beeley Hill Top and became a gamekeeper on the Chatsworth Estate of the Duke of Devonshire. William's mother, Emma Jones, was born at Market Bosworth, Leicestershire, but came to Derby to work in service and it was at Derby that the pair met.

They married, and William was born at Baslow in 1908, whilst his sister Marjorie was born there in 1910. However, before the Great War, Percy and his family moved into the Stand (The Hunting Tower) at Chatsworth and Percy continued in his employment as gamekeeper. It was at the Hunting Tower that their third child, Sylvia, was born in 1913.

William attended Edensor Boys School, whilst Marjorie and Sylvia went to the girls' school at Pilsley. The head teacher of the boys' school, Mr. Wragg, was noted for his severe regime. William was unhappy within this environment and was pleased when the school closed and he and the other lads began attending Pilsley School.

After leaving school, William served a five year carpentry apprenticeship at Chatsworth and then went to work in Derby for the building firm of Messrs. Ford and Sons. By this stage, the family had moved down from the Hunting Tower and into Pilsley, to live at the house above "Bun Alley", next to the Post Office and bakery run by the Simpson family.

His sister Marjorie went into service as a Still Room maid to the Duke and Duchess of Devonshire (Victor Cavendish and Evelyn Cavendish), travel-

William Stone of Pilsley
Ann Salmon

ling with them to Lismore Castle in Ireland and Carlton Terrace in London (the Still Room was where cakes and pastries were served). Sylvia eventually became a post woman in Pilsley, serving in the shop and delivering the mail, before working as a children's nurse in Haslemere in Surrey.

William Stone, Emma Stone, Marjorie Stone
Ann Salmon

William Stone in army uniform, at Edensor
Ann Salmon

William played cricket for the Chatsworth team until he had some teeth knocked out during a game and then gave it up. His childhood girlfriend was a Pilsley girl, Ethel Jackson. She was musical and gave Sylvia piano lessons. William was in the Territorial Army prior to the war, serving with the Derbyshire Yeomanry (Armoured Car) Company and enlisted in early 1940, joining the 50th Royal Tank Regiment, Royal Armoured Corps.

During the wartime years, his father Percy began working at the DP Battery Company in Bakewell, helping in the munitions work which saw the production of batteries for submarines. When the war ended he then went back to Chatsworth, but as a gardener in the House gardens, rather than as a gamekeeper.

In October 1940 the 50th Royal Tank Regiment made a move to a base at Blundellsands, at the coast on Merseyside, and here the first Mark 3 (Valentine) tank arrived. For the next three years the Valentine was to become home and shelter for the men of the 50th RTR.

In November 1940 the Regiment became part of 23 Armoured Brigade and they moved to Whitby. By March 1941, however, they were on Salisbury Plain and here troop training went ahead and entraining and harbouring exercises were carried out at night, before moving to Castlemartin in Wales for ten days battle practice and range firing, before being stationed at Crowborough in Sussex.

On December 2nd orders were given to paint the tanks yellow, fit sand flaps and prepare to move overseas. Departure, however , was postponed and it was not until May 1942 that the Regiment finally left Crowborough to embark at Glasgow (on May 1st the Regiment had been inspected in Sussex by King George V).

The 23rd Armoured Brigade had become part of 8th Armoured Division and embarked on the troopship "Mooltan", leaving the River Clyde on May 11th and linking up with a convoy. Arriving at Capetown on June 6th they were allowed five days shore leave before sailing, and arrived at their destination, Port Tewfik, Egypt, on July 5th 1942.

When 50th Tank Regiment went into action in the Western Desert they were joining a battle that actually began on July 2nd, known as First Alamein, at Miteiriya Ridge. Rommel's Afrika Korps had been checked near El Alamein and British and Empire forces counter-attacked, with 50th RTR taking part in the latter stages.

By July 19th they had travelled near to the coast by the Alexandria – Sollum road. On July 20th the men moved forward by lorry and the tanks on transporters at night. Wednesday July 22nd saw the inexperienced Regiment going into action for the first time, in the area of Ruin Ridge (part of Miteiriya Ridge), in support of an Australian Infantry Brigade.

SS 'Mooltan', which carried personnel of 23rd Armoured Brigade to North Africa May - July 1942. She was a former P and O ship, being converted into an armoured merchant cruiser 1939 but in 1941 was used as a troopship

The concentration area, the night before the battle, was surrounded by a salt marsh and in the darkness five tanks were lost when they became bogged down. They were to support the Australian infantry and were given the task of attacking Ruin Ridge that evening, at 18-45 hours.

A creeping artillery barrage preceded the attack, but two miles from the objective, the Regiment was subjected to intense artillery fire from the right flank and the leading tanks were under fire from anti-tank guns at very close range. Vehicles suffered casualties from this fire and from a minefield they entered.

Visibility in the centre was now almost nil, since the tanks were attacking with the sun full in their faces and into the dust and smoke of the enemy defensive fire. The climax of the battle came with the whole of the Regiment milling around on and just short of the objective, engaging anti-tank and machine-gun positions and waiting for the infantry to consolidate.

24 out of 47 tanks rallied inside the minefields and came back into leaguer that night, but the losses had been heavy. Further along the Ridge, the remainder of 23 Armoured Brigade had almost been annihilated in a grossly mismanaged attack. They left a trail of wrecked machinery, losing well over 100 tanks and over 200 men in actions charac-

terised by supreme gallantry.

Other men had been taken prisoner by the Germans and Italians on the Ridge as their tanks were destroyed and went up in flames. One of these men was William Stone. Captured by the Germans, he was taken to an Italian POW camp at Benghazi, arriving two days later. The food was terrible, sanitation poor and many men went down with dysentery.

My dear, MOTHER.

(post mark date)
(L'ata del timbro postale)

I am alright (I have not been wounded (or) I have been slightly wounded). I am a prisoner of the Italians and I am being treated well.

Shortly I shall be transferred to a prisoner's camp and I will let you have my new address.

Only then I will be able to receive letters from you and to reply.

With love   W. Stone   (signature)

The telegram sent by William Stone to his parents, telling them that we was a POW

Ann Salmon

On August 17th, an Italian convoy left Benghazi, escorting a large party of Allied POW's to Italy. On board the Italian transport ship "Nino Bixio" (7137 tonnes) were 2000 prisoners, including men of the 50th RTR, and they were protected by the destroyers "Da Recco" and "Saetta", along with the torpedo boats "Castore", "Orione" and "Polluce".

Dysentery on board the ship was bad. The POW's were down in the holds and men were allowed to go three at a time up on deck. There was a gap in the rails of the ship and on the side of the ship was a plank. Holding the rail, the men slid along the plank and, as one prisoner reported, "dropped it in the sea."

Sailing northwards in the Ionian Sea on August 26th, close to the southern Greek coast, the small convoy was attacked by the British submarine "Turbulent" (herself sunk the following March), captained by Commander Linton.

The "Nino Bixio" was hit by two torpedoes, one in the forward hold, killing many, and one in the back. The injured, including William Stone, were brought up on deck and attended by medical staff, but William died from his wounds sometime later. The ship capsized and the survivors and the wounded were taken on board the other ships. However, 336 men perished on August 26th, including William.

His body was brought to the Greek coast and he was buried in grave 5, Pilos Orthodox Cemetery, on the Peloponnese coast, southern Greece. After the war, his body was removed and re-buried in collective grave 7.D. 1 – 10 Phaleron War Cemetery, Athens.

It is interesting to record that in 1947, the family was in correspondence

The grave of William Stone in Greece
Ann Salmon

Percy and Emma Stone of Pilsley, in later life
Ann Salmon

with one of the German soldiers who guarded William, immediately after his capture, and he wrote to tell them what happened during that period. He told them that William's tank was forced to surrender by the bullets of a heavy machine-gun. When the crew came out of the tank, its commander, a teacher by profession, as was the German soldier, was killed. William and another crewman were unhurt. The German took them to regimental headquarters, where an officer told the German guard to take them to the field kitchen and provide them with bread and butter.

William and the guard talked during the night and William gave the German his address and invited him to come to England after the war. When William was about to be taken away at dawn, the guard provided him with a blanket and field water bottle. Some days later, the German guard was himself taken prisoner and eventually was taken to England.

TELEGRAPHIST GEOFFREY GILBERT No. C/SSX32419
DUTCH SHIP "ISAAC SWEERS" ROYAL NAVY
DIED NOVEMBER 13TH 1942 AGED 22

Geoff Gilbert was the eldest of ten children of Charles Henry and Alice Gilbert. Charles was born at Pineapple Cottage, near Newholme, Bakewell, and married Alice Goodwin, a Bakewell girl.

Around 1933 the Gilbert family moved to Baslow, where they lived at Alma House (a converted pub), a dwelling on School Lane, which could accommodate a large family.

Charles Gilbert was working on the Chatsworth Estate as a woodsman (later he would work for Glebe Mines at Eyam) and when Geoff left Baslow School, he joined his father as a woodsman.

Geoff Gilbert was called up early in the war and joined the Royal Navy, in which he trained as a radio telegraphist. In June 1941 he joined the crew of a former Dutch destroyer, the "Isaac Sweers", at Southampton, the ship leaving for trials at Greenock, before entering Scapa Flow in the Orkneys, where her crew got their training throughout July.

Geoffrey Gilbert of Baslow, with his new bride, 18 year old Mary Goodall
Bernard Birds

Alice and Charles Henry Gilbert, the parents of Geoffrey Gilbert, of Alma House, Baslow, c1942
Bernard Birds

As part of the 19th Destroyer Flotilla, the "Isaac Sweers" was involved in escorting troopships in convoy, southwards, usually to a position near Spain, throughout August and September 1941.

On September 17th she left for Gibraltar as part of Force "H", to help escort merchant ships through the Mediterranean Sea to Malta. The destroyer had a narrow miss by a torpedo dropped from one of twelve torpedo planes which attacked the convoy. The "Sweers" had two men wounded by shell fragments, one being Geoff Gilbert.

Throughout October and November 1941 the "Sweers" was part of a Freetown convoy, before returning to escort Malta convoys once again, including one to transport 37 Hurricane fighters to the besieged island. It was during this period that the aircraft carrier "Ark Royal" was sunk by a torpedo, close to Gibraltar. During December 1941 and January 1942 other major actions were fought with Italian naval units and aircrafts, and convoys were escorted to Malta.

Geoffrey Gilbert was telegraphist on the destroyer 'Isaac Sweers'. The ship is shown entering Valetta Harbour, Malta

On January 23rd 1942 the destroyer left for the Netherlands East Indies, where the Japanese

*Charlie Gilbert, brother of
Geoff, in India 1942.
He served with the
Chindits in Burma*
Bernard Birds

Geoff Gilbert sits on the gun turret of the destroyer 'Isaac Sweers'
Bernard Birds

were   gaining
successes. It received minor repairs at Colombo, before being attached to the
British Eastern Fleet. After the Japanese fleet attacked Trincomalee, Ceylon
(Sri Lanka) on April 9th, sinking the carrier "Hermes", the fleet left for
Bombay, the Seychelles and finally Mombassa, Africa. It was here that the
"Isaac Sweers" left for England and an overhaul in Southampton through
June to September.

It was during this period of shore leave that Geoff was married to his
fiance, Mary Goodall, from Carr Vale, near Bolsover, Chesterfield. 22 year old
Geoffrey Gilbert married 18 year old Mary at Baslow Church on September
12th 1942, shortly before his embarkation. Mary was the daughter of Thomas
Goodall, a Carr Vale coal miner. She, however, was living at Baslow because
she was working in domestic service in the village, at the home of Dr. Evans.
Shortly after his marriage, Geoff returned to his ship and this was the last
occasion that his new bride and his family saw him.

In October 1942 the "Isaac Sweers" left for Gibraltar as part of the escort of
HMS "Furious" and then made a rendezvous with the troop convoy KMF01,
bound for the beaches of Algeria, and the landing of American, British and
French forces in the invasion known as Operation "Torch".

On November 12th she was at sea to rendezvous with Force "H", the plan
being to refuel underway from Force"R" (two oilers with four
escorting armed trawlers), and by midnight, in the night of 12th/13th she was
ready for action, to the north of Algiers.

At about 0500 hours on November 13th, two torpedoes hit the starboard
side of the "Isaac Sweers", and they put the whole ship ablaze from bow to
stern. The first torpedo hit a fuel tank and burning oil spread over the water,

the second hitting the longroom and officers' quarters. All thirteen officers were asleep at the time and all perished.

The ship had escaped many attacks from aircraft and submarines in the past, but she could not survive the damage now sustained. The "Isaac Sweers" sank due to a U-boat attack by Kapitan-Leutnant Wilhelm Dommes, commanding officer on board U-431. Only 86 men survived from a crew of 194. The trawler Loch Oskaig tried to come alongside the burning destroyer, but had to abandon her plans due to the heavy fires and exploding ammunition.

One of those who was killed was Geoffrey Gilbert. His body was not recovered and his name is commemorated on the Chatham War Memorial and on the Baslow and Bakewell Memorials.

The last casualty for 1942 was a Chatsworth estate gardener, a native of Pilsley, who was living at Baslow.

PRIVATE GEORGE ALLAN HOWARD No. 5890619
5TH BATTALION NORTHAMPTONSHIRE REGIMENT
DIED NOVEMBER 29TH 1942 AGED 30

George Allan Howard was born in a cottage on High Street, Pilsley, just above the Devonshire Arms, on August 31st 1912, the son of Frederick (Fred) and Fanny Howard (née Hibbert). His father, Fred, was a Baslow man but for some time he and Fanny had lived in Sheffield, before they moved to Pilsley, where Fred worked on the Chatsworth estate, in the Builders' Yard.

George's siblings, Francis, Margaret and James (Jim) were considerably older than him. Jim had worked as a coachman at Baslow Grand Hotel and Hydro, taking the carriage and horses to fetch the guests arriving at Hassop Station.

After leaving Pilsley School, young George began work on the Chatsworth Estate, employed as a gardener in the Kitchen gardens under Mr. Chester.

Adjacent to the gardens was the large house, known as Barbrook House, formerly the home of Sir Joseph Paxton, but in the late 1920's and 1930's it was the home of Mr. and Mrs. Gerry Hartopp, an agent for the Duke of Devonshire.

George Allan Howard holds his baby son, Graham, at their home, 'Daisy Bank', at Baslow, in 1939

Graham Howard

George Allan Howard as a member of the 5th Battalion Northamptonshire Regiment
Graham Howard

Howard family group at Pilsley
BACK ROW: *Francis Howard, Jim Howard*
MIDDLE ROW: *Fred Howard, Fanny Howard*
FRONT:
George Allan Howard
Graham Howard

The home of Frederick and Fanny Howard and family on High Street, Pilsley
Graham Howard

It was to Barbrook House that Mary Jane Bradley, a native of Littlemoor near Ashover, came to work as a servant. Her father was a coalminer. George and Mary became acquainted and began courting. On May 2nd 1936, 23 year old George Howard married 19 year old Mary Jane Bradley at Chesterfield Register Office. They began their married life at a cottage in Baslow called "Daisy Bank", just above the old Alma Inn, on Over Lane.

Their first child, Graham, was born in 1938 and a second son, Stuart, was born in 1940. By this time, the war had started and many of the jobs on the estate were counted as reserved occupations. George's grandparents also had connections at Markham steelworks, Chesterfield, and wished to get him a job there. George, though, wished to do his duty and enlisted in the Army, joining the 5th Battalion Northamptonshire Regiment.

In January 1942 the Battalion travelled to Inveraray, on the shores of Loch Fyne, on the western coast of Scotland, for assault landing training. By May 1942 the Battalion became part of 78th (Battle Axe) Division, 1st Army and in September 1942 all ranks were given embarkation leave and stores were packed.

Moving to Greenock, on the Firth of Clyde, on October 16th, the battalion embarked on the 19,000 ton Dutch vessel, "Marnix Van St. Aldegonde". Mechanical transport, including the carriers, were loaded onto another ship.

Two days later the ship moved down the Clyde and on the night of October 20th/21st there was an assault landing exercise on the Isle of Arran. From October 23rd to the 26th many vessels assembled and on October 27th the

George Allan Howard with his Company, in the 5th Battalion Northamptonshire Regiment.
George stands on the fourth row from the front, sixth from the right
Graham Howard

convoy of 49 ships set sail, escorted by the cruiser "Sheffield", an aircraft carrier and a number of destroyers. In the Atlantic Ocean they joined up with an American convoy, sailing past Gibraltar and into the Mediterranean Sea. Operation "Torch" had begun.

The soldiers on board were to take part in an Allied landing in Algeria, then held by the Vichy French. The Allied plan was to occupy the whole of French North Africa, from Morocco to Tunisia and to link up with Montgomery's Eighth Army from the east. Montgomery's forces had defeated the Germans and Italians at El Alamein and were following up Field Marshal Rommel's Afrika Korps as they retreated westwards. The Allies hoped to squeeze the Germans and Italians in Tunisia and bring the war in North Africa to a close.

At dawn, on November 8th 1942, the 5th Northamptonshires, as part of the British 1st Army, landed unopposed, 25 miles east of Algiers. The only casualty was an officer knocked down by a landing craft and drowned. On November 9th they moved to the southern outskirts of Algiers, where the Battalion encamped, during negotiations with the French leader, Admiral Darlan, who wisely decided to end French resistance.

On November 18th the Battalion moved eastwards in motor transports towards Tunis, via Constantine and Testour. When approaching Medjez-el-Bab the Battalion came under fire for the first time. They took up defensive positions and made ready to attack Medjez-el-Bab.

However, the Germans evacuated the town and the Northamptons entered riding on American tanks. They had already been strafed by ME 109's of the German Luftwaffe along the main road to Tunis and had come under ground fire a few miles west of Medjez-el-Bab on the night of November 22nd/23rd, including heavy Italian machine-gun fire. This was soon dealt with by "A" Company. That night, the 23rd, they dug in on a ridge overlooking Medjez-el-Bab, before entering the town on the 24th.

Then followed the traumatic events of November 28th/29th, when they made an unsuccessful dash for Tunis. They actually saw the spires of the city, but they never got beyond Djedeida. The advance, once again riding on Sherman tanks, was brought to a sudden end when enemy 88 mm guns opened up. The men got off the tanks and formed up to attack the village of Tebourba.

Major Vic Hart and Major Ernie Wright were both killed leading their companies. A German counter-attack early on November 29th forced their withdrawal and the remains of the Battalion formed a defensive position at a farm, "Les Romarins". German Mark 111 and Mark 1V tanks came towards them and six were knocked out. However, they had suffered from un-remitting dive attacks by Stukas and ME 109's, with not a sign of Allied air-craft.

They left the farm on December 1st, going back along the River Mejerda and finally reached Oued Zarga. Sadly, many men had been left on the battlefield where they had fallen, and one of these was George Allan Howard. There is no known grave and George's name is commemorated on Face 25 Medjez-el-Bab Memorial, Tunisia, and on the memorials at Baslow, Pilsley and Edensor. We shall find that a few months later, another Chatsworth estate worker would die in the "push" towards Tunis, and his body would be buried at Medjez-el-Bab, a few yards from George's memorial.

Margaret Howard places flowers in honour of her brother, Private George Allan Howard, at the unveiling and dedication of Pilsley War Memorial plaque on Sunday 2nd May 1948. The Duke of Devonshire looks on

Graham Howard

1939 1945

PILSLEY IN APPRECIATION FUND.

Master Graham Howard

On this day, when we the People of Pilsley, celebrate the Victory over the common enemy we remember the Brave Men who made the Supreme Sacrifice, and those who mourn them.

We therefore ask you to accept this small token of our appreciation and heartfelt sympathy.

Each family with a Pilsley connection, who lost a member of the family in the war, received a token from the 'Pilsley in Appreciation Fund'

Graham Howard

THE YEAR 1943

For British servicemen in 1943, the main theatre of operations was North Africa (especially Tunisia), Italy and the Mediterranean, where one man from the Devonshire villages would lose his life. Another soldier perished as a result of the conditions and treatment meted out to him in a Japanese Prisoner of War Camp, whilst a third serviceman lost his life in the skies above Italy, when his plane failed to return from a bombing mission.

CORPORAL CYRIL THOMAS NEAVE No. 4979664
"C" SECTION 2ND BATTALION SHERWOOD FORESTERS
DIED MARCH 24TH 1943 AGED 23

Tommy Neave, in the Sherwood Foresters, 1940
Derek Neave

Cyril Thomas Neave, or Tommy as he was known to family and friends, was born at Market Bosworth in Leicestershire, on November 11th 1919, the second of three children of Fred and Lucy Neave (née Jones). His elder sister was Betty and Frederick Charles (Dick) was the youngest.

Tommy was brought up on the Wentworth estates of Earl Fitzwilliam, between Barnsley and Rotherham, South Yorkshire, where his father Fred was a gamekeeper. It was there that Tommy Neave began training as a gamekeeper, becoming the fourth generation in the family to do so, and it was around 1936/1937 that he came to work as a gamekeeper on the Chatsworth Estate.

Meanwhile, his parents went to live on the estate of Lady Cholmondley at Houghton Hall, Norfolk, bordering the Sandringham estates, with his father continuing his work as gamekeeper.

Tommy lodged at the home of Mrs. Goodwin, an elderly lady in Pilsley. His future wife, Margaret Hulley, eldest daughter of Wilfred and Edith Hulley of Park Lane, Baslow, worked in the laundry at Chatsworth House (her father, George Wilfred Hulley, had been born at Beeley and worked on Home Farm, Chatsworth).

The gamekeepers' gun room was situated underneath the Chatsworth laundry and Margaret and the other girls would see the gamekeepers, including Tommy, gathering in the yard below before going off to work, or to a shoot, and would wave and converse with them from the window. Eventually, Margaret and Tommy began courting.

War now intervened and in February 1940 Tommy enlisted in the Armed

Forces, joining the 2nd Battalion Sherwood Foresters at their Normanton Barracks, Derby, and began his training. Meanwhile, the actual Battalion was in France and Belgium, taking part in the fighting retreat to Dunkirk, and suffered many casualties. It was recruits like Tommy Neave who would make up the numbers in the Battalion.

On October 17th 1940 Tommy and Margaret were married at St. Anne's Church, Baslow, before spending their honeymoon on the Houghton Hall estate in Norfolk, with Tommy's parents. Married life was spent at the Park Lane home of Margaret's parents in Baslow, although Tommy was away most of the time.

Gathering at Sheffield in June 1941, the Battalion travelled three weeks later

The Neave family on the Wentworth Estate of Earl Fitzwilliam, Yorkshire, c1929.
LEFT TO RIGHT: *Dick Neave, Lucy Neave, Betty Neave, Charles Frederick Neave (gamekeeper), Cyril Thomas Neave (Tommy)*
Derek Neave

to Skegness, to take part in the defence of the East Coast. During periods of heavy training, a whole year of this time was spent in the Yarmouth area, up to November 1942. The Battalion moved on two occasions up to Inveraray, in Scotland, for three week spells of combined operational training (including

Cyril Thomas Neave (Tommy) on the Wentworth estate of Earl Fitzwilliam, when Tommy first became a gamekeeper
Derek Neave

Cyril Thomas Neave as a member of the Sherwood Foresters in December, 1940
Derek Neave

Tommy Neave and wife Margaret (née Hulley) on honeymoon at Houghton Hall, Norfolk, October 1940
Derek Neave

running up and down the mountain side carrying full kit).

It came as no surprise in November 1942 that they were ordered to an embarkation concentration area near Carnoustie, in Scotland. Christmas was celebrated at Crieff, and over a period of nearly three months all ranks were despatched on embarkation leave. This enabled Tommy to get home to Baslow to see his baby son, Derek, born on August 4th 1942.

In November 1942, American and British forces had landed in Algeria in Operation "Torch", in order to squeeze the Axis forces between themselves and Montgomery's Eighth Army, pushing from the east. Now, in February 1943, Tommy and his Battalion were about to be "pitched" into this battle. On February 24th 1943 the Battalion entrained at Crieff, arriving at Avonmouth on the 26th, and embarked immediately on the SS "Tamaroa", which sailed on February 27th.

After a pleasant and uneventful journey, the "Tamaroa" arrived at Algiers on March 9th and sailed on for the port of Bone, close up behind the fighting line in Tunisia. It docked at the height of one of the heavy air raids on the port.

The Battalion was to move straight into the line to relieve the 6th Inniskilling Fusiliers in the Bou Arada sector, and moved through the mountains to Teboursouk. The month that followed, spent at Bou Arada, was of great value to the Battalion as they made preparations for the battle to come in late April. The sector was relatively quiet, with the companies disposed on either side

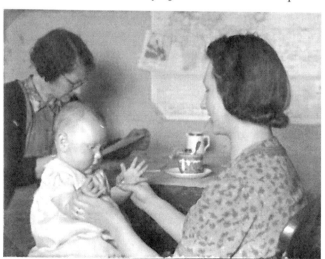 

LEFT TO RIGHT: *Edith Hulley, Derek Neave and mother Margaret Neave (née Hulley) at Park Lane, Baslow, May 1943. Two months earlier, on March 24th 1943, Margaret's husband, Tommy, had been killed in Tunisia. Note the wall map, which families used to trace the progress in the war*
Derek Neave

The headstone of Cyril Thomas (Tommy) Neave in the Medjez-el-Bab War Cemetery, Tunisia
Derek Neave

Land Army Girls in the Kitchen Gardens, Chatsworth, 1944.
Left to right: Miss Palethorpe, Betty, Margaret Neave (née
Hulley)
Derek Neave

Derek Charles Neave, son of Tommy
Neave, on Keepers' Day (Handley
Lane) on the Chatsworth estate 1975
Derek Neave

of the main road running south from the No Man's Land of Medjez-el-Bab, and their positions were in farms on small hills. About half a mile in front was the enemy, positioned on a line of hills.

Considerable patrolling was carried out by the Battalion and experience was gained by the men of living under shell fire, which was sporadic and light. Two outstanding patrols, one by Captain L. Slingsby, "C" Company, and one by Lieutenant Brachi, "D" Company, were carried out into the enemy's lines, gaining vital information of the enemy's forward positions and strength.

Tommy participated in the patrol of Captain Slingsby, together with Private W. Gration, on the night of March 24th/25th, when he was shot and died from his wounds, being reported missing. After the war, his best friend in the Company, Fred Holmes, wrote for an explanation as to what happened on that night reconnaissance and received this reply:

"The patrol had reached the spur running north from Bir Rehel when it was fired upon by a machine gun at 25 yards range. Corporal Neave was hit and did not appear to be initially injured as he started to crawl back to safety. A few minutes later, however, he showed signs that he had been shot in the lungs and appeared to be dying. He could not be brought back owing to the fact that the patrol was under direct fire all the while. Captain Slingsby and Private Gration then made their way back to their Company lines independently."

Just over two months later, Tommy's wife, Margaret, received a letter from Captain Slingsby stating:

"I trust that you will forgive me for having delayed so long in writing. I know that words are but a small consolation but I should like you to know how deeply we all felt the loss of your husband.

"I knew him well as a soldier and as a man and had the highest opinion of him. He and I went out on patrol on two occasions and each time his calmness and great daring was an inspiration.

"On the night in question we penetrated deep into the enemy lines and came under heavy machine-gun fire at point blank range. Your husband was hit, I think in the lungs, and although I remained only a few feet from him I could do nothing to help him as the fire was intense at the time.

"I do wish I could give you more detail but time is so short. I trust you will forgive me.

"I wish it were possible for me to raise your hopes and yet I feel that it is my duty to tell you that to my mind the chances of recovery were very remote.

"I hope one day to be able to tell you more of the unfortunate circumstances but gallant way in which your husband met with his fate. It is only by such valour and devotion to duty that we shall exterminate the enemy.

Yours sincerely, Captain W.L. Slingsby".

Eventually, Corporal Cyril Thomas Neave was buried in grave 2.E.20. Medjez-el-Bab War Cemetery, Tunisia. Later, his wife Margaret met another serviceman stationed in the Bakewell district, who, on departing for overseas service, promised to come back to her. This he did and they were married, Margaret becoming Mrs. Chapman, and they and Derek moved to live in Felixstowe, Suffolk.

At nine years of age, Derek returned to Derbyshire to live with his grandparents and eventually he became a gamekeeper on the Chatsworth estate, like his father, Tommy, and so became the fifth generation Neave to follow this occupation, retiring in the year 2007.

*** *It is sad to report that Tommy Neave's sister, Betty, who married Victor Self, an RAF man, lost her husband in the war. The aerodrome on which Victor was stationed in England was attacked by enemy planes. During the bombing raid he threw himself over a WAAF to protect her from the explosion, but both were killed.*

GUNNER WALTER OLLIVANT No. 1788884
5TH SEARCHLIGHT REGIMENT ROYAL ARTILLERY
DIED JUNE 8TH 1943 AGED 39

Born in 1904, Walter was the fourth of eight children of Joseph William Ollivant (1864 - 1938) and Thirza Ollivant. Siblings Helen (Nellie), William, Charles (a Chatsworth estate worker who lived at Beeley), Thirza, Gladys,

George (Chatsworth Estate worker) and Phyllis completed the family.

Their father, Joseph, became the inn keeper of the Robin Hood Inn, the Old Road, on the outskirts of Baslow, and supplemented their income by working a small-holding from the premises. He kept a few cows, pigs and hens and delivered hay and straw around the district as a hay and straw dealer. He was a tenant of the Duke of Devonshire by the 1920's.

The Robin Hood Inn was a good deal smaller in the days of the Ollivant family and until its refurbishment around 1960, the inn possessed a thatched roof. The large family could not all be accommodated in the inn when it was bed time. The

Walter Ollivant of Baslow
Cyril Robinson

girls slept with their parents in the main building, whilst the lads slept in accommodation above the outside barn.

Walter and the other children attended Baslow School, and one of the highlights of the year was the party provided for the children of Baslow, Edensor, Pilsley, and Beeley by the Duke and Duchess of Devonshire at Chatsworth House, each January.

Walter eventually began working for the vicar of Baslow, Reverend Drew, as gardener and tender of the village graveyard (the verger), a job in which Walter took great pride. He worked there for twelve years, up until the time he enlisted in the Army in 1941.

On April 29th, 1936, 32 year old Walter married a Beeley woman, 45 year old Edith Ellen Grindey, whose father, William was a forester at Chatsworth. The wedding took place at Beeley Church and the reception was held in the village hall.

The couple began married life at Church Cottages, Baslow, but a few years later war

The marriage of Walter Ollivant and Edith Ellen Grindey at Beeley.
They stand in front of Beeley Village Hall (Institute)
LEFT TO RIGHT: *X, Edith Ellen Grindey, Walter Ollivant,*
Phyllis Ollivant
Cyril Robinson

intervened and Walter enlisted in the Army in 1941, being posted to the 5th Searchlight Regiment of the Royal Artillery. His younger brother, George, also joined the Army, in the Pioneer Corps, and thankfully survived the war.

After initial training, his unit embarked for the island fortress of Singapore, in the Far East, travelling around the Cape of Good Hope and onwards to Ceylon.

Singapore was a protected naval base from which a powerful fleet could operate and was defended against attack from the sea by fixed coastal defences. Unfortunately, these guns could not be turned to combat a Japanese attack on the city from the Malayan Peninsula. After the Japanese attack on the American Fleet at Pearl Harbour on December 7th 1941, the Japanese launched its invasion of Malaya on December 8th. A British naval force, consisting of the battleship "Prince of Wales" and

George Ollivant, brother of Walter. He survived the war, ending up in Northern Holland in June 1945. He worked on the Chatsworth estate and lived with his sister Gladys, licensee of the Robin Hood Inn

Cyril Robinson

battle cruiser "Repulse", plus four destroyers, left Singapore that evening to intercept Japanese transports. With no fighter escort cover, both capital ships were sunk the next day.

By the end of January 1942 British forces had been pressed back to the southern tip of the Malayan Peninsula and onto Singapore Island. A Japanese landing was effected in early February. The total strength of the Garrison was 85,000, though many were non-combatants. Very little had been done to put the island's defences in order, morale was low owing to defeats on the Malayan mainland, whilst Japan had air and sea superiority.

The fighting was desperate but short-lived and on February 15th the British Commander surrendered after the Japanese captured the main water supplies for the island. Sadly, the ship on which Walter was travelling arrived in Singapore Harbour as the British and Empire troops surrenedered and he and his colleagues were captured without a fight.

The Malayan Campaign cost the Japanese 3,507 dead and 6,150 wounded. The Allies lost 9,000 dead and 130,000 as prisoners of war, one POW being Walter Ollivant. The captured Allied forces were treated with appalling cruelty and inhumanity by their captors, who regarded them as unworthy of honourable treatment because they had chosen surrender rather than death.

Walter Ollivant was amongst the POW's who were set to work on constructing the dreaded Burma Railway that linked Burma with the Siamese rail network. In October 1942 the Japanese decided to reconstruct the line for military reasons, using labour of mainly Dutch and British POW's and conscript Asian labourers. They worked in appalling conditions, were treated with great brutality and lacked adequate food and medical attention. The railway, over 280 miles long, was completed in November 1943 at the cost of over 63,000 lives (13,000 Allied prisoners and 50,000 Asians) out of a labour force of 150,000.

Walter did not see the completion of the railway, for on June 8th 1943, he died of dysentery and beri-beri in Siam (Thailand), aged 39. For the previous seventeen months Edith had only been informed that he was "missing" and in the first week of June 1943 she received confirmation for the first time that he was a POW. Only after this piece of reassuring news came the devastating information that he had died in captivity.

Walter Ollivant's body was later brought for burial in grave 8.K.67. Kanchanaburi War Cemetery, Thailand, 129 kilometres north west of Bangkok.

The next and final casualty of 1943 was a forester on the Chatsworth estate, who lived at Pilsley.

SERGEANT (WIRELESS OPERATOR / AIR GUNNER) GORDON BOWERING No. 1439758 142 SQUADRON ROYAL AIR FORCE VOLUNTEER RESERVE DIED NOVEMBER 25TH 1943 AGED 24

We have seen that Gordon's father, Allan Bowering, was killed in 1918 whilst serving with the Sherwood Foresters during the Great War. Born in 1919, Gordon was the sixth of seven children of Ruth Bowering (née Beebe) and the family lived at 5 Duck Row, Pilsley.

After leaving Pilsley School, Gordon was employed on the Chatsworth Estate as a forester. Soon after war began in September 1939 he volunteered to serve his country and as he had been interested in aircraft from an early age, he decided to join the RAF. Although volunteering, it was not until October 1941 that he was called up and he began training as a wireless operator and air gunner.

Gordon Bowering of Pilsley
Gordon Bowering

Three other brothers also joined the Armed Forces. Brother Allan had been a regular soldier from 1932 until 1936, serving with the Grenadier Guards in Palestine and Egypt. He came out of the Army at the end of this period and

221

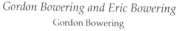

Gordon Bowering and Eric Bowering
Gordon Bowering

Gordon Bowering next to Simpson's Bakery shop at Pilsley
Gordon Bowering

settled in Norfolk, where he became a police constable, until he was recalled to the services when war began and served in the Military Police, first in Gibraltar for two and a half years and then with the 14th Army in Burma. Brother Roy served as an army private with the 2nd Army through Italy, whilst brother Ellis served in England as a leading aircraftman in the RAF.

Gordon eventually began taking part in operational raids over Western Europe and in 1943 joined 142 Squadron, which was equipped with

Members of the Beeley Youth football team in the early 1930s.
Left to right: Gordon Bowering, Ted Bond, Charlie Roose,
Geoffrey Bond, Billie Roose.
Gordon Bowering would be killed whilst serving in the forces
during the Second World War
Gordon Bowering

Gordon Bowering RAF
Gordon Bowering

No. 5 Entry Air Crew Cadets No.4 SS, 1942.
Gordon Bowering stands sixth from the right, fourth row from the back
Gordon Bowering

Wellington bombers. The Squadron had been based near Grimsby until December 1942, when part of the Squadron flew to North Africa to take part in the final stages of the North African campaign and later in the Sicily and Italian campaigns. Thirteen "tropicalised" Wellingtons and crews, plus members of the ground crew, were sent to Blida airfield, near Algiers, to help with Operation "Torch".

It was not until Saturday June 12th 1943 that Gordon Bowering set off from

Allan Bowering as a member of
the Grenadier Guards 1932-1936
Gordon Bowering

Ellis Bowering RAF
Gordon Bowering

Roy Bowering in the Army
during the war
Gordon Bowering

223

England to join the Squadron. They flew from Hurn to Gibraltar and then on to Blida, arriving on June 13th. By this stage of the war, the North African campaign had been successfully brought to a conclusion and Gordon and 142 Squadron now took part in operations over Sicily, as the Allied landings on that island began and shortly afterwards in missions over Italy. By this stage of the war he had been promoted to sergeant.

In November 1943, 142 Squadron was based at Oudna in Tunisia and it was from that aerodrome that Sergeant Gordon Bowering, as wireless operator/air gunner, in Wellington bomber HE929, took off at 1646 hours on November 24th 1943 for a raid on the Italian city of Turin. It was later reported that his aircraft crashed in Italy with the loss of all five crew members on-board.

All five were laid out to rest in the Florence War Cemetery in Plot V. Row J. Collective Grave 7 – 9. By the time of his death, Gordon had taken part in 32 operations over enemy territory.

Sadly, even by June 1944, seven months later, he was still reported as "missing", with all the worries that that entailed for his family at Duck Row, but eventually official notification arrived that he had died in the raid over Turin.

THE YEAR 1944

At the beginning of 1944 the U-boats still menaced the Atlantic and Arctic sea lanes, whilst the embattled German economy was producing war materials at ever increasing rates, despite the ravages from Allied bombing. The war was far from a decision, especially as the Japanese were fighting tenaciously in the Far East theatre of war.

Despite this, the Axis Powers were now on the defensive. The eastern front in Russia was crumbling as Hitler's Russian gamble proved to be lost. Italy's capitulation had taken her forces out of the war, whilst North Africa had been cleared and the sea lanes in the Mediterranean were open. Above all, the burgeoning power of America was now coming to the fore.

The Allies held the priceless advantage of strategic interior lines as they looked across at Europe from their bridgehead in the British Isles. They could, in principle, attack Germany at any point. The invasion of Western Europe, code-named Operation "Overlord", would come in Normandy on June 6th 1944, whilst meanwhile, the difficult assault on the mainland of Italy continued against a well-led and motivated German Army.

One serviceman would die during 1944 and sadly that man was the future heir to the title of Duke of Devonshire, the Marquis of Hartington.

MAJOR WILLIAM JOHN ROBERT CAVENDISH
(MARQUIS OF HARTINGTON) COLDSTREAM GUARDS
DIED SEPTEMBER 9TH 1944 AGED 26

William Cavendish (or Billy as he was known to his family and friends), was the eldest son of Edward William Spencer Cavendish K.G., 10th Duke of Devonshire and the Duchess of Devonshire (the former Lady Mary Cecil). He was born at Arlington Street, London, (now part of the Ritz Hotel), on December 10th 1917, at the time when his father was

The marriage of the Marquis of Hartington and Lady Mary Cecil took place at Hatfield on Staurday April 21st 1917
High Peak News, courtesy of Potter and Co., solicitors

Lord Hartington. His brother, Andrew, arrived two years later, in 1920, and sisters Elizabeth and Anne completed the family by 1928.

Their father, Edward ("Eddie") Cavendish, who had served in the Great War as a Captain at Gallipoli and returned to England after contracting dysentery, became the MP for West Derbyshire in a snap election of 1923 and remained as MP until 1938, when his father, Victor, 9th Duke of Devonshire, died.

For Billy and Andrew Cavendish, their early years were spent with their parents at Hardwick Hall, until they went to live at Churchdale Hall, near Ashford in the Water.

Their grandfather, the 9th Duke, had a stroke in 1925, which changed his character, causing him to become bad tempered and he appeared to take a dislike to the two boys and their mother in his later years. As a result of this their memories of times spent at Chatsworth were not particularly happy ones.

William Cavendish was educated at Eton and Trinity College, Cambridge, but shortly before the ourbreak of war, he left Cambridge to join the Coldstream Guards. He served with the Guards in the British Expeditionary Force in France 1939/1940 and was evacuated from the Brittany port of St. Malo in June 1940, as the Germans completed their

Edward Cavendish,
10th Duke of Devonshire, and
father of William and Andrew
Cavendish
S. Wiltshire

occupation of France.

Meanwhile, his parents were to spend the war years living at Churchdale Hall and his grandmother, Evelyn Dowager Duchess of Devonshire, at Edensor House, whilst Chatsworth became the home to evacuee school girls from Penrhos College, North Wales.

William Cavendish was a popular young man on the Chatsworth estate (a journalist wrote at the time that he had "an entire absence of side") and his coming of age celebrations at Chatsworth in 1939 had been on an extensive scale, lasting two days (Tuesday August 16th and Wednesday 17th). On the Tuesday afternoon there was a county garden party attended by 2,500 guests and on Wednesday evening the Duke and Duchess entertained 3000 tenants and employees from the Duke's estates, not only Chatsworth, but the estates in other parts of the country. He and his parents shook the hand of each guest and the undertaking left the Duchess with her

The Marquis and Marchioness of Hartington and family at Hardwick Hall, c1922.
LEFT TO RIGHT: *Andrew Cavendish, Marchioness of Hartington, William Cavendish, Marquis of Hartington*
High Peak News,
courtesy of Potter and Co., solicitors

The Coming of Age celebrations of the Marquis of Hartington in August 1939, at Chatsworth. A general view, showing guests awaiting the reception, or seated about the grounds
High Peak News, courtesy of Potter and Co., solicitors

Receiving the guests at Tuesday's Garden Party, during the 21st birthday celebrations for William Cavendish, August 1939. On the left is the Duchess of Devonshire, in the centre the Duke, and on the right the Marquis of Hartington

High Peak News, courtesy of Potter and Co., solicitors

arm in a sling.

The Duke said that his own 21st birthday was spent in the Royal Free Hospital, London, where he was a patient for some time after having been invalided home from Gallipoli, where he had been serving with the Derbyshire Yeomanry.

By August 1939, Lord Hartington had been attached to the Coldstream Guards for two months. The celebrations would have taken place earlier but for the death of the 9th Duke of Devonshire, his grandfather, in May 1938, six

The Duke and the Marquis of Hartington, William Cavendish, chatting with one of the guests at the Coming of Age celebrations, August 1939

High Peak News, courtesy of Potter and Co., solicitors

Lady Anne Hunloke, Mr Henry Hunloke, MP, and Lord Andrew Cavendish at the Coming of Age celebrations at Chatsworth, August 1939

High Peak News, courtesy of Potter and Co., solicitors

months before Lord Hartington's 21st.

On Tuesday afternoon the band of the Coldstream Guards played on the South Lawn. On the lawn above, Mrs. Volpre's miniature circus of performing ponies and dogs entertained the guests. The whole company sat down to tea in a large marquee on the lawn adjoining the east front.

The House Party of guests included Lord and Lady Salisbury (his grandparents), the Dowager Duchess of Devonshire, Lord and Lady Harlech, Lord Hugh Cecil, the Marquis of Granby, the Archbishop of York and Mrs. Temple, Lady Jean Ogilvy, Mr. Tom Egerton, Miss Blanche Egerton, Mr. Mark Howard, Mr. and Mrs. Parker Bowles, Mr. and Mrs. Arthur Gore and Miss Mary de Trafford.

Wednesday evening witnessed the attendance of the tenants, and at 6p.m. a presentation of gifts was made from the different estates. The guests were entertained to tea and were taken through the house, whilst the miniature circus and the Coldstream Guards Band again performed.

There was a spectacular wind-up to the celebrations, with a searchlight and torchlight tattoo by the 40th (Sherwood Foresters) AA Battalion, Royal Engineers (TA) and the Coldstream Guards' Band. The main portions of the south and west fronts of the House were floodlit, as were also the Cascade in the garden and the Hunting Tower. There was a magnificent display of fireworks and at the end a portrait in fireworks of Lord Hartington was thrown into the air, with the Band striking up "For he's a jolly good fellow" and the crowd singing enthusiastically.

William Cavendish had fallen in love with Kathleen Agnes Kennedy, second daughter of Joseph P. Kennedy, the American Ambassador to London since 1938. Kathleen, or "Kick" as she was known to family and friends, resided in London for the next year and a half, continuing her education at Queen's College, London and was named "most exciting debutante of 1938". She returned to London in 1943 to work with the American Red Cross in Knightsbridge. However, the marriage was delayed because she was Catholic and the Cavendish family was Protestant, whilst her father was strongly opposed to the marriage. Despite this, the romance continued through the war years.

William's father, the 10th Duke, had remained a minister in Churchill's government and in 1942 was appointed Under-Secretary for India and Burma. In February 1944, William Cavendish was recalled to Derbyshire to contest the West Derbyshire by-election, a political role his forebears had undertaken for nearly 300 years. As a serving officer (Captain) he was barred from fighting an election but the War Office transferred him to the Reserve and granted him leave for the period of the election.

It was bitterly contested. His Independent Socialist opponent, Alderman

The wedding of William Cavendish, 2ⁿᵈ Earl of Burlington and Kathleen Kennedy,
May 1944, at Chelsea Registry Office.
Left to right: Duchess of Devonshire, William Cavendish, Kathleen Kennedy, Joseph Kennedy (junior),
10ᵗʰ Duke of Devonshire
In June 1944, Joseph Kennedy would be killed in action
and on September 9ᵗʰ 1944, William would be killed.

Charles White, turned the issue into an attack on what he deemed to be the "feudal" influence of families like the Cavendishes, on politics. William stood as a patriotic tester for the popularity of Churchill's government.

Churchill wrote to him, "I see that they are attacking you because your family has been identified for about 300 years with the Parliamentary representation of West Derbyshire. It ought, on the contrary, to be a matter of pride to the constituency to have such long traditions of constancy and fidelity through so many changing scenes and circumstances." When the vote was counted, Charles White defeated William Cavendish by a majority of 4561 (it is interesting to note that the girls of Penrhos College, Chatsworth House, were keen that William should win. Groups of girls waited at the boundary of the Park, asking passers by for news of the result and were disappointed when it arrived).

At the declaration of the poll from the Matlock Town Hall balcony, William declared, "It has been a fierce fight. Now I am going out to fight for you at the front. After all, unless we win the war, there can be no home front." It was only a few days later that he and his colleagues in the Guards began their training for the D-Day landings in Normandy, due for June 1944.

However, before the fighting began, William and Kathleen had married in a civil ceremony at Chelsea Register Office on May 6th 1944, with his best man being the Duke of Rutland. Kathleen had been prepared to change her religion in exchange for marrying the man she loved. The Duke and his family were there at the ceremony but the Kennedy parents were absent. One of those who signed the marriage register was the bride's brother, Lieutenant Joseph Kennedy, who shortly afterwards was involved in the fighting on

The marriage of Andrew Cavendish and the Honourable Deborah Mitford, in April 1941
High Peak News,
courtesy of Potter and Co., solicitors

the Normandy front. A few weeks into the desperate struggle, Joseph Kennedy was killed in action when an explosion took place in his aircraft.

Five weeks after his marriage, Lord Hartington embarked for Normandy with the Coldstreams and the Expeditionary Force, and soon after, he was promoted to Major. Some months later, on September 9th 1944, he was killed by a German sniper, a short distance across the French frontier, in Belgium, whilst leading his men ahead of the tanks. Many Guards officers, including William, favoured the wearing of pale corduroy trousers with their battle-dress, marking them out as possible targets. He was buried in grave 1V.B.13. Leopoldsburg War Cemetery, 58 kilometres north east of Leuven, Belgium, the last casualty of 1944 to have connections with the five villages. His sister, Elizabeth Cavendish, later said, "For my parents a light went out when Billy died."

*** *Kathleen remained in England after the death of her husband and in 1948 planned to marry Peter Wentworth-FitzWilliam. The couple sadly died in an aeroplane crash on May 13th 1948, in France, as she was on a trip to her father to gain his blessing. She was brought to Edensor to be buried in the Cavendish family plot in St. Peter's Churchyard.*

William's younger brother, Andrew Cavendish, who was married to the Honourable Deborah Mitford, became his father's heir and eventually inherited the dukedom, on the death of his father Edward in 1950.

From Eton, Andrew Cavendish went to Trinity College, Cambridge in the 1938/1939 term and was not called up until June 1940, when he went for initial training to the Guards Depot at Caterham. He had recently become un-

Andrew and Deborah Cavendish, the future 11th Duke and Duchess of Devonshire,
with their children, Peregrine and Emma, at 'The Rookery', Ashford in the Water, 1945
Jean Blackwell

officially engaged to the Honourable Deborah Mitford, daughter of Lord and
Lady Redesdale.

Discipline at Caterham was severe, but it helped that he knew a number of
his fellow officers and life improved a little when they left for officer training
at Sandhurst.

On April 19th 1941, Andrew Cavendish and Deborah Mitford were married
at St. Bartholomew the Great, in the City of London, and he was then com-
missioned into the 5th Battalion Coldstream Guards. For a while, the newly
married couple lived in Warminster, until the arrival of their first child was
expected and they moved into their first home at "The Rookery", in Ashford
in the Water, where their daughter Emma was born in 1943.

Two and a half years training in England came to an end when, in 1943, he
was posted to the 3rd Battalion Coldstream Guards, who were then taking
part in the Italian Campaign. They had fought in the Western Desert and
Tunisia, suffering badly at Tobruk and had then taken part in the landings at
Salerno, on the Italian mainland. When Andrew Cavendish joined the
Battalion, after a three week voyage to Naples, it was stationed in the
vicinity of Monte Cassino. Between the landings at Salerno and the end of
1943 the Battalion had lost 144 men killed and 350 wounded.

The 3rd Battalion was now involved in severe fighting in the advance on Rome, which they entered in early June 1944, and they pushed on northwards towards Florence. It was during these actions that Andrew Cavendish won the Military Cross for gallantry on the field of battle. It was typical of the man that all he would ever say about the circumstances, was that there were many anxious moments. He was, however, more forthcoming in his praise of the spirit and bravery of his NCO's and men.

The citation for the award of His Grace's Military Cross reads as follows:

"156055 Lieutenant (temporary Captain) Lord Andrew Robert Buxton Cavendish, Coldstream Guards. On 27th July 1944 Number 4 Company 3rd Battalion Coldstream Guards, commanded by Captain Lord Andrew Cavendish was ordered to capture the feature, Point 302, south of Strada.

"The Company, while proceeding to its objective, came under considerable shellfire. Captain Lord Andrew Cavendish, returning from a forward reconnaissance, found considerable confusion amongst his tired troops, several of whom had been wounded. In spite of continuous shellfire, he rallied his men, disposed of the wounded and led his Company gallantly on to the objective. For the next 24 hours, with enemy on three sides of them and cut off by fire on the fourth side, his Company remained in its position without food and water. During this extremely difficult period, Captain Lord Andrew Cavendish kept up the morale of his very tired troops by his endless cheerfulness, energy and disregard of danger. After thirty six hours, his Company was relieved.

"Captain Lord Andrew Cavendish's example and leadership unquestionably was largely responsible for both capturing and holding the feature, whilst his personal gallantry was an inspiration to his men."

It was during a lull in the fighting that he received news from home that a son, Peregrine, had been born on April 27th 1944 (later to become the 12th Duke of Devonshire).

THE YEAR 1945

During the winter and spring of 1945 British forces continued their advance towards the River Rhine and across the mighty river defences into the heart of Germany, whilst Bomber Command crews maintained the pressure on German industry as they pounded what was left of the cities and towns. The German Reich would surrender at midnight on May 8th/9th 1945 and the following day the five parishes back in England were able to bring out the bunting, ring the church bells and light bonfires to celebrate Victory in Europe (VE) Day. Out in the Far East, however, despite the celebrations in Britain, British forces (the so called "Forgotten Army") would continue the desperate fight against the Japanese in Burma, Malaya and elsewhere, until the surrender of Japan on September 2nd.

As the month of April 1945 came to a close, there came news of the final casualty of the war from the Chatsworth villages, that of a man with connections to the village of Pilsley.

PRIVATE SIDNEY LORD No. 4398280
1ST BATTALION GREEN HOWARDS REGIMENT
DIED APRIL 30TH 1945 AGED 25

Sidney's father, Herbert Lord, always known as Tom to family and friends, was born in 1893 at Saltby Heath, to the south of Belvoir Castle, Leicestershire. Tom trained to be a butcher, but then travelled to Thoresby Hall estate, in Nottinghamshire, to become a gamekeeper. It was there that he met Julia Bailey, born in 1900 at Edwinstowe Park Lodge, where her father was the gamekeeper on the neighbouring estate.

After their marriage they moved to Linford, an estate in Lincolnshire,

April 1927. Julia Lord holding Jim with Sidney Lord
Ralph Lord

Sidney Lord of Pilsley, as a member of the Green Howards
Ralph Lord

where Tom was employed as the gamekeeper, and it was there that Sidney was born in 1920. They moved next to the Vale of Clywd, in Wales, and then on to the estate of Sir Ralph Pinkers, near Newport Pagnell. By this time, a second son, Jim, had been born and in 1936, a third son, Ralph.

In his occupation as gamekeeper, Tom and his family moved to the estate of Thorp Perrow, between Ripon and Bedale, North Yorkshire, as war clouds gathered. It was here that Sidney Lord was involved in timber felling in the forestry department. The largest timber felling business in Yorkshire was "Greens", and when they came to fell timber on the estate, Sidney went to work for them when they departed, working mainly in the Ripon area.

In the early days of the war, Sidney enlisted and joined the Green Howards (Yorkshire Regiment) and for the next two years spent most of his time in the

United Kingdom. However, he came out of the Army when "Greens" provided him with a job in a reserved occupation, timber felling on the Thorp Perrow estate.

It was around this period, in 1941, that Tom Lord decided to play his part in the war effort and took his family to live in Nottingham, where he began work at the Raleigh Works, where they were making bicycles for the Army, as

Sidney's face is shown on a card sent to his family whilst he was serving in North Africa
Ralph Lord

well as bullets and shells. When the German bombing of Nottingham resulted in the brewery behind their house being blown up, Tom made his final move with Julia, Jim and Ralph, to work as second keeper on the Chatsworth estate in September 1942 (he eventually became head game-keeper in the 1950's). The family lived at the end of School Row, in Pilsley.

Earlier in 1942, Sidney decided to return to the Army when he saw his former friends home on leave from the Armed Forces. Returning to the Green Howards, he joined the 1st Battalion. By this time he was married to Jessie Middleton, a woman from the Ripon area, who he had met whilst felling timber in the area. She was a divorcee, with a young child, and by 1942, a son was born, who was named Tony. Sadly, the young lad would never get to know his father.

In October 1942, the Battalion was bound for Algeria and Tunisia, as part

of Operation "Torch" and Sidney came to Pilsley on part of his embarkation leave, the last time the family would see him, as they saw him off at the station.

Sidney survived the severe fighting that resulted in the defeat of Rommel's Afrika Korps and was involved in the fighting in Sicily and Italy during 1943 and 1944. With the war in Italy over by early 1945, the 1st Battalion were stationed in Palestine. On February 26th 1945 they sailed from Haifa, their destination again to be Italy. However, when they reached Naples, plans had been changed and they were now bound for the fighting in Germany.

Sidney Lord, Green Howards Regiment, stands on the right, whilst serving in North Africa
Ralph Lord

Landing at Marseilles, in France, they travelled by rail and went into billets at the Belgian village of Schellebelle, between Brussels and Ghent, spending the next few weeks until April 16th in reorganisation and training, the main theme being the practice of "river crossing".

On April 16th, as part of 5th Division, they moved by road and rail into Germany and on April 20th advanced through Celle and Borne, where they arrived on the 21st. They moved into forward positions in the vicinity of Grosse Thorndorf, just south of the River Elbe and 25 miles east of Hamburg. On April 29th the Battalion moved to Hittenbergen, just south of the Elbe. In the early hours of the 30th, an assault was made across the Elbe, in front of the Green Howards, by the Commandos, the 15th Scottish Division and the 6th Airborne Division and by 11a.m. a bridgehead had been established on the northern bank of the river.

At 11a.m. the 5th Division started forward to cross the river in order to enlarge the bridgehead. The Green Howards crossed on a hastily constructed floating bridge at Lauenberg and by 1p.m. were concentrated behind troops of the 15th Scottish Division near Basedow. Orders were then received for the Battalion to advance through the forward troops, and to capture two woods, some 800 yards in front,

The Battalion was to form up in Basedow, and the start line was to be a hedgerow immediately north of the village. The leading companies were "C" Company on the right and "B" Company on the left, with "A" and "D" Companies in reserve. The attack was to be supported by artillery and mortar fire, with machine-guns covering the south-east flank. The attack was launched at 6-30p.m. and by 8p.m. both the woods were in the hands of "B" and "C" Companies. Fairly strong opposition had been encountered and 34 prisoners were taken.

During this action, Lance Corporal Miller of "C" Company led his section with great gallantry against a machine-gun post, which was dug in behind a mound in a hedgerow. Three of his men, including Sidney Lord, were killed, and two wounded, leaving Lance Corporal Miller alone, still about fifty yards short of the post. Single-handed and firing his sten gun, he silenced the post. For his inspiring courage he was awarded the Military Medal.

Sidney Lord's body was recovered and he was laid to rest in grave 1A.A1.12. Hamburg Cemetery.

Just eight days after the death of Sidney Lord, the war in Europe came to an end with the news that the German Reich would surrender at midnight on May 8th/9th and the following day, Victory in Europe Day, celebrations in all the parishes began.

Expectation and excitement were in the air at Penrhos College, Chatsworth. The day before the official celebration, everyone was anxious for news of the German surrender. As the school did not possess a large Union flag, it was decided to let the girls know by raising a large white sheet, hoisted onto the roof of Chatsworth House. The girls were scattered around the grounds, with some playing cricket on the cricket ground. Everyone ran back to the House at the sign and there were scenes of cheering and jubilation.

For the girls of Penrhos College, VE-Day began with an extra hour in bed and continued with a short thanksgiving service. The rest of the morning was given off for free time until 12-30p.m. and some of the girls took the opportunity to bicycle to Pilsley and Baslow to buy pop, even though it was raining heavily. Flags and bunting were strung from buildings and Edensor had done well, too, with a big Union flag flying from the Church. They got cheered by some RAF men in the back of an RAF van and the girls waved their bottles back. At 3p.m. the girls and staff assembled in the Painted Hall to hear Winston Churchill broadcast to the nation, before trooping outside to play ping pong with books and tennis balls, and games of rounders. 5-30p.m. saw the College staff providing an entertainment: "Penrhos from 1939 to 1945", followed by supper of spam, crisps and school made cake with marzipan icing.

At 9-30p.m. a bonfire was lit in the grounds by the head girl, with a dummy of Hitler being consumed by the flames, and the girls sang songs around the fire. Cocoa and biscuits were provided, the School Song was sung and the school retired to bed by 12p.m. Elsewhere on the Chatsworh Estate, there was poetic justice about a huge bonfire which was lighted at Bunker's Hill at 11p.m. For some days the bonfire had been built from brushwood by German prisoners of war engaged in forestry work in the district.

At Beeley, on the Sunday following VE Day, members of the Home Guard, Civil Defence Service, ex-servicemen and serving men paraded to the morning service at Beeley Parish Church. A Thanksgiving Service was held and the collection went to the Merchant Navy.

There was also a Thanksgiving Service on the same day at Edensor. Attending were the Dowager Duchess, the Duchess of Devonshire, Major Lord Andrew Cavendish MC and Lady Cavendish. Lord Andrew read the lesson.

Despite the conclusion of the war in Europe, the conflict continued in the Far East as the Allies battled against Japan. Despite four more months of war, the Devonshire were fortunate that no further losses were incurred by its menfolk.

On August 6th 1945 an atomic bomb was dropped over the Japanese city of Hiroshima, killing 78,000 and injuring 70,000, whilst on the 9th August, a second atomic bomb was exploded over Nagasaki, killing 40,000 and injuring 25,000. The Japanese offered to surrender and on September 2nd 1945, the official surrender took place on board the battleship USS "Missouri", anchored in Tokyo Bay.

At long last the Second World War had come to an end and with it, the villages' participation in five and a half years of dreadful conflict. The people of Edensor, Pilsley and Beeley had experienced the closeness of war with the arrival of the evacuees from the threatened urban areas, the distant views of the Blitz on Sheffield and the activities of locals in the Home Guard and ARP units during the anxious days of 1940/1941, when there was a real threat of German invasion and a perilously fine line between victory and defeat in the Battle of Britain.

It was, however, the involvement of family and friends in combat in the different theatres of war that brought home to the village folk the dangers and perils of the wartime situation. For those who returned home safely, there

The first naval wedding at Beeley Church in September 1945, as the Second World War ended. Evelyn Haynes of Beeley married Petty Officer Leslie Cantrill

Vera Russell

was relief and joy, but for eight families and their relations and friends, there was sadness.

Born just after the conclusion of the Second World War, I have lived through sixty years of relative peace in these islands, without the necessity of being called to fight for "Queen and Country". It is my sincere belief that this is partly due to the sacrifice made by people such as those whose stories are told within this book, and to those who fought alongside them and thankfully survived. This book is dedicated in honour of the men from the Devonshire and Rutland parishes who did not return from the Great War and the Second World War. They will be remembered.

The village of Beeley was fortunate that during the Second World War, none of the residents were killed whilst serving in the forces. The following photographs show some Beeley service personnel who survived the conflict.

Muriel Wragg lived on Brookside with her grandparents,
Mr. and Mrs. Jack Holmes, and her aunty, Ena Holmes
Barbara Hawksworth

Ena Holmes.
Siblings Ena, Madge, Elsie and Byard lived on Brookside.
Ena joined the ATS
Barbara Hawksworth

Edith Hulley. The family moved from the 'Club Yard', Beeley, to Midland Cottages, Rowsley, when Edith's father was an engine driver.
She was a childrens' nurse
Barbara Hawksworth

Marguerite Towndrow (known as 'Biddy')
Her father was a railwayman at Rowsley, but she attended Beeley Church
Barbara Hawksworth

Winifred Spinks. Her father was a gamekeeper on the estate and they lived at Moor End.
Winifred joined the WAAF's
Barbara Hawksworth

Maurice Fearn and his brother Richard (Dick). The family lived on Chapel Terrace (Friendly Row), with their father Harry working on the estate. Maureen Fearn was a gardener at Chatsworth
Barbara Hawksworth

William (Bill) Grindey. He was born at the 'Club Yard', Beeley. He worked in the Chatsworth gardens and played the organ at St. Anne's for many years. He joined the RAF in the ground crew, spending time in the Orkneys and three years in North Africa. He drove a crane and helped retrieve damaged planes from the desert. On his return, he drove a lorry for the builder's yard at Chatsworth
Barbara Hawksworth

Isaac Broomhead. He married into the Hawksworth family. He worked on the local roads for the council, before running a smallholding when he retired
Barbara Hawksworth

Richard Fearn
Barbara Hawksworth

Brothers Bert and Harry Reeve. Their father was Harry Reeve, postmaster and shopkeeper at Beeley. Bert, who lived at Fallinge, was a lorry driver and joined up the day after war was declared. He became a warrant officer in the RAF and flew 46 missions in Halifax bombers. Harry Reeve had farmed a little with his grandfather, Lewis Reeve, at the Devonshire Arms pub, but became a lorry driver. He served in the Royal Army Service Corps, in the North African desert, but was captured by the Italians in 1942, serving as a POW in Italy and then in a German POW camp until 1945

Bert Reeve of Beeley stands on the extreme right. The crew and maintenance crew of the Halifax bomber are with him. He was the rear air gunner
Joyce Gowen

Arthur Towndrow
Barbara Hawksworth

Pilsley

Sunday, 2nd May, 1948
3.0 p.m.

Special Service
for the Unveiling
of a
Memorial Tablet

To honour before God and men the memory of
those members of H.M. Forces from the village of

PILSLEY

who laid down their lives in the service of their
King and Country during the Second World War,
1939—1945.

*The Duke of Devonshire places a wreath on
the newly dedicated Second World War
memorial at Pilsley School
on Sunday May 2nd 1948*
Derek Neave

*The cover of the programme for the
unveiling of the memorial*
Derek Neave

*Unveiling and dedication of the Pilsley Second World War memorial on Sunday May 2nd 1948, by the
Duke of Devonshire. Next to him is the vicar of Edensor, Reverend Hardy*
Derek Neave

British Legion members attending the unveiling and dedication of the Pilsley Second World War memorial plaque at Pilsley School by the Duke of Devonshire on Sunday March 2nd 1948.
LEFT TO RIGHT: *X, Tom Lord, X, X, Donald Bell*
X, X, George Roose (standard), Wilf Deane, Jim Lord, X, Jack Evans, Laurence Bond, X, X, Bill Aveley, X, George Holmes, X, X, Ken Simpson
Ralph Lord

British Legion members at the dedication of the Second World War memorial at Pilsley on May 2nd 1948. The two young children on the right are Owen Jones and John Holmes
Ralph Lord

INDEX